SHELL GAME

Also by J. Michael Veron:

The Greatest Player Who Never Lived
The Greatest Course That Never Was
The Caddie

J. Michael Veron

SHELL GAME

One Family's Long Battle Against Big Oil

THE LYONS PRESS
Guilford, Connecticut
An imprint of The Globe Pequot Press

The Lyons Press is an imprint of The Globe Pequot Press

10 9 8 7 6 5 4 3 2 1

Printed in the United States of America

Designed by Kirsten Livingston

ISBN 978-1-59921-033-9

Library of Congress Cataloging-in-Publication Data is available on file.

For my brother Doug

1953–2004

"Clean up your own mess."

Robert Fulghum,
All I Really Need to Know I Learned
in Kindergarten

"Plaintiffs' counsels' presentation of the case reflect (sic)
the tremendous effort, skill, and knowledge required
of them; the character of the work and the attorneys
themselves are also reflected therein . . . ."

Louisiana Supreme Court,
Corbello v. Iowa Production,
2003-0826 (La. 2/25/03), 850 So.2d 686

"The jury heard ample testimony . . . of how Shell
ran roughshod over the plaintiffs. . . ."

Separate opinion of Justice Knoll,
Corbello v. Iowa Production,
2003-0826 (La. 2/25/03), 850 So.2d 686

ACKNOWLEDGMENTS

This is my fourth book, but my first nonfiction work. It tells the story of my family's battle to clean up my great-grandfather's property, which was badly polluted by Shell Oil Company. I had a particularly good perspective from which to write this story, because I was the lead lawyer who prosecuted the case against Shell.

As I relived the story of this twelve-year-long battle with the second-largest oil company in the world, I was reminded of the judges and lawyers who have been my heroes and role models.

First was my late father, Judge Earl Veron. Dad came from humble beginnings and, when he left a small grocery business to enter college at the age of thirty-two, he became the first member of his family educated beyond high school. After acquiring enough hours to apply to law school, Dad went on to earn a law degree from LSU and become a lawyer at the age of thirty-seven. After eight years in private practice, he was elected to the Louisiana state district court bench in 1967 and then appointed by President Jimmy Carter to the federal district court bench in 1977. He passed away in 1990, and I still miss him every day. I'd like to think he would have been proud of the way I handled the case against Shell.

After my father, men like Joe Tritico, Max Nathan, Judge Edwin F. Hunter, Justice Walter Marcus, Judge Guy Humphries, Judge Don Aaron, Judge James Trimble, and Allen Smith have all exerted a profound influence on my perception of what a lawyer should be. Their legal talent and professional demeanor have been a great source of inspiration to me, although I'm sure that none of them would ever want to be held responsible for all the times I've fallen short of the standards they set.

I would also like to acknowledge the assistance of Tammy Garbarino, my paralegal, who read the first draft of this book and helped me verify historical details. I've been a lawyer for more than thirty years, and I've never met a legal assistant quite like Tammy. She has the instincts of a veteran trial lawyer, an infallible memory, and a wonderful attitude about her work. In addition, my thanks go to Yvonne Hankins, my secretary, for her invaluable help in putting this book together. Tammy and Yvonne have the toughest job around, which is to make me look good. They have been far more successful at it than I ever had a right to expect.

I am particularly grateful to my agent, Jacques de Spoelberch, who conceived the idea of this book and insisted that I tell this story. I have benefited greatly from his keen eye for a good story as well as his editorial assistance.

I must also thank Tom McCarthy, my editor at Lyons Press, for his expert handling of the manuscript. Tom's efforts have made certain that the story of our battle with Shell Oil Company was told in the best possible way. He made *Shell Game* a much better book.

Next, as always, there is my dear friend and literary mentor, Bo Links. I first met Bo in 1998, when the USGA paired us together to speak on legal issues pertaining to golf at the annual Golf Course Superintendents Association meeting. I had read Bo's first novel, *Follow the Wind,* and told him how much I liked it. His response was to challenge me to put my own stories on paper. That led to three novels and now this book. In the process, Bo and I became fast friends. He remains my favorite golfing partner and never seems to mind that I usually do not play to my handicap.

Finally, I am (as always) indebted to my wife Melinda and our children and grandchildren. They give meaning to everything I do, and thanks to them I am a very rich man indeed.

A NOTE ABOUT THE RECORD

As any lawyer will tell you, there is no reality in a trial except what the court reporter records and preserves. If a judge, lawyer, or witness says something, but the court reporter doesn't put it in the official transcript, it never happened in the eyes of the law. Because this book is about a trial, it is important for the reader to understand that the extensive quotes attributed to the judge, lawyers, and witnesses were taken directly from the transcript of the trial.

Of course, I did not have the benefit of a transcript when quoting conversations that were not a part of the trial or were otherwise off the record. When I reported those conversations, I did my best to reconstruct them as precisely as possible. The fact remains, however, that the accuracy of those quotes is only as good as my memory and the memory of those who lived these events with me and were kind enough to read a draft of this book and verify its historical detail.

Beyond that, as a first-person account, this book is necessarily influenced by my own prejudices about the actions and reactions of the various individuals who played a role in this case, from the judge to opposing counsel to witnesses and, finally, to jurors. While I have asked others to verify important historical details about this case, the responsibility for the perceptions and opinions expressed in the pages that follow are mine alone. In presenting this important story, my purpose has not been to offend anyone but rather to portray in more vivid and lively detail the remarkable events of the case as I saw them.

PROLOGUE: MAY 31, 2000

Nothing will make a trial lawyer's gut seize up faster than being told, "The jury's reached a verdict." I don't remember where I was in the courthouse when I got the word. In fact, I don't even remember who brought us the news. But I knew instantly that the waiting was over.

As we hurried back to the courtroom, I checked my watch. The jury had only been out a little over three hours. That wasn't very long, considering that they'd been listening to evidence for two and a half weeks and had a lot of issues to decide. Moreover, I'd asked them to return a verdict against Shell Oil Company that was bigger than anything ever seen in these parts. It seemed like the jury would have taken more than three hours if they were going to come back with anything close to that.

This wasn't the first time I had underestimated what was going on in the case, though. Time after time, our battle with Shell had produced surprises. Of course, I didn't know it at the time, but there would be a few more unexpected turns in the road ahead as well. Before it was all over, I would be roaming the halls of the state legislature with a lobbyist trying to defeat a bill to give oil companies a license to pollute the state. That would land me in the governor's office on the fourth floor of the State Capitol in Baton Rouge, where I would be "asked" to explain myself to his executive counsel and his chief of staff. After that, I would hear one of the leading economists in the state claim that our lawsuit had virtually shut down oil and gas exploration in Louisiana. It was all a crock, of course, but stuff like that happens when you take on the powers that be.

Naturally, I wasn't thinking about any of that as we walked back to the courtroom. Instead, I just consoled myself with the thought that, although the jury hadn't been out very long, they had obviously been hard at work. During their deliberations, the jury had sent no fewer than five notes to the court. Some asked for various items of evidence to be sent into the jury room. Others asked questions about the instructions they'd been given.

Most lawyers claim that it's bad news for the plaintiff if the jury comes back quickly. They say it means that the jury has decided against holding the defendant liable on one of the first questions on the verdict form, which ends their work. Conversely, these same lawyers will say that it's bad news for the defendant if the jury is out a long time. They insist this means that the jury has worked its way past the liability questions and has gotten to the questions on the verdict form asking how much money the plaintiff should be given.

Having been through some forty or fifty jury trials during my career, I had learned that most of this conventional wisdom was nonsense. I had seen juries come back quickly with a verdict for the plaintiff, and I remember one jury that took the better part of two days before returning a "zero" verdict for the defendant. These experiences taught me that the length of a jury's deliberations revealed very little about its verdict.

What *is* revealing is how the jury behaves when they file back into the courtroom. If jurors keep their heads down or look the other way, you're in trouble. If they look directly at you and frown, that's bad news, too. But if they look at you and you're able to detect the slightest trace of a positive expression—a faint twinkle in the eye or the smallest hint of a smile—it's like, oh, baby, we've scored.

As my trial team and I walked into the courtroom and took our places, I wondered what signs I might see. Nervously, I buttoned and unbuttoned my suit coat as I watched the courtroom personnel trickle in. I remember at one point turning around and looking at my mother and her family, my cousins and aunts, who were seated behind us. They had been terrific clients, always supportive and positive throughout what had become a nine-year struggle. I knew they didn't always understand the complicated legal issues in the case, only that Shell had refused to clean up Grandpa Heyd's old farm property after using it for so many years. I was especially grateful that, through it all, they had refused to be intimidated by Shell's hardball tactics and had stood behind my cousin Billy and me every step of the way. I remember thinking, well, they're about to find out if it was all worth it.

It seemed like forever before the bailiff finally stood and said, "Please rise," signaling Judge Patricia Minaldi's entrance. As the judge settled into her chair behind the bench, she looked around to make sure everyone was in place. She then turned to her bailiff and said, "All right, Mr. Day."

That was his signal to bring the jury into the courtroom.

1

Louisiana is known as the "Bayou State," but a better name might be the "Disappearing State." Situated at the mouth of the Mississippi River, Louisiana has been vanishing into the Gulf of Mexico for years. According to experts, the state has lost approximately 1,900 square miles since 1932. That's an area roughly the size of the entire state of Delaware.

The situation is even worse today. Those statistics were generated before the late summer of 2005, when Hurricanes Katrina and Rita pounded the southeast and southwest coasts of Louisiana, respectively, in back-to-back natural catastrophes. The 120 mile-per-hour winds generated by these two storms ripped away untold amounts of the state's coastland and left all of South Louisiana more vulnerable than ever to future storms and other forces of nature.

While coastal erosion is a matter of great concern in Louisiana, the experts will tell you that the Gulf of Mexico is just trying to reclaim land that was under water to begin with. If you look at it that way, I suppose we should be flattered. There's not much else in Louisiana that anyone would otherwise want. With the possible exception of Mississippi, we're usually dead last in education, life expectancy, and just about any other category that's important. In fact, our poor circumstances have moved at least one frustrated state legislator to refer to us as a "banana republic."

He wasn't far from wrong. When you throw in the mosquitoes and alligators (not to mention the heat and humidity), it makes you wonder why you don't need a passport to cross our borders. Of course, our food and music are justifiably considered to be world-class. Beyond that, however, it's hard to find much about the state's geography that's all that appealing. The water off the Louisiana coast is brown rather than blue because of the silt that the Mississippi River empties into the Gulf of Mexico. You won't find any picturesque mountain vistas in the state, either. In fact, the land in South Louisiana leading down to the gulf is so flat that we mark speed bumps as changes in elevation.

Our only consolation is that the geological forces that acted upon the layers of sediment deposited by the ebbs and flows of glaciers in prehistoric times produced massive amounts of hydrocarbons under Louisiana's surface. For you non-chemists, that's oil and gas. Louisiana has always had as much or more of it than any other state in the Union.

Unfortunately, we don't have much to show for it today. It's sad to say, but the vast wealth that the state could have realized from its oil and gas has been almost completely wasted. The causes of this sorry state of affairs aren't hard to identify. Leading the list is political corruption, made possible by an unsophisticated and uneducated citizenry. To put it bluntly, the kinds of shenanigans that would land people in jail in other states are looked upon as a form of entertainment in Louisiana. For reasons I've never entirely understood, the citizens of our state are more amused than upset by elected officials who steal from them.

Perhaps the best example of this is Edwin Edwards, a charming rogue who served four different terms as governor beginning in the 1970s. Throughout his political career, Edwards pursued women, gambling, and other vices with a public gusto that would have embarrassed folks elsewhere.

For some reason, however, Edwards's refusal to be apologetic about his behavior appealed to downtrodden Louisiana voters. In a curious way, they were actually proud when his bad behavior attracted the attention of the producers of *60 Minutes* on CBS, especially when he outdueled TV journalist Ed Bradley in an on-camera interview. For instance, when Bradley asked in an accusatory tone, "Isn't it true you frequently go to Las Vegas to gamble?" Edwards laughed and said, "Why else do people go to Las Vegas?" The folks back home lapped it up. They were actually proud of how "their" governor thumbed his nose at the powers that be because that's probably what they wished they could do. It also seemed that they relished any attention—even negative attention—about their state.

Edwards knew instinctively that being defensive was a sign of weakness, so he perfected the art of deflecting criticism of his bad behavior with a joke. And the more outrageous the joke, it seemed, the better. In one campaign, a voter poll showed him with a huge lead four weeks before the coming election. When asked to comment, Edwards quipped, "The only way I can lose this race is if they catch me in bed with a dead girl or a live boy." In another race, Edwards joked that his opponent was so slow "it takes him an hour and a half to watch *60 Minutes*." In his last campaign, the perennial governor found himself in a runoff with white supremacist and ex-Ku Klux Klan leader David Duke (the incumbent, a reform governor with two Harvard degrees, finished third in the primary and missed the runoff). Edwards poked fun at the "good government" voters of the state—who had always opposed him and his antics—by declaring gleefully, "They might hold their noses while they do it, but they're going to have to vote for me this time." (Edwards wasn't the only one who saw humor in the voters' dilemma. Some wag distributed bumper stickers around the state that read, "Vote for the Crook. It's Important.")

Despite widespread reports of corruption in his administrations, however, no one at the state level ever dared to prosecute Edwards. The federal authorities were a different story. It took them two tries, but they finally got him in the twilight of his career on charges of public bribery in connection with the issuance of state riverboat gambling licenses. Now in his seventies, Edwards is living out his days in a federal penitentiary. In the process, he has become something of a martyr to his blue-collar supporters (as well, of course, to his many cronies who got rich off of state contracts while he was in the Executive Mansion in Baton Rouge). There is even a website dedicated to freeing him from prison, and his supporters have circulated petitions for clemency on behalf of their hero.

Edwards rose to power by marketing himself as a friend of the common man and maintained that image even while making himself and his friends rich off tax dollars. However, he wasn't the first Louisiana politician to pick the state's pocket while pretending to be its savior. The credit for that goes to Huey Long, the populist despot who ruled the state with an iron hand in the 1920s and '30s. Huey was a fiery stump speaker who convinced poor dumb Louisianans that railroads, utilities, banks, and other forms of big business were responsible for their poverty—and, of course, that only he could deliver them from those evil forces. For obvious reasons, the illiterate Cajuns, crackers, and rednecks who made up the state's population at the time preferred to believe that they were poor through no fault of their own and that, when Huey made things right, they would be just as rich as the Rockefellers. It apparently never occurred to them that their inability to read, write, or count to ten might have more to do with their problems than Standard Oil.

Long's campaign slogan—which he persuaded an LSU bandleader to put to music—was "Every man a king." The lyrics aptly expressed Long's bold promise to redistribute the wealth: "Every man a king, every man a king, for you can be a millionaire. If there's something belonging to others, there's enough for all people to share." (Years later, Randy Newman reprised the song on his 1974 album *Good Old Boys*.) "Every man a king" became Huey's anthem, and it obviously struck a chord with the home folks struggling to survive the Great Depression.

Louisiana law at the time prevented a governor from succeeding himself, so after serving his term Huey won election to the U.S. Senate. In his first term in Washington, he quickly launched an ambitious campaign for the presidency. Not surprisingly, Huey's promises of instant wealth met with approval throughout the rest of the country as well, and many historians credit Long with pushing Roosevelt's New Deal policies farther to the left than they otherwise would ever have gone. In fact, a persuasive argument can be made that Huey Long of Louisiana was one of the principal architects of the modern welfare state.

Even after moving to Washington, Huey continued to control Louisiana politics from afar. The average voter still believed that Huey was coming to his rescue by emptying the coffers of big business into their pockets, and his handpicked successors did nothing to disabuse them of that notion. Of course, Huey never did rescue those poor dumb bastards from anything, partly because big business hadn't made them poor or dumb in the first place. However, as a friend of mine likes to say, there is no cure for the dumbass. Certainly, Huey didn't have one, and so all his blustering did in the end was raise false hopes among those who were naive enough to believe his simplistic solutions to what was wrong with their world.

It wasn't enough that Huey did nothing to relieve the average Joe's poverty; he actually made it worse by stealing him blind. Long took over some of the state's most profitable mineral leases and shared them with his friends, who became multimillionaires off oil and gas that rightly belonged to the state and its citizens.

Huey didn't take it all, though, mainly because he was shot to death in the halls of the State Capitol in 1935 before he could finish what he started. To this day, the anti-Long factions, whom Huey ruthlessly persecuted when he came to power, openly consider the assassination to have been an act of good government. Unfortunately, it's not clear who deserves the credit for performing this public service. As most everyone knows, you can't have an assassination without a conspiracy theory, and that's true even in Louisiana. Thus, while most historians believe that Huey was shot by a young doctor who had come to Baton Rouge to avenge the gerrymandering of his father-in-law out of public office, others insist that Huey's own bodyguards did him in. Call it the Cajun version of the grassy knoll.

Unfortunately, the list of flamboyant Louisiana governors doesn't begin or end with Huey Long and Edwin Edwards. After all, this is a state that produced three cousins named Jerry Lee Lewis, Mickey Gilley, and Jimmy Swaggart—all from a little town just across the Mississippi River from Natchez called Ferriday. If that doesn't raise questions about the gene pool down here (or at least the water supply), nothing will. It may also explain, in a weird way, why Louisiana voters can't seem to resist the larger-than-life characters that run for their state's highest office. In fact, when Minnesota elected pro wrestler Jesse Ventura as its governor a few years back, I suspect that a lot of Cajuns were a little jealous (if not downright pissed) at being outdone. If they ever take it as a challenge of some kind, God only knows what might happen.

That's not entirely a joke. Huey Long had a younger brother named Earl who served three terms as governor between 1939 and 1960. Earl was less mean-spirited than his brother, and even more entertaining. Where Huey was fiery, Earl was folksy. (In fact, he liked to call himself "Uncle Earl.") His more colorful nickname was "the last of the Red Hot Papas," and he did plenty to justify the moniker. Like Edwin Edwards, Earl knew the value of a good quip. One year, his runoff opponent had to be hospitalized with a sudden illness. When a news reporter asked Earl if he was concerned for the man's health, he replied, "You're damned right I am. If he dies, they might run somebody good against me." Huey's younger brother was such a great stump speaker that a record album of his political speeches was a big seller in the state many years after his death.

Earl proved to be colorful in other ways, too. In his last term as governor, he engaged in a very public affair with a twenty-three-year-old New Orleans stripper named Blaze Starr. (It later became the subject of a movie entitled *Blaze*, starring Paul Newman as Earl.) As if that wasn't enough, Uncle Earl suffered a meltdown in his final days in office and was photographed pulling a pillowcase over his head as he was being put on an airplane and flown to a mental hospital in Galveston, Texas. Nowadays they would say Earl was a victim of bipolar disorder, but back then they just said he was crazy. Crazy or not, Earl managed to spring himself in time to run for Congress (he wasn't allowed to succeed himself as governor) and, despite all of the bad publicity, won a seat in the House in the first primary, without even a runoff. Unfortunately, he unexpectedly died a short time later, no doubt depriving Washington of one of the most entertaining Congressmen it would ever have seen, Wilbur Mills notwithstanding.

Earl was succeeded as governor in 1960 by Jimmie Davis, whose main claim to fame was that he wrote the classic country song "You Are My Sunshine." Davis loved his image as a cowboy and apparently believed that the public did, too. He even rode his horse inside the state capitol building once, just to have his picture taken there on his mount.

There were others, too. For instance, Governor Richard W. Leche was sent to the penitentiary for public corruption in the 1930s. (One can only imagine what level of corruption Leche must have achieved for it to be a crime in Louisiana.) The point is, there's a lot about Louisiana that's different from any other state in the Union. It's as if our citizens can't shake the Mardi Gras spirit and just have to be entertained by something year-round—and that something might as well be politics.

Some have said that politics is the official state religion of Louisiana. They're not far from wrong. Consider that, in many parts of the state, public offices are closed on All Saints Day, a holy day of obligation in the Roman Catholic Church. Consider also that one of the ceremonies marking the opening of the courts in the fall each year is a Red Mass, attended by judges and lawyers of all religions. If those things don't convince you that religion and politics are indistinguishable down here, nothing will.

In any event, most everyone who knows anything about our fair state agrees that neither Huey Long's thievery nor the antics of our other, equally mischievous governors are entirely responsible for Louisiana wasting its oil and gas. The state legislature certainly deserves a share of the credit, too. Instead of saving (and investing) whatever state-owned royalties Huey and his friends forgot to steal, they chose to use the income to pay the operating expenses of government. Then, of course, each of them went home and claimed credit for keeping taxes low. As a result, generations of Louisiana voters were taught to expect something for nothing, meaning that their roads would be paved and their schools paid for with the state's oil and gas revenue instead of their taxes.

Of course, when oil production began to dry up in the '80s and '90s, leaving the state with no royalty or severance tax income, the voters didn't want to hear that it was time to pay the piper. Any candidate for public office in Louisiana who even hinted that it was time to raise taxes to make up the difference didn't stand a chance of getting elected. To this day, you still can't find a legislator in Baton Rouge who'll go on record as supporting a tax increase. They just keep robbing Peter to pay Paul—which means, as George Bernard Shaw pointed out, they can always count on Paul's support.

In addition to the politicians, the oil companies did their part to keep the profits of oil and gas production out of the pockets of Louisiana citizens, particularly those who owned the land from which the oil and gas were produced. They sent sophisticated "lease hounds," or agents, to get illiterate dirt farmers to sign standard-form leases providing for minuscule royalties. If that weren't enough, these mercenaries often came back and bought what little royalty the farmers had left with cash payments that were small but all too irresistible during the Depression.

What they did was unconscionable, because producing oil and gas from the early fields was a no-brainer. In many parts of South Louisiana, the land was so rich with the stuff you could smell it. According to the old-timers, all you had to do was drive by a farm and sniff the air to know whether or not to lease it. It was like shooting fish in a barrel; these lease hounds and other investors really weren't taking any risks.

That wasn't all. Once the oil companies moved in and set up their oil wells, they showed virtually no regard for the farmer's land. They dug trenches with backhoes and buried toxic chemicals on site because it was cheaper than disposing of them properly. Instead of setting up disposal wells, they ran brine and wastewater into ditches, where it ran into streams that supplied water for irrigation, killing rice crops. When the oil companies were forced to inject brine and wastewater back down into the producing formations from whence it came, they laid pipelines to old oil wells they had converted to disposal wells. Even then, they didn't pay the landowner for a right-of-way for the lines or for a surface lease for the wells. The prevailing attitude was "what the dumb farmer and his family don't know won't hurt them." Later, when the oil and gas stopped flowing, the oil companies simply pulled up stakes and left town, leaving the innocent landowner with polluted land and no money to clean it up.

The irony about all this was that, for once, Huey Long's railings about the evils of "big bidness" were accurate. Unfortunately, however, neither

Huey nor the politicos who came after him did anything about it. Instead of passing laws to prevent the terrible waste of Louisiana's precious natural resources, they quietly accepted campaign contributions from the oil interests while being entertained by their lobbyists with lavish dinners at Baton Rouge's finest restaurants (liquor and women included, of course).

I know this story well. One of the poor dirt farmers who got taken by the oil companies was my great-grandfather, Ferdinand Heyd (pronounced "hide"). Through an agent, Shell Oil Company took a lease from him in 1929 and shortly thereafter brought in the first producing well on his 320-acre farm. By the time Shell sold the lease in 1985, it had drilled numerous successful wells on Grandpa Heyd's farm and made profits that, in today's dollars, exceeded $1 billion. In fact, Shell later bragged that the Heyd lease was the most profitable lease it ever had in Louisiana.

According to the lease, Grandpa Heyd was to receive one-eighth of the market value of all oil and gas produced from the lease as a royalty. His share of production from his land would be worth more than $125 million today. Neither he nor his family ever saw anything close to that.

It took us nearly seventy-five years to get even. This is the story of how we did it.

2

Ferdinand Heyd came to this country around the turn of the twentieth century. He was German by birth, but he actually came here from France. More accurately, he came to the United States from Alsace-Lorraine, a region that has bounced back and forth like a ping-pong ball between French and German rule for hundreds of years. Depending on which period of history you look at, Alsace-Lorraine is a place where Germans lived in France or Frenchmen lived in Germany. Grandpa Heyd was a German who lived in France.

I never knew my great-grandfather; he died before I was born. Moreover, my mother's family wasn't much for oral history, so I was told very little about him or the circumstances of his arrival in Louisiana. My mother does recall that, true to his German roots, Grandpa Heyd was fond of beer and polkas. In fact, one of the first things he did after he got a little money from the oil found on his property was to buy a jukebox and have it installed in his home so that he could play his favorite music all the time.

Grandpa Heyd and a brother sailed from Germany and entered the country at New Orleans. The brother stayed, but Grandpa Heyd found his way over to the southwestern part of the state where he eventually bought a farm.

From what I can tell, Grandpa Heyd had a tough go of things as a farmer. Even during good times, farming is a hard way to make a living, and those weren't good times. Like most of his neighbors, Grandpa Heyd was barely able to pay his mortgage each year after he sold his crop and so was perpetually in danger of losing his farm. Then, in June of 1929, a man named Frank Bennett drove up to Grandpa's modest farmhouse near LeBleu Settlement, a tiny little village outside of Lake Charles, and made him an offer he couldn't refuse: Bennett would pay Grandpa Heyd cash for a mineral lease on his 320-acre farm. In return, Grandpa would give Bennett the right to look for oil on his land. According to the lease, Bennett could pay additional money each year for up to three years to retain this right. If he drilled a well and found oil, he would pay Grandpa a royalty of one-eighth of the production. Meanwhile, Grandpa could still farm his land, as long as he didn't get in the way of the oilfield operations.

To a struggling farmer like Grandpa Heyd, Bennett must have seemed like a savior. And it didn't take long for the news to get even better. Before the ink was dry, Bennett assigned the lease to Shell Oil Company, for whom he had been working, and within a year Shell brought in the first producing well on the Heyd property. Grandpa Heyd was (at least by his standards) a rich man.

He could have been a whole lot richer. Unfortunately, Grandpa Heyd didn't hold onto much of his one-eighth royalty. Over the next few years, he sold off most of it in bits and pieces to different people. Many of them were prominent members of the community who were far more educated than my great-grandfather and understood that Shell's discoveries in the Iowa Field (the area where Grandpa Heyd's farm was located) were big news. They moved quickly to get in on the action, offering many of these poor farmers cash in return for a piece of their royalty.

So did many of the land men who had originally sold leases to the farmers. They, too, knew there was money to be made from Shell's oil production. They returned to the farmers with offers of cash for their royalties, ready to trade on the goodwill they had earned from their past dealings.

Poor people who had lost an entire year's crop to bad weather were no doubt only too glad to take a bird in the hand. They understood all too well that Mother Nature could stop the oil just as easily as she stopped the rain their crops so desperately needed.

But the oil didn't stop. Shortly after the first well was drilled in 1930, the oil started flowing. Rigs were hauled in and set up to drill as many wells as the law allowed. Over the next fifty years, Shell produced as much oil from these leases as from anything in the company's history. (In fact, the 1929 lease on Grandpa Heyd's property is still in effect today, because the oil production has never stopped. It has slowed considerably, but it has never stopped.)

Of course, what flowed out of those wells wasn't pure oil. The typical well stream was a mixture of oil, gas, gas liquids (like gasoline), and salt water. It's hard to believe, but in those early days, gas was considered a waste product, much like the salt water. Thus, after extracting the oil from the well stream, oilfield operators typically sent the gas to a flare, where it was burned.

The flares were huge and, by all accounts, must have been quite a sight. According to folks who lived in the area back then, the flares at night were as bright as the noonday sun, so it was never dark. The only difference between night and day, they claimed, was that at night the burning gas washed the entire landscape with an eerie orange tint.

It smelled, too. If you can imagine the smell of gasoline on your hands, you get an idea of what it was like to live near those massive burning flares. In addition to the gas, other earth minerals burned along with the gas, causing an unpleasant odor that permeated everything from clothes to curtains to furnishings.

Finally, there was the heat. There were dozens of massive flares, sending flames as high as thirty feet, all spaced throughout one area. Some women actually hung their wash on clotheslines at night because the gas heat dried things faster than the noonday sun, particularly during the winter months.

These inconveniences were apparently tolerated without much complaint. After all, the oil brought money to people who sorely needed it, and it didn't matter if they weren't getting as much as those who had taken advantage of them.

Even after Grandpa Heyd sold off most of his royalty, he still had enough left over of his one-eighth that he didn't have to work anymore. While he wasn't a tycoon by any stretch of the imagination, he was comfortable. When he died in the 1940s, his four children all inherited his royalty interest in equal shares, each getting one-fourth of his one-eighth royalty.

John Heyd was the oldest of the four Heyd children, having been born in 1903. He was twenty-six years old and gone from his father's home when Bennett brought Grandpa Heyd a lease in 1929. In fact, John and his teenaged wife, Maisie Johnson, had just had their first (and ultimately only) child, a daughter they named Alverdy, in March of that same year. "Verdy," as everyone calls her, is my mother.

My grandfather (whom I called "Big Daddy") made judicious use of his share of Grandpa Heyd's royalty. By the time I came along in 1950, he had done well enough in real estate ventures, especially developing subdivisions, that he spent most of his time hunting and fishing. The remarkable thing was that he managed to put together this lifestyle with nothing more than a third-grade education.

Big Daddy was not only smart; he had a certain way about him that drew people to him. He apparently never met a stranger and found a way to connect with virtually anyone he encountered. According to my mother, he made an "office" out of a local barber shop on Ryan Street, the main drag in town. He hung out there, visiting with anyone who came by.

Big Daddy even had a brief career in public office. Because of his evident popularity around town, the local sheriff once talked him into running for the police jury, which is the governing body of the parish in Louisiana (parish being what everyone else calls a county). The story is that my grandfather was reluctant to run because he didn't want to campaign and ask people for their vote. The sheriff assured him, however, that he was so popular he would win the election without campaigning.

Which turned out to be the case. Unfortunately, no one had educated Big Daddy about the burdens of public life. It turns out he wasn't prepared for all the phone calls from constituents complaining about trash collection, the condition of the roads in their neighborhood, or the latest zoning dispute. Just two months after taking office, Big Daddy walked into a police jury meeting and informed the assembled group that the job was interfering with his hunting and fishing and therefore he was resigning. With that, he walked out and never looked back.

When I first heard that story just a few years back, I was surprised. Neither Big Daddy nor anyone else in the family had ever told me that he had any kind of political career. I asked my mother if the story was true, and she admitted that it was. I then asked her why she had never told me the story. In a voice that sounded equal parts embarrassment and amusement, she said, "Well, it's not exactly something we're real proud of."

I remember as a youngster being impressed by the fact that my grandfather bought a new car virtually every year. It was usually a station wagon, because that was the best thing to carry all of his fishing and hunting gear when he traveled. It always had the biggest engine you could buy, because Big Daddy also liked to drive fast. I remember my mother lecturing him whenever my brother and me were about to leave on a trip with our grandparents, making him promise to drive slowly.

Big Daddy had a bad speeding habit. To put it more accurately, my grandfather drove like a bat out of hell. The story goes that he was traveling across Texas, in a hurry to get to Mexico to hunt doves. He was apparently rocketing along at 100 mph or so when a state trooper finally caught up to him. Exasperated, the trooper bellowed at him, "Mister, I've been chasing you for damned near twenty miles. What do you have to say for yourself?" Unrepentant, Big Daddy replied, "If I'd have known you were chasing me, you'd *never* have caught me."

This so infuriated the trooper that, instead of issuing a ticket, he made my grandfather follow him into town to face the local magistrate and, presumably, be sent directly to jail. Fortunately, the magistrate was out to lunch at the time. This allowed my grandfather the opportunity to buy the trooper a cup of coffee while they waited for the judge's return. As they sat together at a local diner, my grandfather began asking the trooper about what kind of engine was in his patrol car and invited him to look under the hood of his station wagon. After comparing notes about horsepower and what the State of Texas should provide its troopers so they wouldn't have to chase speeding motorists for twenty miles, the two began to talk about another common interest, hunting. By the time they finished the second cup of coffee, the two were big buddies, and the trooper sent Big Daddy on his way with nothing more than friendly advice about "slowing down."

My grandfather had one brother and two sisters. The brother was named Ferdinand Heyd, Jr. I never heard him called "Ferdinand"; his nickname was "Man" (or, to me, "Uncle Man"). It wasn't just a family pet name, either: There is a dedicated public road named "Man Heyd Road" that runs in front of where he lived. Of Grandpa Heyd's four children, Uncle Man looked the most like him (at least according to the photographs of Grandpa Heyd that I've seen).

Uncle Man and Big Daddy resembled one another enough to look like brothers, but the similarities stopped there. Uncle Man was serious and not as amused by my grandfather's sense of humor as others were. My grandfather liked to vacation at Hot Springs, Arkansas, because the warm springs there were rumored to have great medicinal value. He told his brother before heading there one year that he was going to send him a nice box of cigars from the resort. When Big Daddy arrived in Arkansas, he bought a brick, wrapped it in a cigar box, and mailed it to his brother COD. Uncle Man was so steamed that he didn't talk to Big Daddy for nearly three years.

Big Daddy had two sisters, Rose and Mary. Aunt Rose was more serious, like Uncle Man, while Aunt Mary tended to be more gregarious like Big Daddy. Aunt Rose was a little on the parsimonious side, too, once dropping the newspaper when subscription rates went up, claiming she could no longer afford it. Yet she was very generous to everyone in the family. Aunt Mary laughed a lot, just like Big Daddy. They were all wonderful to me, and I dearly loved them.

My grandfather was the first of the four children to die, passing away in his sleep from a heart attack when I was in high school. He was only sixty-three years old. Uncle Man and Aunt Rose survived him by about fifteen years. Aunt Mary lived well past her ninetieth birthday, into the year 2004.

The Heyds were not prolific. Bid Daddy had only one child, my mother. Uncle Man had two children. Aunt Rose had only one child. Aunt Mary had three children. There was only one advantage to having such a small family: Later, when we took Shell to court, it was easy to keep track of everyone's interests.

3

For me, the whole thing began on May 9, 1991, when Billy Corbello came to see me about what he said was "Heyd family business." My mother's father and Billy's mother Rose were brother and sister.

Billy and my mother were both "only" children, meaning they had no brothers or sisters. Billy is closer to my age, however, than he is to my mother's, and we grew up together. I guess we're proof that opposites attract. We're not much alike, but we've been as close as brothers for many years.

Billy is both tall and big, standing over six feet with arms and shoulders made large from wrestling steers in rodeos and working cattle on his farm. His hands are rough from mending fences and baling hay, and his skin is dark and leathery from a lifetime of exposure to the sun. He moves slowly but confidently, just as you'd expect from someone who's won more belt buckles and saddles than I can count. He talks with the same economy, too, as if there's a tax on the number of words he uses.

I'm roughly the same height as Billy, but that's where the similarities between us end. The only calluses on my hands are from holding a golf club, and my tan is what I would call a George Hamilton golf-course tan, which isn't as deep as one earned from hard work. Not only that, but I talk a whole lot more than Billy (although I probably say much less). I guess it's part of being a lawyer. For whatever reason, I talk as if I'm paid by the word, not charged for them.

Billy's easy manner doesn't fool anyone who knows him. Underneath that "good old boy" demeanor is a keen mind and an iron will. The keen mind came from his dad, my uncle Jeff; the iron will is clearly from the Heyd side of the family. Like many of the Heyds, Billy is generous and loyal to family and friends, but never forgets an insult or a slight. He will give you what you ask for, but never what you demand. As you deal with him, he will deal with you. It is a simple code, but one from which he does not deviate.

For instance, Billy was keenly aware of how the oil interests had taken advantage of Grandpa Heyd, and he was determined never to let it happen again. Not long after I began practicing law, Continental Oil Company (now part of ConocoPhillips) approached Billy about laying a gas pipeline across a corner of his land. During a series of back-and-forth negotiations, my cousin never wavered from the price he wanted in exchange for giving Continental a right-of-way through his property. The Continental representative became frustrated because Billy had rejected what she believed was a very generous offer—more money than they had paid anyone else on the entire route of the pipeline. In exasperation, she told him, "Mr. Corbello, I can't believe you're going to turn down this much money." Billy wasn't going to budge. He just smiled and said, "Ma'am, it's like my daddy used to say, if I didn't have it to start with, I ain't lost nothin'." It didn't surprise me when Billy got what he wanted in the end.

When Billy came to my law office on May 9, 1991, the weather outside was already uncomfortably hot. That wasn't unusual; summer in southwest Louisiana arrives early and stays long past its welcome. Being just thirty miles above the Gulf of Mexico, our area suffers from the twin demons of high heat and high humidity during the long summer months. The only relief comes from an occasional late-afternoon thunderstorm, which brings cool air for all-too-brief a period of time before leaving behind the familiar steamy conditions that drive everyone indoors from May through September.

Billy walked into my office carrying a file. That wasn't unusual, either; Billy often brought documents of one kind or another with him when he came to see me. Typically, it was a mineral lease, a right-of-way agreement, or a commercial lease of some kind, and it was usually marked up with notes he had made. One thing I knew: If the past was any indication, he had read the papers in his hands several times, and he would have some very specific and pointed questions to ask about them.

After we exchanged pleasantries, Billy showed me a lease that Grandpa Heyd's four children had signed many years before. The agreement was with Shell Western Exploration and Production, Inc., which was a subsidiary of Shell Oil Company. It allowed Shell to conduct certain operations on the surface of a 120-acre piece of land that was part of Grandpa Heyd's old farm northeast of town near a place called LeBleu Settlement. Billy and his family lived on a farm nearby.

The lease had been signed on May 10, 1961 and had an original term of ten years. The agreement further allowed Shell to renew its rights for two additional ten-year terms, which it had done. This meant that the lease was set to expire the next day, on May 10, 1991. Billy explained to me that my father, who had died the year before, had called the lease to his attention sometime back.

"Keep an eye on the expiration date," my dad told Billy.

My dad had drafted the lease back in 1961, when he was practicing law before becoming a judge. Until I went to law school, Dad had been the only lawyer in the family and the unofficial spokesman for all the Heyds.

The 1961 lease covered land that was part of the larger, 320-acre farm that Shell had leased from my great-grandfather, Ferdinand Heyd, back in 1929. The 1929 lease was a standard-form oil and gas lease, which meant that Shell was permitted to conduct operations on the surface of the land only as they were necessary to drill for and produce oil or gas from beneath the property. Shell apparently wanted to do more than that on the land and, over the years, obtained a series of surface leases like the 1961 lease.

These ground leases allowed the company to do such things as inject salt water produced from its numerous leases in the area back into the ground underneath the Heyd land. Salt water (or "brine," as it's sometimes called) is a major waste product that comes out of the ground with the oil and gas. Before the oil and gas can be sold, the salt water must be extracted and disposed of in some manner. The best way to do so is to separate it out and pipe it to tanks where, after settling, any remaining oil can be skimmed off the top. The salt water is then injected back into the ground, usually through an old well that no longer produces oil. Thus, it's ultimately is put back into an underground formation much like the one from which it came.

While the 1929 oil and gas lease allowed Shell to do this with salt water produced from the Heyd land covered by the lease, it did not permit Shell to inject salt water produced elsewhere. Rather than build salt water disposal wells, tanks, and other facilities on each lease it held in the entire field, Shell wanted to do it all in one place. The 1961 surface lease allowed it to do that on the Heyd property, so long as the salt water came from wells that Shell operated in the same field.

In addition, the 1961 lease allowed Shell to operate a plant that blended light and heavy oil produced from other wells in the area to produce an optimum "weight," making the end product more valuable than the sum of its parts. Shell called this operation "gravity management," and in the ensuing years had constructed pipelines to connect numerous oil wells in the field to its facility on the Heyd property.

All of this had left the property in a mess. Shell had done little to maintain the maze of aboveground pipelines that crisscrossed the property. Most showed obvious signs of neglect, being rusted and corroded. Some of the lines had simply disintegrated and collapsed. Of course, this meant that whatever went through those pipes spilled onto the bare ground. There was old equipment, also rusted out, scattered across the property as well. Once something was no longer useful, Shell's personnel had simply abandoned it in place.

Billy's farm was no more than a half mile from all this. He regularly passed by Grandpa Heyd's old farm, and he had come to know the people working on the property. Shell had sold its interest in the 1929 mineral lease in 1985, and the property was being operated by a new group of investors. Remarkably, the property was still producing oil, although not nearly in the amounts that Shell had enjoyed in the early years of the lease. At the same time, Shell had not sold its interest in the 1961 ground lease and was still operating its "weighting" facility there.

Billy explained that he saw no sign that Shell was vacating the land. The blending plant, he said, was still in full operation; nothing was being dismantled. And, of course, none of the rotting pipelines and abandoned equipment had been touched or removed. Billy then informed me that he suspected that Shell had been injecting salt water into our property from leases owned by others or from outside the field. Since the 1961 lease only permitted Shell to dispose of salt water into our property from leases it operated in the field that was a breach of the agreement. Finally, Billy pointed out that the 1961 lease obligated Shell to restore the land to its original condition when the lease was up. He said there was a lot of apparent contamination on the property as a result of Shell's operations. As he put it, "I don't know what it is, but it's killed all the grass." Pointing to a provision in the surface lease obligating Shell to restore the property to its original condition at the expiration of the lease, Billy said that we needed to hold Shell's "feet to the fire" and get our property cleaned up.

Billy didn't really explain how he knew so much about Shell's activities on our land. He didn't have to. There were two things about my cousin that I had come to appreciate: He was very tough, and he was very smart. While it would take one of the largest oil companies in the world years to learn that lesson the hard way, it was common knowledge to anyone who knew Billy. As a sign of respect, virtually everyone in the area (including his three sons-in-law) called him "Mr. Billy."

At the end of our meeting, I prepared a demand letter and sent it to Shell. Some lawyers like to posture in their correspondence, huffing and puffing about the other side's "outrageous and malicious" behavior. However, these expressions of mock outrage rarely accomplish anything except to alienate the other side. For that reason, savvy litigators save their chest thumping for the courtroom.

There's a second reason not to be a flamethrower in your correspondence: Letters like that often find their way into evidence. When read by a judge or jury, they cast the writer in a negative light as unreasonable and overbearing. To a jury trying to figure out who's the good guy and who's not, that can be the difference between winning and losing. More than once, I've hung an opponent's indiscreet writing around his neck like a millstone.

For that reason, I was careful about the tone of my letter to Shell. After identifying the lease and explaining that it was set to expire the next day, I wrote:

> It has recently come to our clients' attention that the lease agreement was breached by Shell in several material respects. First, it is their understanding that salt water and other waste from fields other than the Iowa Field were transported onto the leased premises and injected beneath the surface. Second, the property now consists of a maze of pipelines, equipment, and appurtenances that must be removed. Needless to say, our clients reserve the right to seek legal redress, including the attorney's fees provided for in the agreement, if these matters are not satisfactorily addressed.
>
> We would appreciate hearing from you as soon as possible regarding your plans to remove all equipment and appurtenances placed on the premises during the lease, for the restoration of the surface, and for the redress of the breaches of the lease described herein.

The letter was sent by certified mail. The "green card" receipt came back several days later. It showed that Shell got the letter on May 12, 1991—two days after the lease had expired.

Smart lawyers will tell you that a demand letter should be taken not so much as a threat but as a first opportunity to settle a dispute. Our letter plainly informed Shell it had three problems: It was trespassing on our land, it had probably violated our agreement on salt water disposal, and it needed to clean up our property. The trespassing and need to clean up were undisputed, because the terms of the 1961 lease were clear. And Shell could have verified whether it had violated the agreement on salt water disposal just by checking its records. Thus, in a very short time, Shell should have known that our claims were justified, and the tone of our letter should have told them that we were willing to solve them without a lawsuit.

Shell's response was quick but noncommittal.

> We have received your letter of May 9, 1991, advising Shell Western E&P Inc. (SWEPI) of the May 10, 1991 expiration of the above referenced Surface Lease and Right-of-Way Grant. Please be advised, that this matter will be taken under immediate review by the appropriate departments and a response will be forthcoming in the near future.

The letter was signed by Paul D. Lair and identified him as being with SWEPI's "Land Department." Since my law firm had represented oil companies for many years, I knew this meant that Lair was a "land man"— someone who acquired leases and represented the company on matters pertaining to the land on which the leases were located. He was essentially a property manager.

I sent another letter, reminding Lair that Shell and/or SWEPI was trespassing as of May 10, 1991 and should take immediate steps to vacate our clients' property. He eventually called me and said that SWEPI had sold its interest in the surface lease to another company, which he identified as Rosewood Resources out of Dallas. Lair then followed that conversation with a letter dated May 30, 1991, in which he enclosed copies of various surface leases, rights-of-way, mineral leases, and royalty deeds pertaining to the Iowa Field and reiterated that SWEPI had sold all of its rights in these instruments to Rosewood Resources in 1985. Again, he promised that the "appropriate departments" were reviewing our claims and that a response was "forthcoming."

When I shared Lair's response with Billy, he laughed and said, "If Shell sold the surface lease to Rosewood, why are they still operating an oil terminal on the property?" It was a good question—and a reminder not to take anything we were told at face value. In a follow-up letter, I asked Paul Lair the same thing. His response was to admit that Shell had *not* sold the surface lease when it sold its other interests in the Iowa Field in 1985. In fact, he even sent a letter to the present operators of the mineral lease warning them that they had no interest in the surface lease and therefore were not authorized to conduct any operations on that basis.

By now, Lair and I had spoken with each other several times on the telephone. While our conversations were always cordial, I warned him that Shell's continued presence on our land long after the lease expired amounted to trespassing. It was remarkable to me that the company had apparently made no plans before the deadline either to renegotiate the lease or to dismantle and move its facilities.

"If something is not done, we will move to evict," I told Lair.

That brought a telephone call from a Shell lawyer in New Orleans named Howard Smith. I had known Howard for a long time. Like me, he was an alumnus of Tulane Law School, and, like me, he was a fan of the university's Green Wave athletic teams. I wouldn't go so far as to call us bosom buddies, but we were friendly acquaintances. I knew vaguely that Howard had been in private practice for a period of time before "going inside" with the Shell legal department. He was a few years older than I was and had been with Shell long enough to be within hailing distance of a comfortable pension.

Although I wasn't sure, I didn't think Howard had done much litigation. My impression was that he was more or less a transactional lawyer, drafting leases and contracts and presiding over sales and acquisitions of property interests.

Howard was obviously a worrier. From our first conversation, he fretted about everything. He was trying to understand our complaints, he said. He was trying to find someone in the company who was knowledgeable about this property. He just didn't know how soon he could respond to our request for information. He also hinted that Shell and SWEPI were having an internal squabble over which entity was responsible for the operations on our property.

I was a little surprised at all the hand-wringing. From my perspective Shell was letting the tail wag the dog. I had often been in Howard Smith's shoes, representing companies who were being sued for any number of reasons. In fact, that's the side I was on 90 percent of the time. I knew from experience that the smart thing for Shell to do was to satisfy us and make this problem go away. Management needed to clean up the property and, within reason, compensate us for breaching the salt water agreement and for trespassing. Once they made us go away—and had a signed release in their hands—Shell and SWEPI could spend whatever time they wanted arguing between themselves about whose books the expenses should count against. Instead, they acted as if we should share their concern over their inability to get their act together and be willing to wait indefinitely while they decided whether they wanted to be bothered with us.

Ignoring Billy Corbello was not a good strategy. Billy had done the math in his head a long time ago and had made up his mind that Shell hadn't treated Grandpa Heyd (and, therefore, the rest of the family) right. He wasn't about to cut Shell any slack, and he had no interest in standing by while Shell and SWEPI debated which of them should respond to our claims.

Despite Billy's misgivings, however, we delayed suing Shell for over a year because Howard Smith claimed that the company was interested in working out our differences. This included negotiating a new lease on the land so that Shell could continue to operate its oil blending plant. After a series of fits and starts, we finally agreed to a meeting in Lake Charles.

That's when Howard Smith and Paul Lair introduced Billy and me to Mike Maier and Lloyd Deuel. Maier was with SWEPI. He appeared to be in his early fifties and, as I understood it, was a manager of some kind. Of the four representatives from Shell, Maier said the least during the meeting. Deuel, we were told, was an environmental scientist from Texas A&M. He also worked as a consultant for Shell, offering advice on how it could best clean up its old oilfield sites. Deuel was more forthcoming than Maier. His talkative demeanor later proved very helpful to us when we took his deposition.

In hindsight, I now realize that Shell intended this first meeting to be nothing more than a "test the waters" conference. As I later learned, Shell knew a whole lot more about what had gone on at the Heyd property than it was letting on at the time. Smith, Lair, and their compatriots didn't come to Lake Charles to share that knowledge but rather to see how much we knew.

We met for several hours and then toured the property. Lair and Smith seemed to be in charge of the meeting and did most of the talking. However, none of Shell's representatives shared any real information about contamination of the property, salt water disposal, or the terminal business. Instead, they just offered vague assurances that they wanted to work with us in negotiating a new surface lease. Even when we pressed for details about that, however, they gave no details of what they were willing to pay, begging off that they didn't have any specific authority from "upper management."

At one point, Billy asked a direct question about the profits made through the gravity management facility, saying that we couldn't calculate the rental for a new surface lease unless we knew how much money Shell was making from the use of our property. That's when Maier spoke up, saying that he didn't have the information but that, even if he did, he couldn't divulge it because it was "proprietary."

Billy was having none of it. When the meeting broke up and we walked outside to his truck to leave, he turned to me and said simply, "They're bullshitting us."

I understood immediately what he meant. Billy's language tends to be salty, and he makes liberal use of what the late Cajun humorist Justin Wilson referred to as "expletives." Simply put, he cusses a lot. In fact, he's been an expert at it ever since we were kids.

If the function of language is to communicate, Billy can't be faulted for his choice of words. Frankly, two law degrees from Tulane and Harvard haven't given me a vocabulary nearly as effective as his. When Billy says that something is "bullshit" or that someone is a "son of a bitch," you know exactly what he means, and no further explanation is needed. To tell the truth, I've always envied his directness about such things. Billy doesn't soft-pedal anything, because he means what he says and stands by it. There are many times when I've wanted to confront a deceitful witness with the same kind of bluntness, but calling someone a "lying son of a bitch" in open court is frowned upon, even in Louisiana.

Anyway, Billy immediately saw that Shell was stalling.

"Those promises to meet with management and get back to us aren't going anywhere," he told me straightaway. I wasn't quite as sure as he was at the time and was willing to take Shell at its word for the time being.

"Let's wait and see what they come up with," I said.

Over the next few weeks, a series of telephone calls made it evident that we had reached an impasse. Maier reiterated that Shell would not release information about the profits made at the oil terminal. We made it just as clear that we could not negotiate a new surface lease without knowing what the use of our property was worth to Shell. As I tried to explain, the most common form of commercial lease is a "net" lease in which the rental is based on a percentage of profits. Still, Shell wouldn't budge, even after I explained that we could certainly obtain this information with a simple subpoena if we moved forward with the lawsuit against them.

Shell was stonewalling us on an issue it was certain to lose. That seemed dumb to me.

4

In October 1992, we sued Shell in the Fourteenth Judicial District Court in Lake Charles. That's when Howard Smith introduced us to James Blazek, an attorney with a large New Orleans law firm known as Adams & Reese. Howard explained that he would continue to represent Shell Oil Company but that Blazek would henceforth represent SWEPI.

My first impression of Jim Blazek was that he seemed rather amiable. He stood about five-feet-ten or so, was perhaps a little older than I was, and had a ruddy complexion and light brown hair. Beyond his appearance, Blazek had a low-key demeanor and spoke in a soft monotone that made it hard to gauge his conviction or sincerity. He expressed himself the same way about both trivial and important issues, never revealing through voice inflections whether or not he considered the subject at hand to be particularly urgent.

Blazek used this low-key demeanor to avoid confrontations—so much so, in fact, that it was damned near impossible to engage the guy directly about anything. In textbook passive-aggressive style, his first response to any request for information about Shell's activities on the Heyd property was that he wanted to be helpful and cooperative and would therefore "look into it." In the end, though, he rarely came back with anything of substance. When we complained, he would then shrug his shoulders, apologize for not understanding our demands, and claim to be confused. Every conversation with the guy seemed to include the disclaimer, "Mike, I'd like to help you with that, but I really don't know what you're talking about."

As Blazek continued profess his bewilderment, I remember wondering at one point why Shell had chosen a lawyer who apparently understood so little about this kind of case. Adams & Reese had more than a hundred lawyers; it seemed to me that there had to be someone there who knew a lot more about this kind of litigation than Blazek did.

Although I later learned that Blazek's professions of ignorance weren't totally disingenuous, at the time I assumed that he was just following Shell's strategy of responding to our requests for information with nothing more than smiles and promises of cooperation. To a certain extent his tactics—intentional or not—worked. I became very frustrated by Blazek's repeated claims that he didn't understand us. He and Howard Smith kept telling us that we should direct any complaints about the condition of the property to two other companies, Rosewood Resources and Iowa Production Company, because they had bought Shell's interest in the mineral lease. They said that the environmental problems we had identified were caused by the mineral lease operations, and these companies had assumed responsibility for those problems when they bought the mineral lease.

I had to remind Smith and Blazek that we were making claims under the surface lease, not the mineral lease. They were acting as if the surface lease had been part of the deal in which the mineral lease was sold. This was the same mistake that Paul Lair had made. Once again, I pointed out to them that Shell had stayed on the property operating an oil terminal after selling the mineral lease in 1985. If, in fact, it also conveyed the surface lease at that time, then it had been trespassing for the last six years and not just since May 10, 1991.

When we pressed forward with the lawsuit, we got introduced to what my senior partner described as the "tall-building-lawyer treatment." A common litigation tactic of big firms like Adams & Reese is to bludgeon smaller opposition into submission. All of a sudden, Blazek had drafted several young lawyers from his firm to begin bombarding us with paper. First, they sent us interrogatories asking numerous questions about things we couldn't be expected to know. Then they served requests for all kinds of documents that we couldn't be expected to have. Then they requested depositions of all our witnesses. In the middle of all this, they filed motions to dismiss our case on various grounds.

The battle was on.

The lawyers for the other defendants took a different approach. The Rosewood interests were represented by a lawyer named Matt Randazzo. Randazzo was originally from New Orleans but at the time was practicing with a prominent Baton Rouge law firm. Although his firm could have supplied him with plenty of manpower, Randazzo chose a less adversarial posture. From the very beginning, he approached us differently, providing candid and open disclosure of what he knew about his client's involvement with the Heyd property. As he explained, Rosewood had bought the mineral lease from Shell in 1985, operated it for four years, and then sold it in 1989 to a group of California investors headed by a man named Kreuger for less than half of what they paid for it. Kreuger had operated the lease ever since.

According to Randazzo, the Heyd lease was never a profitable deal for Rosewood, but they had operated the property in a very safe and environmentally responsible manner. In fact, Randazzo produced detailed daily records documenting every aspect of Rosewood's operations. He made a persuasive case that any problems on the property existed before Rosewood bought the lease from Shell. (In fact, Rosewood's records even showed that the company spent its own money cleaning up leaks from wells that Shell had allowed to deteriorate for years.)

The Kreuger interests were initially represented by a lawyer from Lafayette named Mark Sikes. (He was later joined by another Lafayette lawyer named Paul Hebert.) Like Randazzo, Sikes was experienced in oil and gas law. The two were about the same age, both being perhaps five to ten years younger than I was. In fact, they were old friends, having served in each other's weddings. Not surprisingly, Sikes took the same low-key approach as Randazzo. Like his friend, Sikes produced documents showing that all of the problems we had identified existed long before his clients bought the lease from Rosewood.

In addition to Rosewood and Kreuger's operating records, there was other evidence supporting what Randazzo and Sikes were saying. For one thing, we had obtained aerial maps of the property dating back to the 1930s. These maps, which were on file with governmental agencies, showed the various pits on the property that were the primary source of the contamination. They established that Shell had dug the pits and used them to collect and contain waste long before either Rosewood or Kreuger came on the scene.

In hindsight, both Randazzo and Sikes showed experience beyond their years. They understood that litigation was first and foremost about people. They knew that the biggest mistake a lawyer could make was to get in his opponent's face and try to force him to back down. No lawyer worth his salt will retreat under those circumstances, because it's too humiliating. All he will do is harden his resolve to beat you.

By approaching us in such a forthright manner, Randazzo and Sikes disarmed us. We thus became more willing to trust them as they explained to us that their clients had not acquired any interest in the 1961 surface lease and that, in any event, all of the contamination on the property had occurred before they came on the scene in 1985.

Randazzo and Sikes both understood, before we did, that Shell was ultimately responsible for our complaints about salt water disposal, cleanup, and trespassing. Both of them also knew that Shell's "scorched earth" litigation strategy would only make us more determined to carry things through. For that reason, Randazzo and Sikes repeatedly made it clear that they were not partnering with Shell in its paper blitzkrieg and didn't want us to judge them guilty by association. Simply put, both lawyers could see that war was coming and knew it was not in their clients' best interests to fight on either side. As Randazzo put it, "When this thing blows, we don't want to be hit by any shrapnel."

I knew that they weren't speaking out of fear. In particular, Randazzo was an experienced litigator who had tried a number of big oil and gas cases. I knew about that because he was a law school classmate of one of my partners, and they had remained good friends over the years. But good trial lawyers pick their fights and don't drag their clients into court when smart negotiating will keep them out. The candid discussions we had with Randazzo and Sikes were a marked contrast to the "bob-and-weave" conversations we had with Shell, and we responded in kind to them.

As a result, Shell remained our target and the center of our attention.

5

At Tulane Law School, I made the law review and was elected to The Order of the Coif, and I actually intended to teach law rather than practice it. In fact, that's why I obtained an LL.M. from Harvard Law School in 1976. Before I was finished there, I had received a generous offer to join the faculty at LSU Law School, but a wonderful Lake Charles lawyer named Joe J. Tritico persuaded me to return home instead to help him defend our longtime local sheriff, Henry A. "Ham" Reid, Jr., against numerous criminal charges.

Joe was the best-known lawyer in my hometown when I was growing up. He was entering the twilight of his career, and the prospect of working with him on such an interesting case was too good to pass up. Besides, as he explained to me, the whole thing was a political vendetta by the local district attorney, and I "owed it to the community" to help set things right. I took the job immediately, feeling too guilty even to ask what it paid, and moved back to Lake Charles in 1976.

It didn't take long for me to realize I had landed in the middle of something big. My first court appearance was the sheriff's arraignment before a courtroom jam-packed with news media and spectators. From that day forward, Joe let me stand in the spotlight with him every step of the way. Before long, I was answering questions from reporters and being quoted in newspapers around the state. It seemed that every motion and every hearing brought a new wave of questions from electronic and print reporters. It was the kind of experience you couldn't buy for a million bucks.

From our perspective, the case against the sheriff was all about politics. Ham Reid had been the sheriff of Calcasieu Parish for more than thirty years. Before him, his father had been sheriff for eighteen years. One of the Reid's top deputies, Jack Hebert, wanted to be the next sheriff and apparently grew tired of waiting for him to retire. He and a number of other deputies attempted a *coup d'état* of sorts by becoming witnesses for the prosecution in an odd collection of criminal charges. Thus, the case had the sexy features of a district attorney and rebellious deputies taking on a political dynasty. It wasn't often that two prominent public officials squared off in such a public way, and the media couldn't seem to get enough of it.

The overriding theme of these charges was that the sheriff had "stolen" from the public by having deputies perform personal services for him. One of the indictments charged that the sheriff had committed theft by supposedly forcing deputies to work on an antidrug book called *The Marijuana Story.* Various deputies contributed to the content and artwork of the book and did tours around the state touting it to local officials and schools. Given that the purpose of the book was to warn young people against the dangers of using illegal drugs, it was hard to understand how the prosecution could expect a jury to be upset about the project. Another indictment alleged that the sheriff had committed a theft of public services by having a deputy serve as security at his farm residence. However, there was never any evidence that the deputy worked as a farmhand or otherwise did anything to benefit the sheriff personally. It was telling that not one of the twenty-six charges accused the sheriff of actually taking any public money.

For two years, I was at the epicenter of one of the great criminal cases that the state had ever seen, and I studied every move that Tritico made. I learned how to play the "what if" game, anticipating every possible eventuality that might occur in the case by asking myself questions about what might happen and, if it did, how we could best respond to it. I learned how to craft cross-examinations that forced witnesses to make critical admissions about my case and to contradict themselves, thus destroying their own credibility. I learned the fine art of rhetoric and how the right words, delivered at the right time to the jury, could pack persuasive power that our opponent couldn't match.

I also learned about the most important part of the trial: jury selection. There's an old joke about a Georgia dirt farmer who was observed in a compromising position with a goat on his farm. He was promptly charged with having committed a crime against nature. Lacking the money to hire the best lawyer in the area, the poor farmer was forced to retain a broken-down old drunk who, despite his flaws, nonetheless enjoyed a reputation for knowing how to pick juries. At trial, the prosecution's first witness was the police officer who witnessed the crime. The farmer squirmed in humiliation while the officer described his unnatural coupling with his goat. When the officer testified that, in the middle of the crime, the goat turned around and licked the farmer's hand, a juror in the back row nudged the fellow next to him and said, "You know, a good goat'll do that."

At the first trial involving our sheriff, Joe showed me that he was every bit as good at jury selection as that drunken Georgia lawyer. We were getting down to the end of our allotted peremptory challenges when the next prospective juror, a pleasant-looking middle-aged woman, was called forward. Our research indicated that she was probably unfriendly to our client.

I remember whispering to Joe, "What are we going to do with her? We only have one peremptory strike left." He just smiled and said, "Watch this." He then stood to question her in what is referred to as "*voir dire,*" which is French and roughly translates to "to see and to speak." The term originated as a reference to the oath that prospective jurors take before being examined, but the phrase is sometimes used to refer to the entire process of jury selection.

In his gentle and friendly way, Joe began by asking the woman about her family. She said she had two children. Joe asked about their names and ages. When she answered, Joe took note that the lady had a daughter the same age as his older daughter. Smiling at her, he said, "Where did your daughter go to high school?"

She returned Joe's smile. I thought, this lady may not like the sheriff, but she's starting to like Joe Tritico. "LaGrange," she said, referring to one of the two largest public high schools in town.

Joe nodded his head agreeably. "I thought so," he said, continuing to smile at her. "Was she in my daughter Marietta's class?"

The juror now was leaning forward. "Why, yes, Mr. Tritico, I believe she was."

Joe nodded. "She visited Marietta in our home, didn't she?"

This lady was now beaming at being recognized as within Joe Tritico's social circle. "Yes, I believe she did."

Joe gave her a final smile. "Please give her my best." Turning to the judge, he said, "Your Honor, we have no further questions."

In an instant, the prosecutor was on his feet. He was so convinced that Joe and this lady were long-lost buddies that, instead of asking the woman whether her daughter's friendship would interfere with her ability to serve as a juror in the sheriff's case, he simply announced, "Your Honor, we'll excuse Mrs. So-and-so with our thanks."

I whispered to Joe, "Why didn't you tell me you knew that lady?" He covered his mouth so no one else could hear him tell me that he had never seen her before in his life.

I realized at that instant that Joe had used his instincts to find a connection with the juror and in the process get the other side to dismiss her with one of *their* challenges. It was a terrific maneuver.

Needless to say, I tried to absorb everything Joe did, and I learned as best I could. Over the course of two years, we went through two major trials and won two acquittals before the discouraged prosecution dismissed all remaining charges. In the first case, the court allowed television cameras inside the courtroom to broadcast the jury's verdict live. It was the first time that had ever been done in Louisiana. I cannot imagine a more exciting—or better—way to start a career as a trial lawyer.

It was also a great way for Joe to end his.

With Joe's blessing, I approached another local law firm in 1978, and they invited me to join them. Even after I did, though, Joe and I partnered on a number of cases over the next several years. It was a great loss to me when he died a few years later. I cried through much of the eulogy I delivered at his funeral.

The years thereafter did a lot to polish the shape that Joe gave me. No lawyer can get better without what I call "airtime," meaning time spent on your feet in court. I've always been blessed with lots of opportunities to try cases. There's a saying in golf (my favorite game) that you can't get better unless you play against better players. I learned that's true in litigation as well.

My first civil jury trial was a good example of that. I represented a widow who had been left a sizeable sum of money by her husband, a physician who died at a tragically young age. The money had been placed in trust with a local bank. Unfortunately, the bank's trust officers had badly mismanaged the account. We sued the bank for breach of trust.

The bank was represented by a lawyer named Fred Sievert. I didn't know him well at the time, but he had a reputation as perhaps the best defense lawyer in our part of the state. At least that's what my dad, who was a judge, told me. At every stage in the case, I saw many of the same things in Fred Sievert that I had first admired in Joe Tritico. Like Joe, Sievert was courtly, with a great courtroom demeanor. Like Joe, he kept things simple, always phrasing the issue in a way that favored his side of the case. I was impressed—and more than a little intimidated.

Still, I had learned a lot from Joe. I kept things simple, too. Noting that one of the jurors was a dental hygienist, I persuaded the jury that the bank's mishandling of my client's trust funds was no different than a dentist who pulled the wrong tooth: It was a mistake, pure and simple, and the bank needed to make things right. The resulting verdict did just that.

Of course, things didn't always work out the way I hoped. While my memory is somewhat hazy about the details of the cases I've won, I can recall virtually every detail of any case I've lost. J. B. Jones, a gifted trial lawyer whom I greatly respected, once told me that, "The lessons I learned from cases I lost were the ones I remembered the most, not the ones I won."

I was no different. Any time I came up short, I spent several sleepless nights figuring out why to make certain I never made the same mistake again.

When it comes to litigation, there is no substitute for experience. Fortunately, most of my experiences were good, and my confidence grew as I became more and more successful over the years. While I often joke that my trial experience is the result of my inability to settle cases, the truth is I learned to trust my evaluation of cases. If the other side didn't agree with me, I was comfortable trying the case. That's something that comes only with "airtime" in the courtroom.

It served me well when Shell thought it could buy our case cheap.

6

The first consideration in any lawsuit is where the case will be filed and tried. My cousins got to choose where to file suit, and when Shell got served with the suit papers, it had to decide if it wanted to try to move it somewhere else. While most people probably don't think about such things, I was keenly aware of whether a particular community and its courts were liberal or conservative, and I knew that the forum could make the difference between winning big and losing big. We wanted to be in the Fourteenth Judicial District Court in Lake Charles.

While liberal and conservative courts can be worlds apart in that respect, it has always amazed me how close they can be to one another physically. The Civil District Court in Orleans Parish, where New Orleans is located, has historically been a very liberal place for jury trials. Since the population there is mostly black and blue-collar, jurors there will award big dollars against large businesses, even where the claims are extremely suspect. Drive ten minutes to neighboring Jefferson Parish, which is a white-collar, mostly Republican suburb of New Orleans, and it's a different world. Jefferson Parish is as conservative as Orleans Parish is liberal. The same car accident case that might produce a $500,000 verdict (or more) in Orleans Parish may only be worth $100,000—or nothing at all—in Jefferson Parish.

Lake Charles, where I live and work, is a community of about 80,000 located in southwest Louisiana. It's only thirty-five miles east of Texas and 125 miles east of downtown Houston. If you head in the opposite direction, it's 200 miles to downtown New Orleans. Lake Charles has a large petrochemical industry, which is the staple of its economy. In fact, many *Fortune* 500 companies operate chemical plants in the area. These plants have historically employed a sizeable population of engineers. Thus, in addition to our native Cajuns, Lake Charles has a mix of Texans from next-door and professional engineering folks from around the country.

This cross-pollination of Cajuns, Midwesterners, and Texans has produced a diverse gumbo in our area. Maybe this lack of inbreeding explains why our politicians don't seem to be as crazy as those in the rest of the state. I'm not saying our area politicos are necessarily smarter than anyone else's, but there's not a country singer among them, and we've never had one wear a pillow case for a hat. Consistent with that, Lake Charles has a reputation as being somewhat "middle-of-the-road" when it comes to lawsuits, with no pronounced liberal or conservative tendencies.

While Lake Charles may not be touched by quite as much madness as the rest of the state, it has produced more than its share of genius. Dr. Michael E. DeBakey, the world-renowned heart surgeon, was born and raised in Lake Charles. On many occasions, Dr. DeBakey has credited much of his success to his upbringing in his hometown, where he says he was fortunate to have demanding teachers and access to an exceptional public library. In 1993, Lake Charles received widespread acclaim when two of its citizens won Pulitzer Prizes. Native son Tony Kushner won the Pulitzer Prize for Drama, and Robert Olen Butler, a professor at McNeese State University in Lake Charles, won the Pulitzer Prize for Fiction in the very same year.

For whatever reason, Shell was apparently comfortable with the forum we chose for our lawsuit. Because the area had strong historic ties to oil and gas interests, Shell must have assumed that judges and jurors in Calcasieu Parish would be inclined to favor the industry side of things. As a result, Shell didn't attempt to remove the case to federal court or otherwise to change its venue.

We had a grand total of six plaintiffs. My Aunt Mary, who was still living at the time, had a one-fourth interest in the property. She lived in Jeff Davis Parish, which was adjacent to Calcasieu Parish, where Lake Charles was located. Uncle Man's two children, Lawrence (no one called him that; he was "Pick" to everyone, another family nickname I never understood) and Bernice, shared his one-fourth interest. Pick worked as a heavy equipment operator and lived in the area. Bernice, who was born the day after my mother and was my godmother, lived with her husband in Orange, Texas, just across the Sabine River from Louisiana. My grandmother and my mother owned my grandfather's one-fourth interest. Of course, they both lived in town. My cousin Billy had inherited his mother Rose's one-fourth interest. He lived on his farm near LeBleu Settlement, just inside the parish line.

None of the Heyds was very talkative. They were mostly farmers who knew from experience that work, not talk, was what brought the crop in. They also knew from experience that Billy always did his homework. Thus, when he told them about the extensive contamination on Grandpa Heyd's land, the way Shell had used the land for improper salt water disposal, and how Shell was still operating its oil blending plant on our land even after its lease had expired, they didn't question whether he knew what he was talking about.

Like any lawyer who has practiced for very long, I've had difficult clients from time to time. Some folks just don't like to be told what they don't want to hear. If I sense that a client is ignoring my advice, I like to explain that I'm not a cheerleader. If that's what they want, I recommend that they fire me and hire a cheerleader, because cheerleaders are cheaper. My job, I tell them, is to offer independent, objective advice about their problems. Of course, sometimes that's the last thing people want to hear. Other times, clients don't intentionally ignore their lawyer's advice; they just don't listen well. (In fact, that's often how they got into trouble in the first place.) Perhaps that's the reason I've been told more than once over the years that a lawyer should never represent his family. Family doesn't treat you as their lawyer, but as their brother, son, cousin, nephew, or whatever relation you happen to be. There's no professional distance.

But with my family, there was a level of trust and confidence throughout our case against Shell that was, if anything, even stronger than with other clients. It started with Billy. He's always been very thorough, meticulous even, and he thinks things through. Once he was convinced that I took care of things the same way, we clicked as a team. Throughout our saga with Shell, we never really disagreed on anything. It was the same way with the rest of the family. Even as we spent several hundred thousand dollars of their money documenting the contamination on the property, none of them complained or even questioned me about whether the expense was worth it. Each paid his or her share every step of the way.

I have no doubt that was a large part of the reason we were able to give the case our best shot.

7

There's an old saying about the wheels of justice grinding slowly. Most cases take over a year, sometimes two or three, to get to trial, because that's how long it takes for both sides to complete their discovery. Based on that, I figured at the outset that it would take at least a couple of years for us to get the Shell case ready for trial. It ended up taking a lot longer—nearly eight years after filing suit, to be exact. The lengthy delay in getting the case to trial was due to a number of things.

First, the case against Shell had a lot more moving parts than anything I had ever handled before. We had a large number of different potential claims to assert on behalf of the family—everything from possible unpaid royalties to salt water disposal to contamination to trespass. For the longest time, I didn't do a very good job of sorting them out. The different issues seemed to run together in my mind. Moreover, we had a number of contracts between Shell and the Heyd family, starting with the 1929 mineral lease and progressing through several surface leases over the years, with the 1961 lease being the final one. The complexity of it all made it too easy at times to put the case aside and tend to other, more pressing matters.

Other things slowed us down as well. A.J. Planchard, the judge to whom the case was assigned, was even more unfamiliar with oil and gas matters than I was. He was a dear man, and he had been a close friend (and law school classmate) of my father's, but he had never before handled a case like this, either as a lawyer or a judge.

In simple cases involving automobile accidents, the evidence consists mostly of eyewitness accounts about who ran the red light. Discovery in these cases is simple: You get a list of the witnesses from the police report of the accident, take their depositions, and go try the case.

In our case against Shell, however, we had to investigate business activities that spanned over fifty years. Many of the individuals who had worked on the Heyd property for Shell were deceased or retired. Those who were still around couldn't be expected to remember much in the way of details about things that had happened half a lifetime earlier. Besides that, while a car wreck is a dramatic event that everyone remembers, there was nothing particularly memorable to Shell field hands about many of the activities in question.

If we were going to get to the truth about what happened all those years, it would have to come from whatever records Shell had kept. Given that Shell was a sophisticated major oil company, we naturally expected it to have documented its activities on the property, if for no other reason than to track its revenues and costs. But every time we asked for these kinds of documents, Blazek and his cronies would shrug and say they either never existed or had long since been destroyed.

We had the same problem getting Shell to identify anyone who had ever worked on the Heyd property and might still be around to tell us about it. When we asked for the names of individuals whom we might depose, Shell's lawyers would again give us that increasingly familiar apologetic look and explain that, since Shell had sold the mineral lease in 1985, there just wasn't anyone around anymore who knew anything about its operations back then.

The legal remedy for this kind of discovery "stonewalling" is a motion to compel the other side to produce the information or face sanctions. Just the threat of these motions is usually a deterrent to bad behavior, because no litigant wants to be dragged before a judge and exposed as uncooperative or hiding evidence. But the threat only works if the other side thinks it's real.

When we finally realized that we were never going to get any help from Shell's lawyers, we filed a motion to bring the issue to a head. The idea was to get Judge Planchard to order Shell to give us the information we sought and to threaten it with sanctions if it failed to cooperate in exchanging information in the future.

In retrospect, I have to give Shell's lawyers credit for doing their homework. They had apparently discovered that the judge had little experience with this kind of case. Instead of fearing his reprisals for not being cooperative, they took advantage of his unfamiliarity with the technical aspects of oil and gas production to offer confusing and complicated arguments about why the records didn't exist, couldn't be found, or had nothing to do with the case.

Judge Planchard did not see through Shell's maze of explanations for holding out on us. Since he wasn't certain that Blazek and his colleagues were lying, his answer to the problem was to direct the lawyers to go out in the hall and try work things out. Of course, once Shell's lawyers realized that the judge wasn't going to crack the whip on them for failing to allow discovery, they had little incentive to agree to produce anything on a voluntary basis. Instead, they continued "stonewalling" us without fear of repercussions. This effectively stalled the case. Without the information we needed, there was no way to understand fully what Shell had done on the Heyd property all those years. This was 1995, the case was more than two years old, and Shell appeared to have won.

We did have one hope: Judge Planchard was nearing retirement. In less than two years, a successor would be elected and installed. Perhaps, we thought, a new judge would see things differently. Until then, we would be forced to nibble around the edges of the case, turning over the few loose stones we could find on our own.

It was worth the wait. In 1997, a local assistant district attorney named Patricia Head Minaldi was elected as to succeed Judge Planchard. Our new judge was originally from Connecticut, but had come to Louisiana in the early 1980s to attend Tulane Law School. Upon graduation, she remained in

New Orleans to serve as an assistant DA in the office of Harry Connick, Sr., the district attorney for Orleans Parish (and the father of the famous singer/musician). After just a few years, the young prosecutor moved to Lake Charles to join the staff of Richard Ieyoub, the district attorney for Calcasieu Parish. Patty Head, as she was then known, quickly earned a reputation as a hard-driving felony prosecutor, first under Ieyoub and then, after Ieyoub's election as attorney general of Louisiana, his successor Rick Bryant.

Along the way, she met and married Thad Minaldi, a Lake Charles lawyer who was general counsel for Burton Industries, Inc., a business headquartered in the area and owned and operated by descendants of W.T. Burton. Burton was a former tugboat pilot who acquired vast holdings in oil and gas in the early part of the twentieth century on his way to becoming one of the richest men in the state. (Perhaps not coincidentally, he was also a close friend and confidante of Huey Long, who was governor of Louisiana at the time.)

Thad Minaldi was born and raised in Lake Charles and was well liked by everyone. An All-State football player in high school, he had gone on to play fullback and linebacker for the LSU Tigers, where one of his teammates was another area native named Jack Lawton, Jr. Lawton's family had inherited Burton Industries when W.T. Burton died. After graduation from law school and a brief stint in a local law firm, Thad reunited with his old friend to become the general counsel for the family business.

Thad Minaldi's popularity and his close relationship with the Lawton family did nothing to hurt his wife's chances of being elected to the state bench. In fact, it's doubtful that the young prosecutor would have even considered running for elective office if not for her husband's local roots. At the very least, her husband's relationship with the Lawtons certainly made it much easier to finance her campaign for the bench. Beyond that, the Lawton family's connections no doubt opened doors in southwest Louisiana that otherwise would have been closed to a relative outsider from Connecticut.

I didn't know our new judge well, mainly because we had worked in different areas of the law and had no cases together. The only time our paths had really crossed was when she briefly joined a group of us who jogged out of the downtown YMCA during the lunch hour. Patty Minaldi's commitment to fitness was a reflection of the pride she took in her entire appearance. She always wore well-tailored clothes, with dressy high-heeled shoes that matched the colors of the business suits that were her uniform as a prosecutor. As part of her no-nonsense look, the new judge also kept her hair cut short in a spiked style that some women would regard as severe but most men would find appealing.

While I didn't know much about Patty's work as an assistant DA, what little I did know I liked. For one thing, I knew that she tended to be committed and emphatic about her court cases. Thus, after she was elected, I hoped this would make her a decisive judge who would move our case forward.

Our only real misgiving about the new judge was that she had been a career criminal prosecutor. In practical terms, this meant that she had little, if any, experience with the discovery process that was so critical to civil cases. For instance, Judge Minaldi had never participated in a deposition. Moreover, as a prosecutor, she began each case with all the information she needed, because the police had given it to her. Unlike civil litigants, she usually had no need to obtain information from the other side.

For these reasons, the new judge would not be familiar with the games Shell's lawyers were playing to frustrate our search for information important to our case. In particular, I doubted that Judge Minaldi would appreciate the ways in which lawyers played "hide the ball" from their opponents in answering discovery requests or the subtle (and improper) ways in which lawyers coached witnesses with speaking objections during depositions or used breaks to tell them how to answer hard questions.

Still, the old saying that a "new broom sweeps clean" offered us the hope that Judge Minaldi would bring new energy to the case and move it forward toward trial. That's when I decided it was time to retain an expert who could help us understand the information we were gathering and separate the wheat from the chaff in our case.

While handling a case for Amoco, I had met a contract employee at the company's Houston offices named John Coalson. Coalson was a burly, affable guy about my age who had been hired to audit records pertaining to "outside-operated" properties, meaning oil and gas wells operated by someone else but in which Amoco owned an interest. During the course of one of his audits, Coalson had discovered that another company had failed to reassign several leases in a profitable gas field to Amoco in violation of their contracts. This led to a lawsuit for breach of contract, and John naturally became an important source of information for us as we proceeded with the case.

I met with John on several occasions during the Amoco lawsuit and grew to like him. He seemed very honest and sincere. Like me, he had a law degree, although he had spent his career as a land man rather than as a practicing lawyer. He was also a golfer, and we even played golf together once while he was in town to work with us on the case.

John had mentioned to me more than once that he was a temporary contract employee and was interested in working on any additional projects we might have. It seemed logical to ask him if he wanted to assist us with the case against Shell. After I explained the "bare bones" of the case to him, he said he could help us. We quickly struck a deal for him to consult with us.

We then met with John several times on the Shell case, and with his help I began to understand how Shell had used our salt water disposal system to get rid of salt water from other operators' wells (in violation of the surface lease) for next to nothing in return for the operator sending all of its gas to a plant that Shell operated nearby. That's where Shell made its money: It kept the valuable gas liquids that it stripped from the gas as a processing fee. It was able to make this profit by using our land to dispose of its customers' salt water. And, of course, Shell kept this profit to itself, never paying the Heyds anything for its unlawful use of their property.

Then, suddenly, Coalson stopped talking to us. His contract with Amoco had ended, and he had hired a lawyer in Houston to sue the company over his termination. The lawyer apparently told him not to talk with us about our case against Shell. I spoke with the guy several times on the phone, and it became clear that he was trying to barter Coalson's assistance in our case against Shell in return for our intervention on his behalf with Amoco.

I was insulted by that. I had not been retained by Amoco to defend Coalson's case and wasn't involved in it at all.

"It's unethical as hell that a lawyer would try to sell his client's testimony," I told him.

That's when the guy really went over the edge. Coalson had already been deposed in the case we were handling for Amoco about his role in discovering how the other side had failed to reassign certain leases. Coalson's lawyer took it upon himself to contact the lawyers for IMC and Mallinckrodt, the defendants in the Amoco case, and suggest that, if they would depose Coalson again, his testimony might be much more favorable to them this time. Of course, they immediately called me about re-deposing Coalson and, in the course of asking for a "second bite at the apple," explained why they wanted to do so.

Essentially, Coalson's lawyer was suggesting either that his client had lied in his original deposition and would now recant that sworn testimony or that his client was *now* prepared to change his previously truthful testimony by lying. Either way, the guy was setting Coalson up for perjury charges. He apparently hoped that this threat would somehow force Amoco to give him a big settlement on the wrongful termination claims. The really remarkable thing was that, when I called the guy, he admitted as much.

Fortunately, Judge Don Aaron, who was handling the Amoco case, refused to allow the other side to take another deposition of John Coalson. Unfortunately, that didn't solve our problem in the Shell case. We were obviously through with Coalson and would have to drop him from the case. I felt badly about it. Not only were we out an expert witness, but John's lawyer had effectively deprived him of what would have been a handsome paycheck over the next several years.

I never spoke with John Coalson again.

I had some anxious moments at that point. I had never been forced to replace an expert witness so deep into a case. How, I wondered, would we ever find someone willing and able to walk into the middle of this mess and make sense out of it?

After I floundered around for a bit, one of our friends at Amoco mentioned Bill Griffin, a petroleum engineer who was retiring from the company. We had worked with Bill on other Amoco matters and really liked him, so I gave him a call. It turned out that he was already familiar with the case. John Coalson had been pumping him for help in understanding the issues and had been regurgitating many of Bill's ideas to us as his own. Bill said he'd be happy to work with us on the case.

It was the best thing that could have happened.

8

Bill Griffin was born and raised in west Texas. Although he left there years ago, he still speaks with a good old boy drawl that immediately tells you he's not from New York. He's also built like a west Texas cowboy, with big, loping shoulders, a barrel chest, and a belly that screams, "I love beer!"

And he does. Bill Griffin can drink more beer than any man I know, including Billy Corbello. Believe me, that's high praise. He's also got the down-to-earth touch of someone who's more at ease with boots and belt buckles than coats and ties.

Bill matriculated, as they say, at Texas Tech in Lubbock, where he earned a degree in chemical engineering back in the early 1970s. After a couple of brief stints with smaller oil companies, he ended up at Amoco, where he spent more than twenty-seven years working as a petroleum engineer. Most of that time was spent in Houston, where he worked on a wide range of projects. That's where I met him. We worked together on another case I was handling for Amoco.

Bill had a lot of experience as a witness, but it was primarily from testifying before regulatory agencies in various states where Amoco had oil and gas interests. While that kind of experience is great in most respects, it does have a negative side: The testimony can get very technical. For that reason, Bill's experience with these proceedings didn't necessarily prepare him for courtroom testimony before a judge and jury who had no background in oil and gas matters.

It turned out, however, that Bill had great natural instincts for litigation. For one thing, he had a knack for understanding legal theories. (In fact, the joke was that we had to remind Bill on occasion to leave the lawyering to us.) He was also adept at playing the "what if" game, anticipating what the other side might do to challenge his testimony. It didn't take Bill long to begin making helpful suggestions about ways to improve our presentation of the case so that the jury could more easily understand our position. He also became invaluable in reviewing the reams of documents we had gathered.

Beyond that, Bill understood instinctively the importance of being prepared before taking the witness stand and identifying key records that supported our claims. He had great pride in his work, and he wasn't about to let any lawyer make him look foolish by surprising him on cross-examination with information that contradicted something he said. Thus, he did his homework religiously, arming himself with facts, figures, and evidence to support any opinion he formed in the case. Bill eventually went to the Heyd property more than fifty times, walking the entire 120 acres so often that he knew every inch of the place.

Bill made it clear early on that he intended to learn more about Shell's operations on the Heyd property than anyone on the other side of the case. He filled in gaps in our records by digging through files at the Louisiana Office of Conservation, where he became familiar with the production history of every oil well ever drilled on the Heyd land since 1929. In addition, he pulled monthly disposal reports going back to the 1950s that Shell had filed with the Office of Conservation so that he could also identify the source of every barrel of salt water ever injected into the disposal wells on the Heyd land. He reviewed the operation of Shell's gravity management plant and determined how much profit Shell was making by staying on the Heyd land and continuing to operate after the lease expired. He then investigated the gas processing plant that Shell operated next to the Heyd property and documented how Shell sent salt water from that plant into the Heyd disposal wells without permission. In order to confirm his figures, Bill visited other gas plants of similar size and scope and checked to make sure they produced similar amounts of salt water.

As he worked to teach us what he was finding, Bill became increasingly comfortable abandoning engineering language and discussing technical aspects of the case in plain English without distorting their meaning. I couldn't have been more pleased, because Bill's role in the case was vital. We needed someone the court would accept as an expert. In particular, we needed someone who could explain from the witness stand how the production from a well was separated into oil, gas, gas liquids, and salt water. We needed someone who could explain how the oil was marketed and how the gas and gas liquids were sent to a gas processing plant where they were separated and then sold. We needed someone who could explain to the jury how salt water, or brine, was a waste product that had to be disposed of in an economical and environmentally safe way, either by trucking it out or by injecting it back beneath the surface through a disposal well. Ideally, we needed one person who could lay all of this out for the jury in a clear and understandable way.

As a petroleum engineer, Bill had "been there and done that" for many years. He had spent his career helping produce oil and gas in the field. He knew all of the mechanics of oilfield production, and he knew its economics as well. And he could describe it in a way that any juror could understand.

As helpful as Bill was, I knew that we also needed more legal manpower on our side if we were going to compete against the onslaught that Adams & Reese was mustering against us. I turned first to Richard Gerard, my immediate senior partner. Richard had a wealth of experience with oil and gas matters as well as litigation in general. Because of that, I had gone to Richard early in the case to get him to help me with the technical aspects of oilfield production. Over time, I began to seek his help more and more as the case got bigger and more complicated.

Richard was the most congenial lawyer in the firm. In fact, his unflappable demeanor had earned him the office nickname "Smooth." Moreover, his laid-back personality offered a nice contrast to mine, which was sometimes fiery and often impatient. Richard's paralegal, Bridget John, would be a valuable addition to our team as well. Bridget was extremely well organized (actually, well-regimented might be a more accurate way to describe the level of intensity she brought to her work). She would help us manage all the documents that we would be gathering from the defendants.

I envisioned Richard taking the lead role in the litigation as we steered the case to trial.

"Representing my own family is awkward," I told Richard. "If things don't go to everyone's satisfaction, it could make for some tense holiday gatherings in the years to come."

Besides that, I worried a bit about whether I could remain objective, since my mother had such an important stake in things.

Richard graciously agreed to serve as the steward of our team. He and Bridget led our effort to obtain records from Shell and the other defendants so that we could better understand what went on in the field for so many years. They went on more than one wild goose chase trying to find records that they knew existed but that each defendant initially claimed were in someone else's custody. But they stayed on the trail and eventually located twenty or so boxes of records in a warehouse in Houston that contained what would become some of our most important trial exhibits.

Despite Richard's efforts, Billy was never comfortable with anyone besides me handling the case. He had, over time, become increasingly frustrated by the delays in the case as we waited for a new judge to be elected, and he felt that part of the problem was that Richard wasn't as aggressive as I was. While I was very happy with Richard's laid-back style (he had nearly thirty years of trial experience), Billy wasn't, and nothing I said persuaded him otherwise. I guess that, deep down inside, he believed that only a family member could pursue the case with the passion he felt it needed.

For these reasons, it really didn't surprise me when Billy came to me and asked me to take back the lead role in the case. Since Billy was clearly the individual most responsible for helping us discover the problems that the litigation was intended to correct, I didn't see how I could turn him down. What if I said no and things didn't turn out well? The family would feel that I had abandoned them. Besides, Richard would still be available to help.

Still, we needed more firepower, so I asked one of my younger partners, Patrick Gallaugher, to be my second chair on the case. Pat and I had often worked together in the past, and we were handling a number of pending cases together at the moment as well.

Pat and I were a good team. First, we were polar opposites (and therefore an effective counterbalance) of each other when it came to litigation. Pat was a worrier whose glass was always half-empty. Give Pat a set of facts, and he would see an unlimited number of arguments favoring the other side. Fortunately, the other side rarely had counsel as talented as he was, and so they didn't see what he saw. As for me, where Pat saw disaster lurking, I saw opportunity. Even if my glass was empty, I was damned glad to have the glass. Besides, I figured, I could always fill it up with something later. Where Pat worried, I brimmed with confidence. He summed it up well one day when, after I continued to be rosy about a situation he thought was bleak, he laughed and said, "If I ever have cancer, Mike, I want you to give me the news."

Regardless of his worrisome nature, I knew that Pat Gallaugher had a world of talent. We had known each other since high school. While I had gone directly to law school after college, Pat had taken a different route. After graduation from college, he went through a variety of jobs, including a stint as a reporter for our local newspaper, the *Lake Charles American Press*. Pat also found time somewhere along the way to obtain a master's degree in philosophy, which satisfied his intellectual curiosity about the meaning of life but gained him zero additional earning power. (As he pointed out, there just weren't enough people who required the services of a philosopher on a regular basis.) He finally decided to go to law school in his early thirties and enrolled at Tulane Law School, where he immediately found success by making the law review after his first year. Upon graduation, he returned to Lake Charles and joined our law firm.

I've often said that Pat was the one person you want to sit next to at dinner, because he could converse knowledgeably about virtually any subject.

While we both played in garage bands in high school, Pat continued to play music in local clubs for many years thereafter. He still owned several guitars, including a twelve-string Rickenbacker like the one used by his all-time favorite band, the Byrds. If need be, Pat could wax eloquent about virtually any musical genre since the 1960s.

As you might expect for someone with a graduate degree in philosophy, Pat could also speak intelligently about any philosopher from Plato to Kierkegaard—that is, if he could find someone willing to listen. Beyond that, Pat was a voracious reader and was particularly a fan of satirical writing. He could quote the works of H. L. Mencken, P. J. O'Rourke, and Woody Allen with equal aplomb. Top it all off with a mean Rodney Dangerfield impersonation, and you were sure to be thoroughly entertained at dinner regardless of whether the food was good or bad.

In Pat Gallaugher, I had a younger partner who was complicated, bright, pessimistic, and accomplished. It was a combination that made him a perfect addition to our litigation team.

The next—and perhaps most critical—member to join our team was Austin Arabie, who became our environmental expert. Austin owned his own consulting firm in Lake Charles called Arabie Environmental Solutions. After receiving a graduate degree in environmental science from McNeese State University, he began his career working for the Louisiana Department of Environmental Quality. After several years, he went to work in the private sector. Before long, he saw an opportunity to build a business providing remediation, or cleanup, services to industry and governmental agencies. That's when he started his own company. In a relatively short time, he had earned an enviable reputation as pragmatic, reliable, and honest, and he had an impressive list of clients within the local petrochemical industry.

Austin's scope of work in our case was to identify any and all contamination on the property that was attributable to oilfield operations, and then devise a program for cleaning it up as required by the 1961 surface lease. Since Shell had refused to clean up the property, our clients would ultimately bear the expense of this program. For that reason, Austin would also be asked to calculate how much his cleanup plan would cost, because that was the amount of damages we would seek from the jury.

I briefly wondered if Austin would be reluctant to become involved on the landowners' side of a contamination case for fear of offending his industry-side clients. I soon realized, however, that he approached his work with the simple conviction that, if he stuck with good science, his results would be the truth no matter which side he was on.

In terms of temperament, Austin couldn't have been more different than our other expert, Bill Griffin. Austin was very quiet by nature. He never answered questions quickly. Instead, he carefully chose his words to make certain they were accurate. In contrast, Bill liked floating trial balloons during brainstorming sessions and wasn't offended if they were shot down. He said testing ideas in that fashion was the best way to arrive at the truth. But, considerations of style aside, Austin and Bill had much in common: They knew what they were talking about, were very thorough in what they did, and communicated well.

In another stroke of good fortune, Tammy Garbarino came to work for me around this time. She was a paralegal with great experience and ability, having worked for more than fourteen years at another firm in town. Her reputation was such that there was hardly a lawyer in southwest Louisiana who hadn't heard of her. She had better litigation instincts than most lawyers and the ability to outwork them as well.

Tammy's timing couldn't have been better. She arrived at the firm in 1999, just as we were beginning to prepare the Shell case for trial. It didn't take long for us to realize that Tammy's reputation was well deserved. In particular, I was impressed by two things. First, Tammy never forgot a piece of paper once she read it. If she saw something in another document weeks later that was related in any way (particularly if it was contradictory or inconsistent), she could go back and find the earlier document in seconds and compare the two. Second, she had insights that one would only expect from an experienced (and very talented) trial lawyer. She knew how to read between the lines of documents to find the real story they told. She also knew how to put evidence together that contradicted the testimony of opposing witnesses and destroyed their credibility. When she came on board, our side of the case starting moving even more quickly.

Our team was complete.

9

One thing every trial lawyer learns early on is that cases rarely settle without a trial date. The reason, obviously, is that a defendant is not going to pay money to settle a case until it has to. Until our case had a trial date, there would be no real urgency on Shell's part to settle the case.

The closest we ever came to working things out in our case against Shell was back in 1995. After some haggling back and forth, Shell offered us $300,000 to settle all of our claims. It was the only firm offer we received over a nine-year period. My grandmother, who was still living at the time, was very excited, because her share of the settlement would be one-fourth, or about $75,000.

For reasons that neither Jim Blazek nor Howard Smith ever disclosed, Shell backed out at the last minute. After that, Shell began playing hardball and didn't raise the subject of settlement again. If we expected Shell ever to get serious again about resolving the case, we needed a trial date.

In state court, a case is not placed on the trial docket until a party (almost always the plaintiff) requests it. We hadn't requested that our case be fixed for trial because we hadn't been able to complete discovery. After Judge Minaldi took over the case when she took office in 1997, we renewed our efforts to discover information that would support our claims against Shell, and Shell's lawyers continued to do their best to frustrate our efforts to learn what went on out at the Heyds' land.

In 1998, we sent interrogatories asking Shell to provide the names and addresses of those employees who had worked on the property. Given that Shell had operated a mineral lease on the Heyds' land from 1929 to 1985 and thereafter operated the surface lease on the land until 1991, we naturally expected a long list of individuals whom we could then depose. Jim Blazek responded by giving us one name: Thomas "Buster" Brashear.

When we pressed him for more information, he shrugged and said that Shell couldn't locate any more names. He said that everyone had retired or left the company and there was no way to locate them. However, when we took Mr. Brashear's deposition, he regurgitated name after name of his fellow coworkers from the Heyd lease and even told us where most of them lived. It turned out that these guys all belonged to a Shell retirees' club that met once a month at a local cafeteria.

It then dawned on us that Shell had had their names and addresses all along, because it was mailing each of them a monthly pension check. Shell's failure to provide this information when directly asked was a serious breach of its duty to respond honestly to any discovery request. Jim Blazek was sitting right next to Brashear as he gave this testimony. I found it hard to believe that he hadn't known about it all along.

We then filed a motion to compel Shell to review its records again and provide names and addresses of any employee who had worked on the property. On the day of the hearing on our motion, Judge Minaldi met with us in her chambers. She looked at Blazek skeptically and asked him directly why he couldn't supplement his earlier answer and provide us with additional names and addresses.

"There are too many people who worked at Shell over the years for Shell to name them all," he told the judge with a straight face.

Apparently, his position was that, if there were too many to name them all, he should only have to name one. I nearly laughed out loud. Shell had gone from saying it didn't have any names but one to saying it had too many names to list.

A lot of judges would have held Shell in contempt for such a transparent refusal to comply with discovery. Judge Minaldi didn't go that far, but she at least ordered Shell to give us all of the names and addresses it could find. It eventually did, and the information led us to find some of the most important witnesses in the case.

In the hall outside the courtroom where we entered the judge's order on the record, I lost my cool with Blazek. Getting directly in his face I said, "I don't trust you," adding that this latest episode was proof positive that he wasn't being truthful about what Shell knew. I found it difficult to believe that no one had bothered to ask Brashear about other Shell employees who worked at the Heyd property with him. It seemed clear to me that they *had* asked and then deliberately withheld the information. "Put everything in writing to me from now on," I told him. "Your word is no longer any good to me." I must have said more, because I remember Blazek asking me not to call him names.

Once we got the list of additional witnesses and deposed them, we were able to request a trial date, and in early 1999 we finally received notice from Judge Minaldi's office that our case would be set for trial in November of that year. As usually happens, that prompted a flurry of activity on both sides. We wanted to make sure we had gathered all of the information we needed and had deposed all of Shell's likely trial witnesses. On Shell's side, the preparation was even more fundamental: It changed lawyers. While the company didn't fire Blazek and his firm, it added Tom McNamara and Pat Gray, who were with the Lafayette law firm of Liskow & Lewis.

There was some irony there. Liskow & Lewis had originated in Lake Charles. In fact, Cullen Liskow, one of the founding partners, had first practiced with our firm back in the 1930s before striking out on his own to form a partnership with another local product, Austin Lewis. The two men quickly forged a reputation as the foremost oil and gas lawyers in the state. A third lawyer soon followed. His name was Richard E. (Dick)

Gerard, Sr.—not coincidentally the father of one of my partners, Richard E. Gerard, Jr. When they were joined by Arthur Shepard, the fledgling firm became known as Liskow, Lewis, Gerard & Shepard. As it continued to add lawyers, the firm's name reverted to Liskow & Lewis.

While Cullen Liskow and Austin Lewis were the early stars of the firm, it didn't take Dick Gerard long to catch up. A tough-as-nails World War II veteran who had participated in D-Day, Dick Gerard was blessed with a sharp mind that matched his two senior partners.

Louisiana property law is based on European civil law concepts that are very different from the Anglo-American common law of property. Because Louisiana was one of the first states to develop an oil and gas industry, Dick Gerard and his partners were responsible for many early landmark decisions by the Louisiana courts that skillfully applied these property concepts to oil and gas production. This body of law was eventually codified into the Louisiana Mineral Code, which has since served as a model for the oil and gas laws of other states. If you talk to old-timers in the Louisiana oil and gas industry, they'll tell you that much of that legal handiwork can be traced to Dick Gerard.

In the late 1960s, much of the oil and gas business in Lake Charles moved 70 miles east to its sister city of Lafayette, Louisiana, which had actively courted oil companies and the businesses that served them. Lafayette's business leaders had put together a business district called the Oil Center, where various companies associated with the energy industry located their headquarters, and literally stole the oil business out from under Lake Charles's nose. Liskow & Lewis moved from Lake Charles to Lafayette to follow its clients. The firm also opened an office in New Orleans.

Only one lawyer in the firm refused to move: Dick Gerard. He informed his partners that he would quit (or retire) if they insisted that he move. The members of the firm wisely told Dick that he could stay in Lake Charles if that's what he wanted. And, of course, that's exactly what he did. When Cullen Liskow and Austin Lewis died in the 1970s, the firm's leaders approached Dick and again asked him to leave Lake Charles and move to Lafayette to head the firm. He again rejected their overtures. They even named their main conference room in their New Orleans office (at One

Shell Square) the Richard E. Gerard, Sr., Conference Room. He was not impressed enough to reconsider.

It was my privilege to know Dick Gerard. As the father of Richard, my law partner, he was a familiar face around our law firm. He no doubt forgot more oil and gas law than I'll ever learn, but he was down-to-earth, friendly, and courteous to everyone he met. In the short time I knew him (he passed away in the early 1990s), I understood why everyone at the Liskow firm held him in such high esteem.

Tom McNamara and Pat Gray were partners in the Lafayette office of Liskow & Lewis. They were both approximately my age, having graduated from LSU Law School around the same time I came out of Tulane Law School. I later learned that Shell had hired the two of them because they had teamed together successfully to defend a similar case in federal court in Lafayette just a year before, winning a verdict in the company's favor that denied the landowner plaintiff any recovery on claims that were much like the ones we were asserting in our case.

I already knew Pat Gray. He and I had been on the same side in a couple of cases over the years. In fact, he had just a few months earlier referred a client to me in a complicated case involving regulated gas tariffs. At the outset at least, I had a "warm and fuzzy" feeling for Pat.

McNamara and Gray were, in appearance at least, a "Mutt and Jeff" combination. McNamara was a squat Irishman with the freckled complexion of his forebears from the Emerald Isle. He had a quick wit, which he used to disarm his opponents.

"Check your wallet whenever Tom tells you a joke," I told Pat Gallaugher, "to make sure he's not picking your pocket at the same time."

Pat Gray was a tall, dark-complected Cajun from Morgan City who was clearly proud of his good looks. He, too, liked to joke, but it seemed that his humor always had a sarcastic edge or was at someone else's expense. As I later learned, he was also very quick to anger when things didn't go his way.

The two lawyers from Liskow & Lewis formally enrolled in our case in mid-1999, just three months or so before the November trial date. One of their first formal actions was a motion to continue the trial. Of course, we protested vigorously. This was an old case, having been filed in 1992. We didn't want any further delays. In the end, however, Judge Minaldi was uncomfortable forcing lawyers who were new to the case to go to trial on short notice, so she granted their motion and upset the trial fixing. At the same time, she set a new trial date for May 1, 2000. Thus, while things were put off, the delay was only for six months.

It was a hectic six months.

Gray and McNamara were racing to put together a roster of experts who could testify on Shell's behalf at trial. They borrowed the experts who had earlier been retained by the Kreuger and Rosewood interests and, in addition, hired some of their own. When we eventually settled with Kreuger and Rosewood, Shell had redundant experts. It was like Noah's Ark: They had at least two of everything. To testify about cleanup, they had Lloyd Deuel (the Texas A&M professor), Don Sagrera (a farm expert), Mike Pisani (an environmental consultant), and Calvin Barnhill (a petroleum engineer and experienced oilfield operator). To testify about gas plant operations, they had Dick Jones (an experienced gas plant operator) and John Berghammer (a gas marketing expert). In all, McNamara and Gray identified a total of eleven experts for the case, claiming that they needed them all in order to defend Shell against our claims.

The law in civil cases does not allow a party to cumulate evidence by calling redundant or repetitive expert witnesses. Simply put, the law says that witnesses are weighed, not counted, and neither side is allowed to trot out witnesses who give the same testimony over and over, just so they can argue that more experts supported their side than their opponent's. Otherwise, trials would last forever, with each side trying to outlast the other by calling the greater number of witnesses on any given issue.

In contrast to Shell, we had a grand total of five expert witnesses: Bill Griffin, Austin Arabie, Dan Cliffe (an economics expert who would convert our past losses from illegal salt water disposal to their present value), Benny Miller (a local contractor who estimated the cost of clearing the surface of overgrown brush), and Everett Dillman (an expert on punitive damages who would explain how the jury could equate everyday sums of money to a company that was Shell's size). Since we had the burden of proof, our short list of experts was a telling sign that Shell certainly didn't need its entire gallery of experts to defend our claims. For that reason, I fully expected Judge Minaldi to order Shell to pare down its list and name only one expert in each area of expected testimony.

This was important because it would cut down on the amount of time we spent preparing for trial. We needed to depose each expert that Shell listed, digest what we had learned, and then prepare to cross-examine each witness at trial. That was difficult enough under ordinary circumstances. Requiring us to depose several witnesses who covered the same subject matter raised the degree of difficulty and imposed a needless hardship on us. In fact, in many courts it was a matter of local rule that you couldn't list more than one expert in any particular area. Thus, I was confident that Judge Minaldi would force Shell to identify who would be its "cleanup" expert, who would be its economist, who would be its petroleum engineer, etc.

However, Judge Minaldi both surprised and disappointed us on this score. Being unfamiliar with civil cases, she didn't fully appreciate how much time and effort went into deposing an expert in a civil case. Forcing us to depose all of the experts Shell listed would take an enormous effort and—as Shell's lawyers no doubt intended—keep us busy when we needed that time to prepare our own case for trial. It also made it possible for Shell to ambush us at trial by holding back on which expert it would call to testify about each particular phase of the case. That was decidedly contrary to settled law, which prohibited trial by ambush or any other kind of "hide the ball" tactics.

In the end, the judge denied our pleas to force Shell to shuck its redundant expert witnesses. Still worse, she allowed Shell to wait until the last minute to produce its experts for depositions. I prevailed upon Richard Gerard to travel with me to Liskow & Lewis's offices in Lafayette for four consecutive days to depose all eleven experts, many of whom had not produced any reports or other evidence of their expected testimony beforehand.

I assume the point of this tactic was to deprive us of meaningful preparation for the depositions. I don't exactly fault Gray and McNamara for this ploy; lawyers are paid advocates for their client's side of the case. It was a smart strategic move to try to cram their experts down our throats. I'm not sure I would have thought of it, because I had never known a judge who would sanction that sort of thing. Nonetheless, the Liskow lawyers continually complained to Judge Minaldi that, being new to the case, they really didn't know exactly how they might use their experts and didn't want to be caught shorthanded. This whining eventually persuaded Minaldi that forcing us to depose all of their experts in such a short period of time was neither unfair nor prejudicial.

The German philosopher Friedrich Nietzsche once said, "That which doesn't kill you makes you stronger." In the end, despite enormous stress and sleepless nights, Richard and I pulled it off, deposing all of Shell's experts at Liskow's offices within the limited time that we were allowed. Not only that, but we did damned well in those depositions, too. As a result, we had transcripts of testimony that would be very useful in preparing cross-examinations of these witnesses at trial. Better still, we did so well with a number of Shell's experts that we effectively eliminated them as witnesses. Simply put, we got them to admit so much of the "good stuff" about our case that Shell's lawyers became reluctant to call them at trial for fear that their testimony would be more helpful to us than to their own client.

At the same time, we also had to finish deposing Shell's fact witnesses as well. That's when I really began to see Pat Gray's dark side. We were in Houston deposing Paul Lair, the former Shell land man. As we grilled Lair on Shell's failure to leave the property or clean it up, Gray became upset at the damning testimony we were getting from the witness. Finally, he let me have it, saying that he objected to my "trick questions." It was an interesting comment, because there was no such thing as objecting to a question because it was "tricky."

"I'm not paid to ask questions you like," I said to an agitated Gray.

In any event, as we continued to get damaging answers from Lair, Gray couldn't take it anymore. After I asked another question that I suppose he deemed "tricky," Gray stood up before Lair could answer and announced, "We're taking a break." With that, he literally grabbed Lair and took him out of the room. After a few minutes, they reappeared. Suddenly, Lair had pat answers to my questions that mimicked the party line.

I knew that most courts (especially federal courts) prohibited lawyers from discussing testimony with a witness during any break after he started testifying. The rule, in other words, was that you couldn't coach the witness once the game started. Obviously, Gray had coached Lair during the break. I then asked Lair about it, and he freely admitted that Gray had discussed his testimony with him during the break. I then lodged an objection on the record, explaining that we objected to any coaching of the witness based on the customary rule.

Gray exploded. Among other things, he said in a loud voice, "I don't believe you. You're making that up. There is no such rule."

I was taken aback, both at how quickly he erupted and how easily he lied. Anyone with his litigation experience had to know about the rule against coaching. It was inconceivable to me that Gray didn't fully understand the basis for my objection. I had just gotten an unpleasant glimpse at a lawyer's ugly side that I knew I wouldn't soon forget.

As the trial date approached, McNamara and Gray were deposing all of our witnesses at virtually the same time as we were deposing theirs. We were pleased at how the depositions of our expected trial witnesses turned out. Shell's lawyers were unable to shake any of our experts or expose any real weaknesses in their opinions. It became clear that, despite all of Shell's maneuvering, we were ahead in terms of readiness for trial.

It must have been just as clear to the lawyers at Liskow & Lewis, because they moved for another continuance. This time, though, Judge Minaldi was less sympathetic. She seemed to understand that Shell had had this case for nearly eight years at that point and that its decision to change lawyers shouldn't work to the detriment of the plaintiffs, who had waited long enough for this trial date. To our relief, Judge Minaldi decided that one continuance was enough and denied Shell's motion for another delay of the trial.

We weren't quite there yet, but we were getting close.

10

As we entered the last few weeks before trial, I was finally able to boil the case down to its essentials for presentation to the jury. Although much of what Shell did on my family's land violated the 1929 oil and gas lease, I had pretty much eliminated that as the basis of our claims and focused almost entirely on Shell's violations of the 1961 surface lease.

For one thing, the 1929 mineral lease was a needless complication that didn't add anything to our case. Simply put, the mineral lease didn't provide any legal remedies that we didn't already have in our favor under the 1961 surface lease. There was no point in confusing the jury by asking them to consider whether Shell's actions breached two different contracts, especially if it didn't benefit our clients.

Besides, we were better off under the surface lease, for several reasons.

First, it contained an explicit promise from Shell that, at the end of the lease, it would restore the property "as near as possible" to its earlier condition.

The mineral lease had no specific language about restoration, and some cases suggested that the duty to restore land imposed by a mineral lease didn't arise until the lease ended, when the oil company was obligated to return the land to the owner. Our lease was still producing, so it hadn't terminated yet. Shell could (and eventually did) argue that any cleanup claim under the mineral lease was therefore premature. They couldn't make that argument about the surface lease, which expired by its own terms on May 10, 1991.

Second, the 1961 surface lease limited Shell's salt water disposal rights only to wells operated by Shell in the Iowa Field. Despite this specific limitation, we discovered documents in which company officials deliberately took on salt water in violation of the contract—either from others who operated wells in the Iowa Field or from wells (both Shell's and others') that were not in the Iowa Field. The documents we had obtained showed that this was a calculated decision or, as Shell officials put it, "an acceptable business risk." (Obviously, if what you're doing is legal, there is no "risk" involved. The "risk" of doing something illegal is that you might get caught.) In any event, Shell's attitude about salt water disposal was directly contrary to the terms of the surface lease.

Third, the surface lease terminated Shell's rights to occupy our land on a fixed, set date of May 10, 1991. Yet they stayed on the property, operating their profitable gravity management facility, for an additional twenty-two months. This was a clear case of trespassing, and I thought it would motivate the jury to send Shell a message. ("Imagine, ladies and gentlemen, how Shell would react if a trespasser chose to occupy one of its chemical plants without permission for nearly two years.")

Fourth, the surface lease provided that we could recover, in addition to all other damages, our attorney fees and costs. The mineral lease contained no such provision. Absent a specific statute, Louisiana law did not allow the prevailing party in a lawsuit to recover his attorney fees unless the other party agreed to it in a contract. If we proceeded under the surface lease, we could obtain attorney fees. If we proceeded under the mineral lease, we could not.

I now knew that our case was simple: We were suing Shell for trespassing, for unlawful salt water disposal, and for refusing to cleanup our property. And we had them dead to rights on each count. Remarkably, however, Shell was still making no effort to settle the case. Since I was more accustomed to being on the defense side of litigation, it made me wonder if I was missing something.

A good trial lawyer must be a touch paranoid. He must never relax, no matter how good he thinks his case is. The worst thing that can happen to a lawyer is surprise, because he cannot prepare in advance for something he didn't anticipate. Looking at Shell's side of things as I normally would in defending cases, I couldn't understand why it wasn't making serious settlement overtures. More than once, I asked myself if I had missed some defense or secret evidence that Shell was waiting to spring on us. In the end, I decided I hadn't and that Shell was simply being shortsighted by not pursuing a settlement that would avoid the trial. Of course, I couldn't force them to make an offer, so I just kept my head down and continued working.

There was one rather interesting complication in my life at that time that could have been a distraction. My first novel, *The Greatest Player Who Never Lived,* was published in March of 2000, just two months before trial. It was (to me, at least) a completely unexpected success. My story of a heretofore unknown player in the 1930s who was befriended by golfing great Bobby Jones somehow struck a real chord within the sports-writing fraternity, who gave the book wonderfully generous reviews. Pulitzer Prize winner Dave Anderson of the *New York Times* devoted an entire Sunday column to the book, calling it "golf's literary rookie of the year." *USA Today* called me a "master of fiction." (The joke around the office was that opposing lawyers had been calling me that for years.) *T & L Golf Magazine* did a feature article on me entitled "The John Grisham of Golf."

As part of promoting the book, my publisher took me to Augusta in April for the Masters, where I was taken to the Butler Cabin and, at the annual golf writers' dinner, met many of my heroes (I'm referring to the writers, not the golfers). Still, I couldn't do everything he wanted me to do, because I was immersed in preparing for trial. It was difficult for my publisher to understand how, in the midst of all the hoopla over my book, I was too busy to give interviews. He was especially put out when I turned down an invitation to appear on the Golf Channel because the date fell during the trial.

We soon learned that Shell's failure to make a settlement offer wasn't due to any eagerness on its part to try the case. Remarkably, its lawyers again moved to continue the trial, even after Judge Minaldi had rejected their last attempt at delay. This time, Shell claimed that it was simply unable to be prepared to start the trial as scheduled on May 1. Reciting what had been Jim Blazek's mantra, Pat Gray moaned over and over that he just didn't understand our case and needed additional time to prepare. He said that depositions had only recently been concluded and that our experts had testified to damages of nearly $50 million. No party, he argued, should be forced into trial without being fully prepared when the stakes were so high.

Leaving aside that the late depositions were largely Shell's own doing, it was a persuasive argument. Judge Minaldi became concerned that she was, indeed, forcing Shell prematurely into a very serious trial. At the same time, she seemed intent on holding the case to its schedule. Instead of granting an outright continuance and moving the case to a future jury trial docket (which would have caused a delay of at least six months), she gave Shell's lawyers an additional two weeks to prepare, moving the trial from May 1 to May 15. By acting as she did, the judge was able to keep the same jury pool, informing them to report two weeks later than originally scheduled. She also made it clear that trial would begin on May 15 and that no further delays would be tolerated.

That finally got Shell's attention. A few days later, Tom McNamara called me and asked if we were willing to discuss settlement with the assistance of a mediator. A mediator is someone who is trained as a "go-between" to preside over settlement discussions and try to cajole each side into meeting the other in the middle. In essence, the parties get together at a given place and time and, after opening statements, break off into separate rooms and communicate with one another through the mediator, who goes back and forth between the parties in the lawyers' version of shuttle diplomacy. Needless to say, mediation is very popular with judges because it disposes of cases that they would otherwise have to decide.

I agreed to McNamara's proposal, and we settled on meeting at our office on the Thursday before trial. We also agreed to use a local lawyer named Allen Smith as the mediator. It was a good choice. I had known and admired Allen for many years. He was a senior partner in a prominent local law firm and a veteran—and very accomplished—trial lawyer. In addition, he was trained as a petroleum engineer and had worked briefly as one before law school. He had spent over thirty years trying cases, and he knew how a jury would react to a given set of facts. I was confident that Allen would understand the value of our case and communicate it in a meaningful way to Shell's representatives.

When I told Billy about the mediation, he reacted in a lukewarm way. He had long ago decided that he wanted a shot at Shell in the courtroom, win or lose. The idea of coming this far and then shaking hands and settling the case turned him off. He wanted nothing short of victory over Shell. In his mind, we couldn't win the case if we settled. What worried him, though, was that the rest of the family didn't necessarily share his resolve and might want to take whatever money was offered in settlement. Still, he agreed to attend the mediation with me.

I did impose one condition on Shell, however.

"Don't come to the mediation without authority to sign for eight figures," I told Tom McNamara. "Otherwise, we're wasting our time." He agreed.

Given our history with Shell, it shouldn't have surprised me when McNamara brought an in-house Shell lawyer named Charles Raymond with him to inform me that he was authorized to settle the case for a total of $1 million. Of course, that was nowhere close to eight figures. Allen Smith did his best, but Shell wouldn't budge. After haggling for a couple of hours, that remained Shell's best offer to end the case.

I was angry at still another Shell deception, but Billy was strangely pleased. As he put it, "Well, they made it easy." What he meant was that Shell hadn't come with enough money to tempt us into settling. We believed our case was worth well more than $1 million, so Raymond's offer was easy to reject.

The curious thing was that, when I turned down the offer and terminated the mediation, Raymond acted almost offended. As he left, he turned to me and said, "We'll see you in court on Monday." He made it sound like a threat of some kind.

I laughed to myself. I had learned a long time ago that there were only two kinds of lawyers: Those who were afraid to go to trial—and those who made the other side afraid to go to trial. I had no trouble figuring out which group Charles Raymond belonged to. Come Monday, he would be sitting in the very back of the courtroom at trial, as far away from the action as he could get. It was easy for him to stick his chest out. As I watched Raymond strut to his car, I said softly, "Bubba, that's what I do."

The day of reckoning was finally at hand.

11

There is nothing like the electricity of the opening morning of a trial, when the parties, their lawyers, the judge, court personnel, and prospective jurors convene in the courtroom together for the first time. There's a palpable tension in the air, because no one—not even the lawyers—knows exactly what's going to happen.

The litigants are especially wary of what lies ahead. The fact that they're about to go to trial means that they have failed to find a common ground for settling their differences. Inevitably, as each side realizes that its fate will now be decided by twelve strangers, there is no small amount of second-guessing about the wisdom of rejecting the other side's last settlement offer.

Even the judge is a bit nervous as he or she makes a last-minute study of the case file and ponders what unexpected challenges the lawyers might present that morning. No one likes to appear stupid, but smart judges understand that there is no way to anticipate every legal maneuver, motion, or issue that might come their way. As a result, they learn to be comfortable in uncharted waters and are never afraid to admit they don't know the answer to every legal problem that lawyers dump in their laps.

Although I've never been a juror, I have to assume that, of all the folks who are gathered there, they are the most apprehensive about the coming trial. Unless they have served on a jury before, they have no idea what to expect and have to wonder how they will manage to make the right decision, if called upon, about something they know nothing about.

To be sure, we knew more about the prospective jurors summoned to the Calcasieu Parish Courthouse on that muggy morning of May 15, 2000 than they knew about us. As was customary, both sides had been furnished a list of the individuals who had been randomly selected from the parish voter registration lists for possible jury duty in our case. Our office had then researched courthouse records to determine whether any of these people had prior criminal records or had been involved in lawsuits of any kind. We also circulated the list throughout the office so that everyone could give comments about any person they knew. Finally, the prospective jurors filled out a questionnaire at the courthouse when they first arrived that morning, giving background information about their education, occupation, and families. This information was furnished to the lawyers to assist them in jury selection. When we put all of this together, we had a profile of every prospective juror.

Our initial impression was that this jury panel (or venire, as it's called) was a mixed bag. There were numerous prospective jurors whom we believed would be unfavorable to our position, but there was an equal number whom we felt would be favorably disposed to our side of the case.

We had little controversy in selecting the jury for our trial against Shell. Both sides must have felt that the jurors who were called into the "box" would be fair, because neither side used all of its peremptory challenges. In fact, Shell accepted the jury early during the second day of the trial, while it still had two peremptory challenges left.

We were particularly pleased to have two men on the jury who had worked for a number of years in local chemical plants. They would be familiar with much of the technical evidence we would be presenting. We also expected Shell to excuse much of its bad behavior by claiming it acted in accordance with "industry custom and practice." We felt that anyone who worked in our local chemical plants would know that violations of environmental rules were never justified by "industry custom and practice."

Once the jury was selected, they were sworn in. Each juror gave an oath promising to be fair and impartial and to judge the case solely on the evidence and the law. Judge Minaldi then called a fifteen-minute recess and instructed us that opening statements would begin immediately after our break.

12

There are important differences between opening statements and closing arguments. Opening statements allow the lawyers at the beginning of the trial to tell the jury what they expect the evidence to show; closing arguments allow them at the end of the trial to argue what the evidence *did* show. The big difference between the two is that you're not supposed to argue the case in the opening statement, just preview what the evidence will be. The fact remains, however, that the opening statement presents a golden opportunity to sway the jury to your side of the case. You just have to know how to do it without being argumentative.

It's not easy to describe the line that separates a proper opening statement from an improper argument. It has as much to do with a lawyer's tone of voice and body language as it does with what he says. The trick to staying on the safe side of the line is to let the facts speak for themselves and save the more colorful language and table pounding for closing argument.

A good opening statement requires a lot of preparation. I learned early on that you should deliver your opening statement without notes, if at all possible. You can't make good eye contact with the jury if you're reading from notes, and you cannot expect someone to believe what you're saying if you don't look them in the eyes.

Unfortunately, that kind of preparation takes time, and time is at a premium right before trial. You're trying to set up the order of your witnesses, make sure they're all available when you need them, prepare your *voir dire* questions, consider last-minute pretrial motions, and deal with an unlimited number of other eleventh-hour surprises that seem to be a part of every trial. So, when Judge Minaldi gave us a fifteen-minute recess before opening statements, I spent the recess running through my remarks one last time before facing the jury.

As the plaintiffs, our side would speak first when court resumed. I had enough experience from past cases to know that I was ready. When Judge Minaldi brought court to order and nodded to me to proceed, I turned to Pat Gallaugher just before I stood up to begin and whispered in his ear, "I'm gonna kick their ass."

I don't know exactly what possessed me to thump my chest like that. Looking back, I guess it was a way of challenging myself. Unlike any other case I had ever tried, I was representing my mother and her family on this one. And they were all there in the courtroom watching: aunts and cousins I'd grown up with, people I really cared about. When I said what I did, it was as if I had thrown the gauntlet down at myself. The message was: no excuses, no turning back.

Even though I talked for the better part of an hour, it felt like a lot less. I didn't need or use notes. Not every sentence was grammatically perfect, but words spoken with conviction while looking a jury straight in the eye carry more power than the most perfect prose read from a book. I just looked directly at the jury and spoke with them as if we were having a quiet conversation—albeit a one-sided one, given that I was doing all the talking.

"Ladies and gentlemen," I began, "I can only imagine that when you finally became aware that you were going to sit in judgment on this case you developed some apprehension about how you were to decide something that we probably made sound pretty complicated yesterday. . . . Well, I hope to allay your fears during this brief time I'm going to talk to you to tell you that I think that when this case is over and it's submitted to you for you to make a decision, you're going to find that it's really a pretty simple case."

Making eye contact with each juror, I continued, "It's going to come down to good old-fashioned right and wrong, and I think you're going to be very, very comfortable deciding who was right and who was wrong . . . and what's the proper way to right the wrong."

I then began to sketch out the background of the case. "This case is about some things that occurred on property owned by the Heyd family in a little area north of Iowa known as LeBleu Settlement. The property has been in the Heyd family since my great-grandfather purchased it, around 1915. This case is about some things that Shell did on the property in violation of the Heyd family's rights." I then said that it would be "extremely clear . . . and without much dispute that Shell did some things that were wrong. . . ."

I knew that it was important to explain what we expected the jury to do with this evidence of wrongdoing. In effect, I was making a contract with the jury. I had already asked them in jury selection if they could render an award in the millions of dollars if the evidence justified it. I wanted to remind them that they promised they could do so, because this case involved the largest sum of money any of us (them or me) had ever dealt with. I wanted to dispel any "sticker shock" the jury might have, and I wanted to make it clear that they shouldn't be reluctant to award any amount, no matter how large, if we produced evidence that would justify it. Thus, after saying that we would show what Shell did wrong, I told the jury that "the law will give you much discretion in determining what amount of money will right that wrong. And, in fact, will right several wrongs."

I then explained the "several wrongs."

First, I told how the 1929 mineral lease came about and how it covered 320 acres. I then described the history of oil and gas production from that lease. I explained how salt water came out of the well along with any oil and gas that was being produced and how it had to be separated out and disposed of. I then explained how the mineral lease allowed Shell to dispose of any salt water produced from wells on Grandpa Heyd's property back into his property, but that Shell obtained the 1961 surface lease in order to have the right to dispose of salt water produced from its other leases in the Iowa Field onto the Heyd property as well.

"In the early years of the mineral lease," I told them, "Shell just flowed salt water into open, unlined pits dug on the Heyd property."

Apparently, the idea was that the salt water would just evaporate without the need to do anything more. But that idea had several flaws. First, Louisiana typically experiences heavy rainfall, which caused the pits to overflow, spreading salt water into ditches that flowed into a nearby waterway known as English Bayou. The problem there was that area rice farmers drew irrigation water from English Bayou. The salt water killed their rice crops. Second, the wells began producing more and more salt water with the oil and gas over the years. Thus, even if the rainwater hadn't caused the pits to overflow, the increased volumes of salt water flowing from the wells did. When the overflow was released into ditches and then into English Bayou, it produced additional crop kills. Finally, to make matters worse, the unlined pits leaked. The brine in the pits then migrated underground. The problem there was that the clays that separated and protected groundwater aquifers were cracked (a common feature of the area, according to the U.S. Geological Survey), which allowed the salt water to invade the underground aquifers.

Using a projector (called an "Elmo" for reasons that escape me), I then showed the jury some documents we had obtained from Shell's records. When any document was placed under the camera of the Elmo, it appeared on a large television screen in front of the jury, as well as on monitors in front of the judge, the witness, and the lawyers. Thus, everyone in the courtroom could instantly follow any witness's testimony about a particular document, including maps, diagrams, and photographs.

In particular, there was a report describing how law enforcement authorities had filed criminal charges against Shell personnel for contaminating irrigation water supplies and destroying rice crops in the area in the 1930s. One of Shell's employees had been convicted, and the report said the district judge was so incensed by the destruction of rice crops that he threatened to jail every Shell field employee, up to and including the superintendent, if it ever happened again.

"That prompted Shell to begin injecting the produced salt water back into old oil wells that were no longer in production."

The idea was to return the brine to the producing zone from which it came. Shell wanted to centralize its salt water disposal facilities on one lease, rather than set up facilities on every lease it was operating in the area. That's why Shell approached Grandpa Heyd's four children in 1961 to ask for a surface lease on 120 acres within the 320 acres that were under the mineral lease. The oil company wanted to take salt water from all of the various leases it was operating in the Iowa Field and dispose of it in the salt water disposal facilities on the Heyd property.

The Heyd children had no problem agreeing to take salt water that was produced from their neighbors' land. After all, they were farmers, and all the farmers in the area were used to helping one another out. Shell didn't offer them much money for this surface lease: They paid each of the children $1,000 a year for a lease that gave Shell the right to use their land for any and all business purposes, not just salt water disposal. Through my father, who was practicing law at the time, the Heyd heirs demanded only one thing in the lease: They wanted Shell to promise that it would restore the land as near as possible to its present condition when the lease expired. That's why, I explained, the lease contained just such a provision.

The lease was originally for a single ten-year term, but it allowed Shell to renew for two additional ten-year terms at the same price. Not long after signing the lease, Shell began its salt water disposal operations in earnest. Taking advantage of its bargained-for right to use the land for all business purposes, Shell also constructed an oil gathering facility on the Heyds' property, where oil from various sources, with different weight, was blended to an optimum weight before it was delivered into a pipeline. Shell called this, I explained, a "gravity management" system.

"This case started," I explained to the jury, "when we sent a letter to Shell on May 9, 1991—the day before the lease was to expire at the end of its third and final ten-year term. And while Shell had always been careful to notify the Heyds when it was time to renew the surface lease, it didn't seem to care about when the lease was finally going to expire. So we sent a letter asking Shell about its intentions."

As I explained to the jury, our letter complained that, although the lease was about to terminate, we had heard nothing from Shell about its intentions to vacate the property. Our letter also disclosed that we had recently received information that Shell may have been disposing of salt water into the Heyd property that was not from Shell's other leases in the Iowa Field, which would have been a violation of the terms of the surface lease. Finally, our letter asked Shell about its plans to restore the property as required by the lease.

I knew I had to tie this to the law so the jury would understand its significance. "This case is about a breach of contract. That's the legal term. And all that is, is a fancy way of saying, you broke your agreement, you broke your promise. The law says that when you breach an agreement, you must respond in damages and that's what you're here to decide," I said.

"We knew going in," I told the jury, "that Shell had breached the contract by failing to leave when the lease expired. Shell stayed on an additional twenty-two months after the lease was over, operating its oil blending facility, before we sued them. Once we filed suit and served subpoenas seeking information, we discovered a second breach, which was that Shell had been taking salt water from third parties and from leases outside the Iowa Field and injecting it into the Heyd property. Neither was permitted by the surface lease," I explained.

"But that wasn't all," I said. "We discovered a third breach. The agreement that Shell signed with the Heyd family said that at the conclusion of the agreement Shell would reasonably restore the property as near as possible to its present condition, meaning the condition it was in 1961. . . . Shell has not cleaned up the property. To this day, nine years later, Shell still has not cleaned up the property, has not done anything, despite the fact that it retained an expert who came out and tested the property in 1991 and reported to Shell 'you have got oil contamination here. You have got heavy amounts of salt, you've got problems in the pits, you have got heavy amounts of oil and grease and benzene, cadmium, lead, and silver.'"

While I didn't have time to explain the toxic qualities of these materials, I said, "You test for [these materials] because you want to know if they're there because if they're there they need to be 'remediated.' That's a fancy word for 'cleaned up.' Shell had that report. To this day [they] have done nothing."

Continuing, I said, "Now, all of that is what we're here to fix. We couldn't get Shell to do it, so we're here and we're asking to be awarded an amount of money that will allow us to do what Shell failed to do when it failed to keep its promise."

At this point, I knew that I needed to motivate the jury to be as generous as possible in making its award. I wanted to be sure they didn't feel any sympathy for Shell that might cause them to underestimate our damages. I knew the best way to destroy *any* possible sympathy for Shell was to make it clear that Shell's actions were deliberate. It was time to show the jury some of the documents we had gotten during the years of hide-and-seek discovery games we were forced to play with Shell's lawyers.

I looked directly at the jury. "You're probably wondering, well, you know, how could all of this happen? Well, the sad truth is we're going to show you that what happened here was not accidental, because as we dug into this, we discovered some remarkable documents that indicate that over a period of time Shell repeatedly and deliberately admitted . . . that it was doing things that it didn't have a right to do, but that 'let's not approach the owner. Let sleeping dogs lie.'"

"In 1945," I said, "Shell was talking about how whenever it had a salt water disposal well, it would take a little one-acre lease on the property to dispose of it. Presumably, because they could argue we shouldn't pay you much, we are only taking an acre." I paused. "In a memorandum written by the field people, in typing, to management they said, 'Look, for ten years now, we've been taking one-acre leases around disposal wells. We've never gone to the landowner for a right-of-way to lay the pipelines that take the salt water to the injection well. We think in view of the fact that the landowner hasn't complained, doesn't know about it, that we shouldn't bother them now when we get new leases to get rights-of-way in the future. But what do you think?'"

I paused again, looking at the jury to make sure they were all following me. When I was confident they were, I continued. "Well, the natural expectation would be that management would say, 'Well, no, you can't lay pipelines without rights-of-way. You go back and do it the right way and go to the landowner and get their permission and compensate them for this.'" I then shook my head, as if in sad disbelief. "Well, management writes back: 'We agree with you that it is an acceptable business risk not to approach the landowner and obtain a right-of-way. Moreover, in view of the fact that you haven't been getting rights-of-way, why are you even bothering to get surfaces leases for these salt water disposal wells?'"

Looking up and down each row of jurors, I said, "I wish I could tell you that was isolated, but if you fast-forward a few years into 1960 there's a Shell document that says we want to plug and abandon this salt water disposal well because it leaks—the casing leaks a lot. Of course, you're drilling through drinking water aquifers. It's leaking a lot and the salt water is leaking and can contaminate anything it leaks into. So we are going to plug and abandon this well. . . . We want to convert this well on the property into a salt water disposal well to take its place. It's not on the surface lease, but we don't want to obtain a new lease to take this in because they are hard to get from the landowner and it would prove too costly . . . so we'll just do it."

I pointed out the Shell documents from 1964 in which Shell officials discussed buying gas from a producer who had a well south of the Heyd property. The producer's name was Tuten, and he wanted to process his gas in Shell's gas processing plant. In order to pipe his gas to Shell's plant, Mr. Tuten needed to cross the Heyd property. He asked Shell if it could grant him a right-of-way to do so. In the first memo, the land department asks the law department if it can grant Mr. Tuten such a right-of-way. In reply, the law department writes back: "No, you don't have the right under our surface lease to let other people lay pipelines to our plant."

Shell's law department went into an incredible rationalization in which it told the Shell land people: "You can, however, issue a permit to the extent that you have the right to give them permission."

As I explained to the jury, a permit is something the government gives, such as a building permit. There is no such thing as a "private" permit given by a third party to cross someone else's land. It was clear that Shell was going to great lengths to avoid having Mr. Tuten contact the Heyds for permission to cross their property, because that might alert the Heyds and cause them to discover that Shell had been using their property without leases and rights-of-way for many years. So Shell concocted the notion of a private "permit."

I could tell the jury was impressed with what they were learning about Shell's lawlessness. I knew it would get better, because I had more.

"Unfortunately," I said to them, "it doesn't stop there. In 1984, Shell was preparing to sell the mineral lease on the Heyd property. . . . Shell was leaving the Iowa Field. . . . As part of it, it had some pits it had been using to put waste in on the Heyd property. It brought in this man to test the pits to see what needed to be done to clean it up. As part of that process, Shell issued a prognosis saying, 'This pit is so contaminated you are going to need to excavate the soil. . . .' The testimony will be that you don't get third party bids for removal of soil unless somebody in Shell's environmental department says the soil can't be reworked with chemicals, it's got to be excavated. And Shell went to Campbell Well Service . . . over in Jennings, and got a bid for what it would take to excavate a lot of the soil. . . . Campbell Well Service said for one pit alone . . . it's going to cost you $1.1 million. Shell just dropped that. It eventually went to one corner of the pit . . . and took out two feet of soil there when the contamination was below two feet. Just taking out two feet there it cost Shell $220,000. So, they stopped there and did no further work on the property."

It was important for the jury to know who "this man" was that Shell has brought in to assess the Heyd property. "His name is Lloyd Deuel, who was sent out in '91 and who documented there's still contamination here. To this day Shell has done nothing more."

Referring to some comments Shell's lawyers had made the day before, during jury selection, I said: "Now, yesterday you heard some talk about others sharing responsibility. I want to make one thing clear to you: Shell may have transferred the mineral lease, but there was never, ever, anyone else on the land lease, the thirty-year land lease, and that's what our case is based upon, because Shell in that land lease said, 'We're going to cleanup your property.' It didn't say 'We're going to cleanup your property unless we can blame it on somebody else. . . .' It didn't put conditions. That was the right that was bargained for."

I continued to look at each juror, one at a time. They were looking back at me intently. I was encouraged, and I felt that I was connecting on every point. I wanted each juror to understand how important the cleanup provision in the surface lease was to the Heyd family, so I said, "That may be the very reason why the Heyd family took so little money in return for a provision that said 'our property is going to be cleaned up.'"

It was time to turn the jury's attention to our damages. "Now," I said, "we're going to introduce evidence of how valuable the rights are that Shell took without permission." Referring to our trespass claim, I said, "We're going to introduce evidence of how valuable it was to stay on that property without permission and operate an oil terminal. You're going to hear that it was very profitable." Referring to the damages arising from Shell's failure to cleanup the property, I said, "We're going to introduce evidence of what it will cost the Heyd family to do what Shell has failed to do. You know, the problem is we can only come here once; if we don't get the amount of money it will take to clean it up, we can't come back. You're going to hear some very interesting evidence about the extent of the contamination and how the contamination is so severe that it threatens drinking water supplies. . . . Even Shell's own people have said it is possible." Finally, referring to the damages from unlawful salt water disposal, I said, "You are going to hear evidence about how valuable it was for Shell . . . to take in salt water from others and dispose it in the Heyd property for nothing and charge people for it as well as bring their own from as far away as the Kings Bayou Field 45 miles away—and they pass two of their own disposal sites on the way—to trucking it in for a solid year to the Heyd property." I didn't give the jury any damage numbers, mainly because I had already asked them several times during *voir dire* if they could award as much as 100 million dollars if the evidence justified it.

I was nearing the end of my remarks. Before I was through, though, I wanted to fire a preemptive strike and talk about Shell's defenses just in case the jury was wondering how Shell was going to justify its conduct.

After a pause, I turned to the jury and said, "What is Shell going to say? Well, first of all, they may tell you that it's industry custom and practice [to do what they did]." I continued to look at each juror, up and down, front to back, as I faced them. Their eyes were still locked on mine, indicating they were following closely. Measuring my words carefully, I said, "Our position is that, first of all, it's not industry custom and practice to break the law. It's not industry custom and practice to stay on property when the lease is up. It's not industry custom and practice not to cleanup your mess. It's not industry custom and practice to come here and to tell you they are going to clean it up after they haven't done so for nine years. It's not industry custom and practice to use other people's property for salt water disposal and charge third parties for it and never inform the landowner. . . . At bottom, our position is this is a grown-up version of the excuse I used as a youngster whenever I was caught doing something wrong. . . . You know, 'everybody else was doing it, too.' My dad would look at me and say, 'I don't care how many other people did it. If it was wrong, it was wrong.'" Several of the jurors smiled, no doubt remembering their own childhood attempts to escape punishment with the same excuse. Concluding, I said, "That's our position on this, that saying it's industry custom and practice when it's a violation of the law just isn't a valid excuse."

I shrugged. "What else will Shell say?" I knew that Shell would argue that we weren't entitled to the profits they made from their unlawful salt water and gathering terminal operations and that we should only get what we would have gotten in rent if they had signed a lease with us. I wanted to hit that argument head-on. Shaking my head, I said, "You will hear their lawyers over there saying we are trying to take all their profits. What they are really telling you is 'We want to keep the profits' because we said this was an 'acceptable business risk' and now that we have been caught we want to tell you, 'Why don't you just make us pay these people what we would have had to pay them if we had gone to them in the first place and done the honorable thing?' Of course, the problem with that is: They *didn't* go. They *didn't* ask permission. They can't say that the Heyd family would ever have agreed [to let them use their property for additional salt water disposal]. . . . It's a little late for that. But they . . . want to keep their ill-gotten gains."

I wanted the jury to remember that, no matter what numbers Shell presented, the amount of damages to be awarded in the case was strictly up to them. "In the end, ladies and gentlemen, it will be your decision, your decision alone, and the court is going to tell you, you will have 'much discretion' in deciding what is the value of the rights taken. Shell is going to tell you, well, the underground of the property wasn't harmed. We submit that isn't the point. The point is Shell . . . made a lot of money taking things that didn't belong to them and now they want to keep it. And they want to stand here and tell you that they should keep it because they deliberately planned . . . to take what they termed an 'acceptable risk.' Now, I don't know about you, but I've always understood that you take no risk if you don't do something wrong. The 'risk' is the risk of getting caught [doing something wrong]."

Referring to what I anticipated might be other excuses Shell would offer for its bad behavior, I concluded my remarks by saying, "Now, you may be told a lot of things. I just want you to remember what the real issues are, because, in the end, it's a good old-fashioned case of right and wrong. And it's a good old-fashioned case of doing things the honorable way. And it's a good old-fashioned case of keeping your promises."

I took one last look at each juror, said "Thank you," and sat down.

13

I felt like I had nailed my opening statement. I had been confident and clear in explaining what the case was about. Our objective was to show the jury enough of our case to convince them that Shell had behaved badly. We had done that. They had to be aroused by what Shell had done and, at least for the moment, squarely in our corner.

It was now Shell's turn to respond. The oil company had taken some real hits in my opening statement, and the documents we had shown the jury were damning evidence of Shell's cavalier attitude toward the Heyds. I was anxious to see how Shell's lawyers would repair the damage.

Judge Minaldi turned in the direction of the other table. She had already been told by Shell's trial team that Tom McNamara would make the opening statement on Shell's behalf. Nodding to him, she said, "Mr. McNamara?"

Tom McNamara stood and walked to the podium. He was carrying his reading glasses and a sheaf of notes. That set an immediate contrast to my opening remarks, which had been delivered without notes. McNamara adjusted the podium, placed his papers on it, and put on his reading glasses. He must have sensed that his use of notes required an explanation, because he apologized right off the bat. "Good morning. My problem is I need the podium because I'm probably not as good as he is on my feet. . . . I'm also a little too short to see over it real well, so I hope y'all can see me okay." He was right; it seemed like McNamara's head barely reached over the podium. That was about all of him that the jury could see. This sharply contrasted with our opening statement, in which I stood directly in front of the jury, without a podium between us.

After introducing himself and Pat Gray, McNamara then told the jury that "we are glad to get a chance to talk to you. It's been kind of hard getting here, and we're just glad to be here to have your help to sort out the things in this case."

That remark set the tone for Shell's opening statement. It was apparently Shell's strategy to suggest that, like the jury, it was hearing the Heyds' complaints for the first time and until now was unaware of what had been done on the family's property over the years. It was as if Shell's lawyers were trying to create two "Shells": The "bad" Shell we described and the "good" Shell that was here at trial. To that end, McNamara said, "I want to let you know we are going to be discovering things right along with you in the trial. We are going to be asking some questions. Hopefully they are good questions. Hopefully the same kind of questions that might come out of your mouth."

He then presented Shell's version of its "history" with the Heyd family. Continuing with his theme of the "good" Shell, McNamara claimed that the evidence would show that "the tensions between Shell and the Heyd family are relatively recent. For most of the time that Shell dealt with the Heyd family, they got along fine. . . ." He then said that Shell's history in the Iowa Field "is a good story, filled with some excitement, innovation, . . . progress." In a colorful reference to *The Beverly Hillbillies,* McNamara said that the discovery of oil in the Iowa Field wasn't the result of technology, but rather there "was actually visible evidence of oil accumulation in the form of gas . . . bubbling to the surface," like when "up through the ground came a-bubblin' crude." Apparently, the idea was to suggest that my great-grandfather was an early version of Jed Clampett.

McNamara then said that newspaper stories at the time told of this discovery with "excitement" at the prospect of oil activities bringing jobs to South Louisiana, "put[ting] money in people's pockets and put[ting] the town of Iowa on the map." This was a curious comment, because Shell hadn't listed any of these articles among its exhibits, so I knew they wouldn't be coming into evidence. McNamara also claimed that Ferdinand Heyd's lease was the best producing property in the Iowa Field, with approximately seventy wells being drilled on the 320-acre lease area since 1930. He then told the jury that these wells produced more than thirty-seven million barrels of oil. And, he said, although Shell had sold the Heyd lease in 1985, the Iowa Field "was, and it continues to be, a good thing for the people of the area."

What McNamara was doing was clear. We had learned before trial that Shell planned to present evidence of how much royalty it paid based on the oil production it achieved from the Heyd property. The purpose, of course, was to suggest that the Heyd family had received millions of dollars already from Shell and that this suit was a greedy attempt to get more. At the same time, McNamara was careful not to mention that the royalty was only one-eighth of production, meaning that, if the Iowa Field was good for royalty owners, it was *seven times better* for Shell. Even so, Shell's strategy was to prejudice the jury into thinking that the Heyd family was filthy rich from oil royalties and didn't need to be compensated for anything Shell may have done wrong.

From our perspective, Shell's lawyers should never have been allowed to refer to any of this. The amount of royalties that Shell paid to anyone (Grandpa Heyd included) was irrelevant to the case. We weren't suing Shell for additional royalties, and we weren't claiming that Shell had failed to pay the proper amount of royalties. In any event, all of that was governed by the 1929 mineral lease. We were suing Shell for breaching the 1961 surface lease. Beyond that, McNamara's comments about the royalties paid by Shell were misleading. As he knew but conveniently failed to mention, Grandpa Heyd had sold most of his royalty rights, which meant that all those royalty payments made by Shell largely went to others.

When we realized what Shell intended to do, we lodged an objection before trial, asking Judge Minaldi to prohibit Shell from referring to the royalties. Despite this, Shell's lawyers succeeded in convincing Judge Minaldi that this information was important because it was part of the "history" of Shell's operations on the Heyd property, which they claimed the jury needed to know. As a result, Judge Minaldi denied our objection to Shell's use of this information.

After sensationalizing the royalties paid by Shell, McNamara then expounded on his theme of "landowner greed." Looking down at his notes, he said, "Let me establish some things right away. From the Shell perspective this case has never been about whether we accept our share of the responsibility to cleanup that property. . . . We absolutely do accept that responsibility. We're grown-ups. We accept responsibility. But that's not what's going on here. . . . I think you will conclude from the evidence that what it's actually about, instead of actually cleaning up anything it's about money. . . . Mr. Veron will not . . . agree to simply ask you for specific guidance as to what Shell ought to cleanup and when. He's going to ask you for money instead."

At this point, McNamara had one foot on the pedestal at the bottom of the podium and both hands on its sides, and he was leaning forward against it, almost as if he couldn't stand without it. He then spent several minutes giving an extended explanation of oil and gas production and of Shell's mineral and surface leases on the property, which was largely repetitive of our opening statement and therefore, in my mind at least, unnecessary. He then turned his attention to the salt water disposal issue and told the jury that Shell "may" have disposed of salt water into the Heyd property that "technically" wasn't permitted by the surface lease. After reminding the jury that Shell's rental of the property was a mere $4,000 a year, McNamara told them, "if that's the case [that Shell disposed of salt water illegally], you may have to try to figure out what the additional rent for the disposal might be." He then asserted that the illegal salt water was less than 1 percent of all the salt water injected into the disposal system on the Heyds' property. The not-so-subtle suggestion, of course, was that the additional rental should be one percent of $4,000, or $40 per year.

Of course, there was more to the surface lease issues than just the salt water disposal, and McNamara knew it. Shell had also operated its "gravity management" plant on the Heyd land by virtue of the authority it obtained from the surface lease. In a further attempt to make Shell the victim, McNamara said that Shell had "kept the oil trading facility on the property until 1991. The Shell surface lease expired and Shell suddenly found itself without a lease. You will discover that this entire lawsuit has evolved from that moment of opportunity, the day the surface lease expired. That's when there began to be a rewriting of the history of this lease and a recharacterization of Shell."

Reading from his notes while occasionally peeking above his reading glasses at the jury, McNamara said, "Some very inflammatory terms are going to be thrown at you, and I need to talk to you a little bit about them. . . . One of the main problem terms is pollution or contamination. . . . [T]here's no environmental scientist who is going to come here and tell you that this is a contaminated wasteland. They will tell you that to understand the condition of the Heyd property, you have to understand the history of how they had agreed that it could be used."

I was a little surprised at this. A lawyer never wants to make a false promise of proof. McNamara was telling the jury that no expert in the case would say that this land was contaminated. However, he knew that our primary environmental expert, Austin Arabie, was going to testify that the Heyd property was not only contaminated, but that it could cost as much as $34 million to clean it up. Beyond that, McNamara was suggesting that the Heyd family had somehow agreed to allow Shell to pollute their land. This flew directly in the face of express language in the 1961 surface lease whereby Shell promised to restore the Heyds' land at the end of the lease to its original condition. Since the contract would be a central part of the trial, I wondered how Shell expected the jury to believe what McNamara was saying.

I didn't have to wait long. McNamara essentially told the jury that spills and discharges were an essential and unavoidable part of oil and gas production and that, over the years, there had been numerous such spills and discharges. All this produced, he said, nothing other than some "hydrocarbons" in the soil. "It hasn't caused any harm," he asserted, "that can't be remediated or cleaned up with some digging equipment and a crew of workers going out there and doing some work and then putting the land into agriculture." He then attempted to paint us as sensationalists, saying that "I don't think it's fair using those words [i.e., contamination and pollution] to create a specter of danger when there really isn't any. When the property is no longer used for oil operations, the oil and its hydrocarbon constituents will go away. The same thing for all this talk about cadmium, lead, and silver, these so-called heavy metals."

McNamara then came to the most prejudicial issue facing Shell in the case—one that I hadn't brought up in opening statement, preferring to save it for dramatic effect later in the case. Not long before trial, we had received an anonymous tip that Shell had buried barrels of sludge, asbestos pipe, and other potentially harmful chemicals on the Heyd property, about twelve feet below the surface. Armed with sensitive detecting equipment, we discovered the buried "junkyard." We even found an old Shell gasoline-dispensing pump, the kind you see at Shell gas stations around the country.

We had disclosed this information to Shell almost immediately and had furnished Gray and McNamara all of the photos and other evidence we had gathered to document this discovery. We also posted all of this stuff on our pretrial exhibit list, so Shell's lawyers knew it would be offered into evidence at some point during the trial.

McNamara was smart enough to know he needed to face this issue head-on and try to take some of the sting out of it. "You know, it was normal in oilfield operations to bury some things," he said almost apologetically, "some old concrete and some boards and things like that. . . . We know that burying household trash is common in South Louisiana out in the country, but from the time this issue of old crushed barrels and things being buried came up in this case, every credible witness will tell you that it was against Shell's policy to go out burying barrels and stuff like that. . . . From what we have learned so far, by and large what's buried out there is some metal and other things that aren't toxic and hazardous. It's not going to be so clear who buried all that stuff or when, but the bottom line is this: The materials . . . that are buried, they ought to be taken out."

He then delivered Shell's version of conditions on the Heyd property. "[T]he bottom line is this: It's not an environmental wasteland. Shell was concerned about that. You'll hear from a number of experts who are going to talk about that. . . . You will hear from an environmental expert who specializes in oilfield cleanups and groundwater. You will hear him say that the only problem out there is salt in some of the areas and that's because it affects the surface vegetation, and he will tell you that there's no evidence that anything Shell did on this property affected the drinking water, period." McNamara went on to talk about the soil chemist that Shell would call to testify that the land could be returned to agriculture with very little treatment. He told the jury that Shell would also call a toxicologist to testify that there was nothing on the property that was harmful to humans.

Like some of his previous statements, I was surprised by these promises of proof. McNamara had to know that, when we deposed these witnesses, we obtained some damning admissions about the contamination on the Heyd property. He also had to know that, when he put these witnesses on the stand, we would bring out these admissions during our cross-examination of them.

McNamara next explained Shell's failure to cleanup the property over the previous nine years, between the time the lease expired in 1991 and the trial in 2000. "Mr. Veron suggested that Shell didn't come up and clean the property after it looked at it in 1991. He told you about a man that came out there and studied the property in those years, 1991 and 1992. Well, I think you will see that Shell got sued in 1992 by the landowners." He did not explain how being sued prevented Shell from cleaning up the property. I hoped that the jury also noticed that McNamara didn't claim that the Heyds ever refused to permit Shell to cleanup their property during that time, either.

McNamara then made what I felt was one of his best points about our "history" of Shell's bad behavior on the Heyd property. "Have you noticed that we're talking about 1936 Shell did something, 1945 Shell did something? Seventy years of history yet we're picking out these little bits . . . to throw at you."

Judge Minaldi then informed Shell's lawyer that he had two minutes left of the forty-five minutes allotted to each side for opening statements.

Nodding to the court to acknowledge the warning, McNamara hurriedly described his client's efforts to close pits on the Heyd property, claiming that Shell "generally did a good job of closing pits." In his final comments, McNamara predicted to the jury that, after examining the evidence in the case, it would "conclude that [Shell] dealt with the Heyd landowners in the manner which reflected mutual cooperation . . . in which both the oil company and the landowners got along fine." He then told the jury that he was looking forward "to spending this time together with you and examining this lawsuit," thanked them for their attention, and sat down.

Judge Minaldi declared a fifteen-minute recess, after which we would call our first witness.

14

After an hour and a half of opening statements without a break, everyone piled out of the courtroom, presumably headed for the restrooms. I stayed at our table, looking through my notes to prepare for our first witness. As I worked, I remember wondering if McNamara's efforts to put a shine on Shell's bad behavior had neutralized my opening statement.

I didn't have to wait long to hear one person's opinion on that score. After a few short moments, I heard a familiar voice speak my name. I looked up and saw Judge Minaldi, standing behind her executive chair up on the bench. She apparently had stopped before walking through the door behind the bench that allowed her to come and go from the courtroom. Looking around the courtroom as if to make certain that no one could hear her, she said softly, "Mike, that was a great opening statement."

I was taken aback. It was unusual for a judge to pay a lawyer that kind of compliment, especially in the middle of trial. There certainly wasn't anything wrong or improper about it. This was a jury trial, which meant the judge wouldn't be deciding the facts and was free to share her comments about things with the lawyers as she saw fit. Nonetheless, it surprised me because I would never have characterized us as particularly friendly. To my knowledge, it was the first compliment she had ever paid me. I managed to mumble a polite "Thank you, Judge," as she turned and left the courtroom. I don't know if she even heard me.

In any event, it certainly wasn't a harbinger of things to come. (As a jogging buddy of mine later joked, "She really paid you two compliments at once—the first one and the last one.") I didn't realize until later that Judge Minaldi's comment about the opening statement was in reality the first indication that she was also concerned that the case may have tilted out of balance. She was, after all, the only Republican judge on our eight-member district court bench. She was fiercely conservative and proud of it, which wasn't surprising for someone who had spent her career prosecuting criminals before she was elected to the bench. The idea of a big plaintiff's verdict coming out of her court couldn't have appealed to her.

In addition, the judge's husband worked as inside counsel for one of the wealthiest families in the state. That family had extensive oil and gas interests and had even operated a number of oil wells. Simply put, they wouldn't want our case to establish any kind of precedent that oil operators could be sued for contamination. This wasn't just my imagination. At one point during the first day of trial, the judge thought enough of the problem to call both sides' attention to her relationship with the Lawton family and invite us to raise any objection we might have. Since there was no direct conflict of interest (the Lawtons were not a party to the case), there was no legal ground for the judge to recuse herself, and we did not ask her to do so.

Of course, I wasn't thinking about any of that at that moment. I was too busy concerning myself with whom to call as our first witness. Normally, when I am on the plaintiff's side, I like to open by calling the defendant to the stand. The law allows me to interrogate an adverse party with leading questions, and with the right admissions the case is essentially over.

Unfortunately, I didn't have that kind of witness available to me in this case. Shell wasn't a person that I could put on the stand. Nor did it have a particular representative whom I could call to elicit admissions about Shell's bad behavior. For instance, the documents spoke for themselves, and the fact that Shell hadn't done anything to cleanup the property over the last nine years was undisputed. I really wasn't sure whom I should call first, until Pat Gallaugher suggested that we make Austin Arabie our first witness.

It was a great idea. As our environmental expert, Arabie would lay out for the jury how badly the property was contaminated and what it would take to clean it up. He could describe how he found the barrels of sludge and other toxic materials buried under the Heyds' land. In addition, Austin made a great appearance, was soft-spoken, and was very credible. I reminded myself that the jury would form its first impression of our evidence based on our opening witness. Austin would put a great "face" on our case. We couldn't do any better than him.

When court reconvened, Judge Minaldi looked at me expectantly. "Mr. Veron, you may call your first witness."

I stood. Knowing the jury was watching, I smiled confidently. "We call Mr. Austin Arabie to the stand, Your Honor." With that, a man I would describe as medium-height, medium-weight, and medium-age with a neatly trimmed beard came forward. The deputy clerk motioned for him to raise his right hand and asked him if he swore to tell the truth, the whole truth, and nothing but the truth "so help you God." Austin said quietly, "I do," and climbed the three steps to the chair on the witness stand located just a few feet from where the jury sat.

Witnesses are ordinarily limited to testifying about facts. They may not give opinions unless they are qualified by the court as an expert in a particular field, and even then their opinions are limited to their field of expertise. The first thing I needed to do was establish that Austin was qualified as an expert in the field of environmental science. If I couldn't satisfy the court as to that, he wouldn't be allowed to express any opinions about Shell's contamination of the Heyd property.

After having him identify himself for the record, I asked Austin, "What do you do?"

He replied evenly, "I'm an environmental consultant, environmental scientist with a specialty in investigation of groundwater contamination, soil contamination." Austin went on to testify that he owned his own company, Arabie Environmental Solutions, and that his clients were "industries, businesses, commercial-type companies, filling station owners, and petroleum distributors." He explained that companies generally contacted him if they suspected they had a contamination or pollution problem. He also said that his companies did a lot of work obtaining permits for clients relating to wetlands, discharges, air emissions, and solid and hazardous waste facilities.

I next asked Austin about his formal education. He said that he had originally obtained a bachelor of science degree in animal science, with a view toward becoming a veterinarian. After a stint in the Army, however, Austin returned to school and instead obtained a master's degree in environmental science. As part of his graduate education, he completed courses in soil science, solid waste management, microbiology, toxicology, air pollution, and environmental law.

After leaving school, Austin worked briefly for a food company before finding his way to the Louisiana Department of Environmental Quality in the late 1970s, where he became involved in the investigation of contaminated groundwater. It was during this time, he explained, that the state government first put into effect its hazardous waste regulations. After several years of concentrating in the field of soil and groundwater contamination, Arabie returned to private industry, going to work for a large waste management company as operations manager at a cleanup site known as Willow Springs. Not long thereafter, he opened his own environmental consulting business.

To complete my tender of Austin's expertise, I had him describe how he had previously been recognized as an expert in soil and groundwater contamination in hearings before the Louisiana Office of Conservation. I then turned to Judge Minaldi and said, "Your Honor, we tender Mr. Arabie as an expert in the field of environmental science, with special emphasis on soil and groundwater science, including the remediation of property contaminated by oilfield products."

It was now Shell's turn either to accept the tender or ask questions intended to persuade Judge Minaldi that Arabie should not be recognized as an expert in the field in which he was tendered. Unless he was accepted as an expert, Austin would not be allowed to give any opinion testimony. McNamara rose to ask questions, which led me to assume that Shell intended to dispute Arabie's qualifications.

"Mr. Arabie, do you claim to be an expert in the application of Statewide Order 29-B to oilfield cleanups?"

Austin nodded. "Yes."

"Do you claim to be an expert in the history of the development of oilfield operations in Louisiana?"

Austin shook his head and gave an equally short answer. "No."

"And you are not a registered professional engineer?"

Austin again shook his head. "No."

"Are you a registered professional geologist?"

Austin answered, "No. I have both of those on my staff, but I'm not personally."

McNamara turned to the bench and said to Judge Minaldi, "No objection to the tender."

This took me by surprise. As McNamara knew, Arabie was the witness who had documented Shell's contamination of the property, devised a plan to clean it up, and calculated how much it would cost to administer that plan. McNamara also knew that Arabie would say that it might cost upwards of $34 million to do what he believed needed to be done. I fully expected Shell to wage war over whether Arabie was qualified to put such a big number in front of the jury. Instead, McNamara had asked a few perfunctory questions and then essentially conceded that Arabie had the expertise to say that Shell should be required to pay millions to cleanup the Heyd property.

I suspect it caught Judge Minaldi by surprise, too. Without objection from Shell, she had no choice but to tell the jury that she "recognize[d] Mr. Arabie as an expert in the field of environmental science, specifically soil and groundwater science, including the contamination of soil and groundwater by oilfield products . . . [and] the remediation of property contaminated by oilfield products." Explaining the significance of what that meant, she further informed the jury that Arabie was "thus allowed to give his opinions on issues related to the fields in which he is an expert."

We were now ready to get to the heart of the matter.

15

To start my direct, I asked Austin: "What have you done at the property since becoming involved in this case?"

"I was asked to evaluate the site for oilfield waste contaminants, to look into the sources of that contamination, and to develop a cost estimate for cleanup, if they were there."

Taking each part of his answer one at a time, I first asked him to describe what he did to evaluate the site for contamination. He explained that he began by reviewing some of the historical documents in the case, which included documents from Shell showing previous studies of the property by its own experts. He also viewed the site several times and developed a sampling plan that was designed to "determine whether or not contaminants were there and to give us an idea to what extent they were there."

I knew that an important key toward persuading the jury to believe our experts instead of Shell's would be to show that ours were more familiar with the property. So, I asked Austin how many times he had actually gone to the Heyd property.

"There were at least thirteen visits that I made and members of my staff made."

Austin had already mentioned reviewing documents from Shell's experts about the contamination at the site. This was important evidence, so I followed up.

"Did you read a report by someone named Lloyd Deuel?"

He nodded. "Yes, I did. That was Shell's expert."

I nodded my head in agreement. "Did you take samples from the soil and groundwater?"

He nodded again. "Yes, we took samples of surface soil. We took samples of pits that were on the site. We took samples of the water and of the sediments, and we also took soil borings where we collected subsurface soil samples and also collected groundwater soil samples."

It was time to tie this in to Deuel's report. "Did you see reports from Deuel that showed an analysis of soil samples from the property back in 1984?"

At first, Austin seemed unsure of what I was describing. He said hesitantly, "I don't remember specifically. I'm sorry. I remember him visiting the site in '84."

It's every lawyer's nightmare to have his own witness draw a blank on the stand. Ordinarily, you aren't allowed to ask leading questions on direct examination, so it's hard to prod a forgetful witness's memory. Fortunately, Austin was an expert witness, so I was allowed to ask him leading questions. My next question led him to his answer by asking if he remembered a certain laboratory that had produced the report. He suddenly remembered the report.

"Did you become familiar with the contents of that report?"

He nodded agreeably. He was comfortable again, now that he knew what I was talking about. "Yes, I believe that report showed 35 percent hydrocarbons."

I knew the jury needed some context. "We're going to hear a lot of numbers in this trial and so the jury can put some meaning to those numbers, is that a significant number?"

I could tell that Austin was growing more and more comfortable on the stand. He appeared to become more relaxed. "Yes, the regulatory agency allows no more than 1 percent to be left on site for oilfield waste, so that would be thirty-five times what they would allow."

Our discovery of Shell documents revealed to us that Shell had made only a half-hearted attempt to clean this area, which was part of a pit where oil was collected and skimmed. At the same time, we also knew that Shell was anxious to show that it had made at least some effort to cleanup the property and was likely to talk about what it did. I decided to fire a "preemptive strike" at them.

"We were talking earlier in opening statements about a small area of the big pit that was cleaned up. Is that the area you understand that was cleaned up?"

Austin knew the importance of being precise. "That's—that's where *the attempt* was made." He was not conceding that *anything* had been properly cleaned up.

"All right. Now, Mr. Deuel also returned to the property in late 1991 when this dispute arose, correct?"

"That's correct."

I half-turned to the jury. "Let me ask you this: Aside from this small skimming area, did you find any evidence that any other efforts were made to cleanup the contamination that Deuel's laboratory documented at the time?"

He shook his head. "No."

I figured the jury had to be impressed with Austin. He had all the earmarks of a good witness. He was soft-spoken, appearing to have no ax to grind. He answered questions directly and succinctly, never using more words than required. If a question could be answered with a simple "yes" or "no," that's all he would say.

Shell's expert had issued a second report about the contamination of the Heyd property. It was time to cover that, too.

"Deuel returned to the property in 1991 at Shell's request. Did you become familiar with the report he issued at that time?"

Austin nodded and said quietly, "Yes, I have reviewed that report."

I looked at the jury and then back at him. "Am I correct in understanding that his findings in 1991 from soil samples taken from the property are consistent with what he found in 1984?"

Austin was now taking my cue and looking at the jury when he spoke. "He found very high levels of hydrocarbons, oil, and grease, in that same area, and then he also found high levels of salts."

"Is that associated with oilfield activities?"

He turned again to the jury. "That's the two most common contaminants."

"Is that again consistent with what he found in 1984?"

Austin returned to his one-word answers. "Yes."

I then put up maps and diagrams of the property and had Austin show where Deuel had taken samples and analyzed them. Deuel generally took samples from shallow depths of only three to six feet below the surface. Even then, he did not pull any cores from near the centers of the old waste pits on the property, where the contamination was most severe, instead taking samples from what Austin described as the "periphery" of the pits. Despite this, Deuel nonetheless found numerous contaminants, including benzene and heavy metals, in both the soil and groundwater that exceeded legal limits.

Looking at Austin, I said, "Did Deuel recommend that the soil be cleaned up?"

"Yes," he nodded.

"Was that work ever done by Shell?"

He shook his head. "No."

I pressed on. "Did Deuel recommend that the groundwater contamination be cleaned up?"

Austin hesitated. "His report had no . . . no . . . it did not address the groundwater at all."

"Now," I said, "Deuel has an interesting opinion about groundwater contamination, does he not?"

Austin nodded. "That's correct."

"You're familiar with his deposition testimony on that subject?"

Austin paused. "Yes."

"Am I correct that Mr. Deuel agreed that it was possible that drinking water sources such as wells in the area might be contaminated from the oil waste he found?"

He looked at the jury. "Yes."

"That would include the various things that you described: benzene, cadmium, lead, and other poisons?"

"Yes," he said again.

"But Mr. Deuel said he didn't think Shell should notify anyone in the area who might be drinking that contaminated water, correct?"

Austin shook his head. "That's what he said, yeah."

Shell's lawyers couldn't take it anymore. They were on their feet, objecting to this line of questioning as hearsay. Their problem was that Deuel was testifying at the time as Shell's retained expert, and therefore, his statements were binding on Shell as declarations against interest. As such, Deuel's statements fell under an exception to the hearsay rule and were admissible. Judge Minaldi overruled the objection.

I then asked Arabie if he could be more specific about what Deuel said. That's when he delivered the knockout punch just as I hoped.

"I think the wording I heard at his deposition is that he would wait until somebody complained."

Simply put, Deuel would let the Heyds' neighbors drink contaminated water and hope they never got sick—or, if they did get sick, hope they never figured out it was from Shell's contamination. I paused, letting the callousness of Deuel's comments sink in with the jury.

After a suitable interval, I asked Austin my next question. "Did Shell ever do anything about groundwater contamination?"

He shook his head. "Not that I'm aware of, no."

"Now," I said, "do you agree with Deuel's suggestion that you wait to see if somebody complains?"

Austin again shook his head. He explained that, if you detect contamination in groundwater, you test the next groundwater aquifer and verify whether that is contaminated as well. As he put it, "You determine whether the next groundwater is contaminated or not and proceed like that until you determine whether the drinking water is contaminated or not. That would be the customary practice."

Asked why that was the customary practice, Austin explained that the sole reason for documenting groundwater contamination was to determine whether the deeper aquifer that supplied drinking water for the area was threatened. "It all relates back to public health and the health of the environment."

Shell hadn't been truthful about Deuel's findings when we first asked about them. I wanted the jury to know that. The biggest thing a jury must decide during a trial is whom to believe. If you show that the other side has not been truthful, the jury becomes suspicious of them.

I looked at Austin. "Are you familiar with what Shell said when it was asked in court papers to identify what Deuel found on the Heyd family property?"

Austin replied calmly, "What I've seen defined is oil, grease, and salt."

As I projected a copy of what Shell said onto the various television screens in the courtroom, I said, "Let me show you the answers to interrogatories beginning with this where it says 'Lloyd Deuel in testing done in connection with settlement negotiations identified elevated levels of oil and grease and salt. . . .'" I let the jury read those words on the television screen in front of them.

"Let me ask you this: Mr. Deuel's report found benzene, correct?"

"That's correct."

"Is benzene the same thing as oil, grease, or salt?"

Austin shook his head. "No."

"Mr. Deuel found cadmium, lead, and silver, correct?"

He nodded. "That's correct."

"Is that the same thing as oil, grease, or salt?"

Austin again shook his head. "You can have salts of those compounds, but, I mean, I wouldn't call cadmium salt, I wouldn't call arsenic salt, lead salt."

"Is benzene known to be toxic?"

"Yes."

"In what ways?"

"It's a carcinogen."

I repeated the questions for cadmium, lead, silver, and silver fumes. In each case, Austin confirmed that these materials were toxic and caused harmful health effects to humans exposed to them.

It was now time for another killer question. "Do you have an opinion about whether Shell's answer that Deuel found only oil, grease, or salt is accurate?"

McNamara was on his feet. "Your Honor, I think that we're entitled to have the document reviewed." It was an interesting argument. Shell's lawyers had authored the document, but now they needed to read what they had written before the witness was allowed to comment.

As silly an argument as it was, it worked. Judge Minaldi said, "You will certainly have that opportunity on cross-examination and at other times during the presentation of this case, but I do agree that it is a good time to take a pause. So, we'll break for lunch until 1:30." With that she recessed court—before my witness could answer the question.

I was surprised. When the judge overruled Shell's objection, it meant the question was proper and should be answered. By declaring a recess before the question could be answered, however, Judge Minaldi had effectively sustained Shell's objection, after she had supposedly overruled it. I had never before seen a judge declare a recess while a question was pending.

For whatever reason, I forgot to follow up and repeat the question when court resumed after lunch. Instead, when Austin returned to the stand for the afternoon session, I had him identify various documents showing the results of the different tests he had conducted on the property. While asking a witness to identify documents isn't as sexy or interesting as narrative testimony, it's necessary to get all the paper into evidence. In the eyes of the law, if something isn't in the court record, it doesn't exist. You can't later complain on appeal about something that's not in the record. The only reality in a lawsuit is what is between the brown cardboard covers of the suit record.

After getting this "housekeeping" done, I went back to asking questions that allowed Austin to tell the story of how he determined the extent of Shell's contamination of the property. He indicated that his initial visits to the Heyd property were made just to get an understanding of the layout of the site. He wanted, he said, to identify the major areas of apparent contamination, because that would be where he would primarily take samples for testing and analysis.

It was important to show that Austin had done his sampling, testing, and analysis properly. I didn't want Shell to argue that Austin's results were questionable because he didn't use proper methods. For that reason, I had Austin explain that he performed all of his testing and analysis in accordance with EPA standards.

I then asked, "Did you follow customary procedures that you're familiar with in your profession?"

He looked at the jury. "Yes."

"Did you collect these samples the same way you've always collected samples when you have done work for all of your industrial clients?"

He nodded. "That's correct."

We had enlarged a map of the property to display for the jury. I brought it out, identified it, and set it up for Austin. I then had him show the jury where the various pits were and where he tested for contamination. He first showed the jury where he took borings and explained how that was done. He then explained how he took soil and groundwater samples from each of the eighteen borings he made on the property. He described the depths from which he pulled the samples, how they were marked, and how he sent them to an independent laboratory for analysis.

Again, I wanted to make it clear that Austin had done everything by the book.

"What laboratory did you send this data to?"

He replied, "Gulf Coast Analytical Laboratories in Baton Rouge."

"Is that a laboratory you have used in the past?"

He nodded. "Yes, it is."

"Is it one that others in your profession have used?"

He nodded again. "Yes, . . . they do a lot of business in this area. They have a courier service here. They have a sort of a terminal here where they handle samples and provide laboratory glassware, so they're established in this area."

I figured we had satisfied the jury that everything had been done according to Hoyle. It was time to get to the results. Austin had prepared charts showing the results of the various tests done on the soil borings and the groundwater samples.

His first charts depicted the two groundwater zones beneath the property. Austin explained that the first groundwater zone was approximately eight to ten feet below the surface and the second was approximately twenty to twenty-two feet down. He also explained that these two groundwater zones did not supply drinking water for the area, which generally came from the deeper Chicot Aquifer. He estimated the top of the Chicot Aquifer to be approximately 120 feet down. This would become important later.

The next charts illustrated two sets of measurements, the first by Shell's expert Lloyd Deuel and the second by Austin. The measurements showed the levels of benzene and other pollutants found in the groundwater beneath the Heyd land. It was significant, Austin said, that the concentration of foreign materials was heavier at greater depths. He said this showed that the contamination wasn't of recent origin. This helped us, because Shell's mineral operations had ceased in 1985. This evidence suggested that Rosewood and Kreuger, the two recent operators, were less likely to be the cause of the pollution than Shell.

After describing the extent of groundwater contamination, Austin then presented charts showing the results of his analysis of the soil borings taken on the property. As with the groundwater, the contamination was greater at deeper depths than near the surface. Again, Austin explained, this indicated that it had migrated over time from the surface down through the soil.

The contamination consisted of heavy concentrations of salt, as well as hydrocarbons of various kinds, including benzene, and heavy metals. Austin also explained that, while salt sounds innocuous (after all, we sprinkle it on our food), "it won't support vegetation, won't support growth. It's just an indicator of a problem soil."

All of these materials, he said, were byproducts of oilfield production. The most likely source of this contamination, both in the soil and the groundwater, was Shell's exploration and production activities carried out from the early 1930s until 1985.

Austin then showed charts that matched the measurements he and Lloyd Deuel had taken with the various permissible limits for each pollutant. These charts illustrated that the contaminants on the property all exceeded the limits allowed by regulatory agencies such as EPA, DEQ, or the Louisiana Office of Conservation. The remarkable thing, of course, was that Shell's own environmental expert had documented this for Shell years ago, but the company did nothing.

As I walked Austin through these exhibits, I'm sure that much of our presentation seemed tedious to the jury. Still, it was necessary for him to identify all of the documents that supported his work so that they could be introduced into the record. If not, an appellate court might later say that we hadn't submitted sufficient evidence to support any award we obtained for the cost of cleaning up Shell's contamination. That's where real court proceedings are different from those seen on television shows. No one worries about the court of appeal on television, and trials move along much more quickly—and dramatically.

Austin next explained that, contrary to what Tom McNamara had told the jury earlier, salt water contamination in the soil would not just "go away" over time. In fact, he said, "salt contamination can last for probably hundreds of years." Moreover, although hydrocarbons "degrade" when exposed to air, they will not do so if sealed from the surface. He said this was frequently what he found when he investigated old gas filling station sites that had been closed for years. All of the oil, grease, and other hydrocarbons that had been poured onto the soil and allowed to seep down below the surface were still there after many years. Thus, he explained, all of the contamination he documented would not go away by itself. Someone would have to clean it up.

It was now time to get back to the buried treasure I had mentioned earlier. Turning to Austin, I asked, "Now, beyond the soil borings, did you find anything else on that property that Mr. Deuel didn't look for?"

Austin leaned forward. "Yes, we . . . we had . . . we introduced it earlier . . . an electromagnetic survey done of an area or a couple of areas on the property. That survey used some instrumentation to tell if there was buried metal in the ground."

I showed him an exhibit and asked him to describe what it was for the jury.

"Exhibit P-3 is a report prepared by Geo-Spec, who's a company that specializes in finding buried tanks, buried pipelines, maybe old landfills where drums may have been buried; and so we retained them to inspect or do a survey of two areas out at the Heyd property."

I looked at the jury before asking my next question. "And what did you find?"

Austin arched his eyebrows. "Their report showed buried materials on both areas that we had them inspect, but one area that's been referred to as the old junkyard area had indications of a lot of buried material down to maybe 12 feet deep. So, we went in behind Geo-Spec with some excavating equipment and dug down to see what we would find."

"And what did you find?"

He shrugged. Picking up a set of photographs, he said, "We found a big assortment of things that might be good to . . . to go through these."

As Austin showed the photographs, he explained that the deep trenches in the pictures were dug with a large backhoe. He then showed the jury photographs of one trench and described what was found in it. First, there was an old gasoline-dispensing pump, painted with the distinctive yellow Shell logo. Another photograph showed crushed barrels that were excavated. One had a label that said "triethylene glycol." The label also had a warning that said "harmful or fatal." Another picture showed old tires.

Austin then showed photographs taken of the second trench that was dug. "It contained all sorts of debris," he said. He then described fiberglass pipe, various filters used in oilfield production, and other abandoned materials.

The third trench contained still more debris. There was a yellow-colored drum with chemicals of unknown origin. There were yellow well signs—again, the same yellow used in the familiar Shell logo. Another photo showed still more buried drums.

The fourth trench showed something different. Austin described a dark, thick fluid as "sludge." It ran through the trench and appeared to have leaked from another drum or barrel. Analysis revealed it to be a "gumbo" of hydrocarbons and related chemicals. There were also two crushed tanks that analysis revealed contained lots of heavy metal substances.

Austin didn't mention the fifth trench, but he said that the sixth trench contained an old 500-gallon tank, with some piping and other debris as well. There was an old well sign that had been buried there, too. Another photo showed a second tank in the sixth trench, similar in size and shape to the first. Austin confirmed that they hadn't been used in place there, but had been buried there in order to dispose of them. One of the tanks leaked an oily substance throughout the trench.

It was important to remind the jury of what Shell had said about this.

Referring to a comment made by Tom McNamara in his opening statement, I turned to Arabie and said, "I heard that if I used the word contamination that was going to be inflammatory. Is that an inaccurate term to reflect your findings, contamination?"

Austin shook his head. "No, not at all."

"Okay. So it's not inaccurate in any way when I say that this is about contamination?"

He again shook his head. "That's correct. It's not inaccurate."

There remained one more comment made in the opening statement on behalf of Shell that I wanted to meet head-on.

I turned back to Austin. "I want to backtrack for a second because I did not ask you a question that I should have. All of these photographs of the buried barrels, the triethylene glycol, the gas pump, the Shell sign, and all that. You heard a reference to buried kitchen trash in the opening statement by Shell?"

"Yes," he replied.

"This isn't kitchen trash, is it?"

Austin shook his head. "No."

We then went through other photographs that Austin had taken of the property. In particular, we showed on the map of the property where each picture was taken and described the surface damage that it depicted. There were several photographs of the two large pits on the property, where the contamination was particularly severe. Shell had obtained a bid back in 1984 to cleanup just part of one of the pits for $1.1 million, but elected to do nothing.

I wanted to discuss the groundwater contamination some more.

"Now, let me get back, Mr. Arabie, to your test results. Now that we've been able to look at your results and look at photographs of the things that you saw, in your opinion do your test results show significant groundwater contamination?"

Austin nodded. "Yes, we have borings on each side of the site and over much of the site, and all those showed groundwater contamination."

"Does this contamination possibly pose any threat to drinking water in the area?"

He paused. "I think any time you have contamination of groundwater, then you need to assess that, whether it does or it doesn't, and at this point I would have to say it could because there is contamination there, and it hasn't been documented whether or not it goes deeper or not, whether or not the full extent of it."

I knew that Shell's expert had reached the same conclusion.

"Did Mr. Deuel's results rule out groundwater contamination of the drinking water supply?"

He shook his head. "No."

"Did he test enough to be able to rule that out?"

"No."

"Are you familiar with his testimony when his deposition was taken last month when he said it was possible, he could not rule it out?"

Austin nodded. "Yes. I was there."

"Now, let me ask you this: Could this contamination pose a threat to the Chicot Aquifer, that is, of the drinking water that supplies the City of Lake Charles?"

Austin didn't hesitate. "Yes, this contamination is right over the Chicot Aquifer, and there are some shallower groundwater zones under this that may be contaminated also." Austin then referred to a map from the U.S. Geological Survey showing a "plume" of salt in the area beneath the Iowa Field. He said that the most likely source of that salt was the oilfield production there. He called the "plume" an "anomaly" in that there was no natural explanation for it.

"Do you believe that this kind of contamination should be taken seriously?"

He nodded. "Yes."

"Do you believe that Shell's consultants have taken it seriously enough?"

He slowly shook his head. "There's been no further investigation that I know of, no addressing of it at all that I know of."

I looked at him, then the jury, and then back at him. "You heard Shell's attorney in opening statement make the claim that Shell was ready to do whatever was necessary to clean it up, or words to that effect. Are you aware of any cleanup efforts undertaken by Shell in the nine years since the 1961 surface lease expired?"

Austin shook his head again. "No."

Austin then explained how the clays separating the various groundwater sands in southwestern Louisiana were known to be fractured, or cracked, and how this allowed groundwater to seep downward toward the deeper Chicot Aquifer. Thus, he said, the contaminated groundwater could eventually reach the Chicot Aquifer and pollute the area's drinking water supply.

Now that we had explained the severity of the contamination and the urgency of cleaning it up, I moved toward presenting Austin's cost estimate for restoring the property.

I asked him if he had been able to estimate the cost of restoring the property as Shell promised to do in the 1961 surface lease. He replied, "I was able to prepare cost estimates based on the contamination that we had identified. Probably, you know, one important thing is that I know we have not fully defined the full scope of the contamination, so my figures may be low. But we have prepared some estimates based on what we know at this point."

I knew that Shell would claim that Austin's estimate was "overkill." Shell's experts would present a radically lower cleanup estimate, based on what remediation was required by state regulations, not what our surface lease required. It was important to emphasize the difference.

"The regulations that Shell has been talking about, 29-B and all of that, do they require that you restore property, quote, as near as possible to its present condition, or do they require something less than that?"

Austin answered directly. "The regulations require something less than the contract would."

I then asked him, "Tell the jury how much it will cost the Heyd family to cleanup this contamination that you found and that you attribute to Shell."

16

While Austin had done remarkably well on direct examination, he was clearly drained from being on the witness stand for several hours. As we walked the block and a half from the courthouse back to our office, I congratulated him on a job well done. He just smiled and said thanks.

He didn't have to say more. We both knew that the real test lay ahead, when Shell's lawyers would cross-examine him the next morning. Their objective would be clear: Shell needed to raise doubts about whether the contamination on the property was as severe as Austin claimed and whether his estimate of the cost of cleaning it up was reasonable.

I told Austin to go home and get a good night's rest. It was the best way for him to prepare for his cross-examination. Just before he left, I reminded him that no one knew what he had done on the property better than he did. We then sent him on his way.

When we reconvened court in the morning, Judge Minaldi nodded toward Gray and McNamara. Tom McNamara stood and walked to the podium, indicating that he would handle the cross-examination of Austin Arabie.

The cross began on a light note. McNamara showed Arabie an aerial photograph of the property. Austin looked confused as he studied the photograph.

McNamara asked him, "Do you recognize this to be an aerial photograph taken in the year 2002 of the area of the Heyd property?

Austin seemed puzzled. "I didn't see that photograph, but . . . ."

McNamara interrupted. "Would you take a look at it, please, and see if it appears to be a picture of the Heyd property that you have studied in aerial photographs?"

Austin suddenly brightened. "Maybe if you turn it right side up, I could."

Everyone in the courtroom, including McNamara, laughed.

"Cha-ching," said Judge Minaldi. The expression referred to the sound of a cash register ringing up a sale. It originated with fans of the New Orleans Saints football team, Louisiana's entry into the NFL, who chanted it whenever the team scored a touchdown. (Given the Saints' mediocre record, the cheer eventually died from lack of use.)

McNamara then turned the photograph around.

Austin, who now seemed embarrassed, then said, "Thank you. I believe that's it. Yes."

McNamara then had Austin again point out the areas on the photograph where he had drawn samples and sent them to the laboratory for testing. He seemed to make a point of the fact that Austin pulled samples from the areas with the greatest apparent contamination. I suppose he was trying to suggest to the jury that Austin was attempting to exaggerate the problem. Austin explained, however, that the Louisiana Department of Environmental Quality required environmental investigations to be conducted that way.

The cardinal rule of cross-examination was best expressed by Atticus Finch in *To Kill a Mockingbird*: "Never, never, never ask a question that you don't already know the answer to." For this reason, most experienced trial lawyers don't ask open-ended questions on cross-examination. They know that a smart witness will talk about what he wants to talk about, not what they want him to talk about. If nothing else, the witness will simply repeat what he said on direct examination, giving the jury another chance to absorb it just in case they missed it the first time. Simply put, losing control of cross-examination that way is a rookie mistake.

That's why some of Shell's cross-examination of Austin Arabie surprised me. In the beginning (when the jury was most attentive), McNamara went back over what Austin had done to document the extent of contamination of the property. It afforded Austin the opportunity to conduct a tutorial on how to measure soil and groundwater pollution. If the jury had any doubt about whether Austin knew his stuff, it should have been resolved by the time he got through talking about the equipment he used, how it worked, what regulatory agencies used the same tests, and how an independent laboratory verified his results.

Beyond that, Shell's strategy was to suggest that much of the contamination was within certain regulatory standards (known by such cryptic names and acronyms as 29-B and RECAP) and therefore somehow acceptable. McNamara asked Austin numerous questions about hazardous waste regulations and other environmental standards. The problem was that these regulatory standards sounded complicated and were never really explained. Beyond that, they had little to do with what was necessary to restore the land to its original condition, which is what Shell's agreement with the Heyd family required.

To be fair, McNamara did address a number of instances in which Austin's courtroom testimony appeared to be inconsistent with his deposition testimony. The problem for Shell was that the differences were somewhat technical and thus didn't have the same impact as testimony that was more easily understood by the jury.

McNamara scored real points, however, when he addressed whether the contamination reported by Austin existed before 1961, when the surface lease was signed. This was important, because the surface lease obligated Shell only to restore the property to its "present condition," meaning its condition at the time the lease was signed in 1961. After having Austin acknowledge as much, McNamara showed him aerial photographs taken in the late 1950s and early 1960s. These photos plainly showed that the pits and other surface problems were already present on the Heyd property. To make his point, McNamara then turned to analogy.

"When I go to 'Rent a Wreck' and rent a wreck and I promise to bring the car back in its present condition, that doesn't mean I'm going to bring the car back the way it came off the showroom floor, does it?"

Austin nodded. "No, but you have a record of what the present condition is."

"The lease doesn't say original condition; it says present condition, right?"

Austin agreed. "That's what it says."

It was a point well taken. However, as Austin later pointed out, while the aerial photographs showed surface features, they didn't reveal anything about the groundwater contamination beneath the surface. Simply put, they didn't help Shell prove that the groundwater had been contaminated before 1961, when the contract was signed.

If the pollution before 1961 had been caused by someone else, Shell's argument that it wasn't responsible under the surface lease to clean it up would have been much more appealing. However, Shell had been operating on the property for some thirty years before then, and all of the pollution and contamination that Austin had identified was unquestionably caused by Shell. Thus, Shell was trying to avoid cleaning up its own mess by saying that it had polluted the land before the contract took effect. That, it seemed to me, was a tough sell.

McNamara's next point was one that Shell would stress over and over.

"Have you ever seen a court award money to landowners who said that they wanted to have things on their property cleaned up and they didn't use the money to cleanup the land?"

Austin shook his head. "No, I have not."

A short time later, McNamara returned to the point, apparently hoping to get a different answer.

"If this jury gives them [i.e., the Heyds] money, they can do whatever they want with that money, right?"

Austin answered, "The regulatory agencies at some point are going to require that it be cleaned up."

McNamara wasn't ready to give up. "That's something they would require Shell to do, right?"

Austin didn't agree. "Well, the landowner wants the property cleaned up. I don't know if Shell wants it cleaned up or not."

McNamara persisted. "Do you understand that if the jury gives the plaintiffs money that they are under some legal compulsion to take that money and cleanup the land?"

It turned out to be one question too many. Austin replied, "I feel like they are because that's—I mean, it's a continuing liability that's useless for potential future use. I certainly would not take any amount of money and be stuck with that piece of property."

Shell had suggested in its opening statement that this lawsuit was not about its contamination of the Heyds' property, but about their greed. This was the first attempt by Shell's lawyers to develop that theme, by suggesting that the landowners would not spend any of their recovery to cleanup the property.

Under other circumstances, it could have been a powerful argument. Here, however, Shell had unquestionably polluted the property and then had ignored the recommendations of its own environmental experts to clean it up. It had been nine years since our lawsuit was filed, and Shell had made no effort during that time to cleanup the property. Shell was now arguing that the landowners would behave just as badly if the jury awarded them money to do what Shell had refused to do.

McNamara then turned to Austin's estimates of what it would take to restore the property. In response to questions, Austin conceded that he didn't know all there was to know about the property and that he couldn't be certain of the cost of cleaning it up. Inexplicably, however, McNamara abandoned this line of questioning and began to ask Austin to describe what was pictured in the various photographs we had introduced. I remember thinking that the jury was being reminded of the kinds of damage that existed throughout the property, including our photographs of the buried "sludge" and other junk. After spending a good twenty minutes going through these photographs with Austin, McNamara announced that his cross-examination was over.

That meant it was time for my redirect examination. The rules generally limit redirect to issues brought out on cross. That was fine with me; I had kept careful notes of the things McNamara had questioned Austin about. I would just walk back through the issues he had raised and give the jury what radio personality Paul Harvey would say was "the rest of the story."

The good thing about hearing an opponent's cross-examination of an important witness is that it reveals his plan of attacking your case. When he's finished, you know how to counterattack. Your redirect examination of the witness who was just cross-examined is your first—and best—opportunity to do that.

Tom McNamara had asked Austin numerous questions on cross-examination about different environmental regulations for cleaning up oilfield waste, including Statewide Order 29-B. Those newer regulations did not require the operator to restore the property to its "present condition," as the 1961 surface lease did, but permitted the operator to do something less. The law was clear that the regulations did not affect the agreement between Shell and the Heyds, who were free to agree on more stringent restoration. Because of McNamara's questions, however, I was worried that the jury might be confused into thinking that Shell was only obligated to satisfy the lesser standard, not what it agreed to do in the 1961 surface lease.

I put the surface lease under the Elmo's camera and highlighted the portion in which Shell agreed to restore the Heyds' property to its "present [i.e., 1961] condition" when the lease expired. After having him identify the document, I asked, "Is there anything in this lease that says, 'We will clean it up, but only according to Order 29-B'?"

"No."

"Is there anything in this lease that says, 'We will clean it up but only in accordance with some other rule or regulation'?"

Again, Austin said, "No."

"Is there anything that says we will clean it up but try to shift responsibility to somebody who may have been out there?"

"No."

"Is there anything that conditions this agreement to cleanup the premises at the termination of the lease?"

Once again: "No."

McNamara had also asked Austin about agency standards for closing old pits under 29-B, implying that the standards had been satisfied and therefore Austin's recommendations for cleanup were unnecessary. I needed to clarify that.

"Now, you were asked some questions about pit closure analysis under 29-B, and the difference between that and what you did. You said you did a site assessment rather than a pit closure; is that right?"

He nodded. "That's correct."

"A pit closure just focuses on the pit itself and doesn't really address the area outside of the pit; is that correct?"

"That's correct."

I continued the tutorial. "You were trying to look throughout the property to see if there were signs of contamination outside of the pits themselves, correct?"

"Right," he said and then added, "And that's what we confirmed."

"And did you find contamination outside the pit areas?"

He nodded. "Yes, all over the site."

I pointed to the contract that was on the television screens. "Now, the contract here, it doesn't just say that they will cleanup the pits, does it?"

Austin replied, "No, it says the premises."

"So someone who was just doing a pit analysis really wouldn't be able to render an opinion about what the rest of the premises required under the terms of the cleanup of this contract?"

He shook his head. "No, that's correct."

"Now, this contract also makes no reference to RECAP or DEQ or any of the other letters that we've talked about, right?"

Austin responded quietly, "None, no, sir."

I wanted to make certain it was clear that Austin had done his work in a thorough and professional manner. So I asked him, "And, again, the work you did here and the tests that you did here, did you perform that work and those tests in the way that you have done in the past on other sites in other projects of this kind?"

He nodded agreeably. "Yes."

Next, I brought out some documents that were old estimates Shell had obtained years earlier for cleaning up the pits on the Heyds' property. As is customary, these documents had been numbered by Shell before they were produced to us. Lawyers refer to this as "Bates numbering," apparently because the devices that were first used to number the pages of documents were manufactured by a company named Bates.

This simple procedure shouldn't ever give rise to any controversy, but it did.

Shell had introduced the documents, bundled together, as a single exhibit. The problem was that Shell's lawyers had shuffled the documents and put them in a different order from the way they were produced. When I put them back in the order in which they were Bates-numbered, it revealed that Shell had obtained an estimate to replace soil in one of the pits *after* its own experts had concluded that the soil in the pit couldn't be treated in place, not *before*.

This was important, because it amounted to an admission that we were right all along. Moreover, since this was only for a small portion of one pit, it corroborated Austin's testimony that cleaning up the entire 120-acre site was going to cost millions. Finally, the documents really hurt Shell in the jury's eyes, because Shell took the estimate and did nothing.

I intended to walk through the documents in proper order with Austin. However, as I began questioning him, Shell's lawyers asked to approach the bench. They informed Judge Minaldi that they didn't know how the documents got numbered the way they did, but that it was improper for me to rearrange the order they put them in when they introduced them into evidence. They argued that Austin had no personal knowledge of the proper order of the documents and therefore couldn't comment on them at all.

I didn't think much of their argument. Shell had rearranged the documents, not me. Shell had arbitrarily put them in a certain order in their exhibit, not me. Shell's lawyers even conceded that the documents "may" have been produced in a different order from the way they were arranged in their exhibit.

Despite this, Judge Minaldi told me, "If Arabie doesn't have any knowledge of how those papers were originally organized, then I don't see how he can testify on them having been shuffled." Since Austin had been asked numerous questions about the documents by Shell's lawyers, I didn't see how I could be prevented from responding. They had opened the door by questioning him about this, and now they were arguing he couldn't answer my questions because he didn't have any knowledge.

I leaned toward the judge. "Then we move to strike his cross-examination testimony on that because the ruling of the court is that he doesn't have a foundation to say these things. It shouldn't have been gone into on cross."

Minaldi waved me away. "If you felt that way, you should have objected to it."

In the heat of battle, a lawyer can overreact to things. Even allowing for that, however, I thought the judge's comment was nonsensical. If Shell's lawyers had felt Austin didn't have the knowledge to testify about the documents, *they* shouldn't have asked the questions in the first place. I didn't see how that meant I couldn't address an issue they had raised on cross-examination.

After the court sustained Shell's objection, I suggested to Judge Minaldi that I wanted to proffer what Arabie would say if permitted to answer my questions. This was the standard way in which lawyers show for the record the substance of the testimony that the trial court excluded. Without a proffer, the court of appeal will not entertain a complaint about the lower court's ruling, because the complaining party hasn't shown that the testimony was significant or that its exclusion was prejudicial in any way. In other words, the trial court's ruling, even if wrong, is considered to be harmless error.

I began to state for the record what I expected Austin to say, but the judge cut me off, saying, "No, no, no, no. You make a proffer outside the presence of the jury with the witness. You don't testify as to what he would say."

I tried to explain. "Well, courts have said it's either way, and I've done it either way. I'm not trying to . . . ."

She cut me off. "You've never asked him these questions before. I don't know how you know what he is going to say."

I responded, "It's routine for lawyers to make a proffer that way. I wasn't trying to violate your rules. If you want it always done with the witness, then we'll do that. That's fine."

She cut me off again. "No, no."

I continued, "Just so you didn't think I was doing something irregular. I've been doing it that way for twenty years."

For some reason, that comment offended her. She said sarcastically, "Mr. Veron, I'm very sure that you are very experienced; however, if you have never asked the witness the question before—which I know you have not—I'm not going to let you testify in a proffer as to what his answer is going to be. In those situations, you ask him under oath on the record in a proffer outside the presence of the jury. You don't testify."

With that, I and the other lawyers turned to walk back to our seats. Raising her voice—and speaking only to me—Judge Minaldi then said, "I know not everyone thinks what I say is important, but when I'm talking, I really would appreciate . . . ."

I turned back. "I thought you were through . . . ."

She gave me a hard look. "I was in the middle of a sentence. I don't know how you could think I was through. Obviously, whatever I was telling you is not important enough for you to listen. So, we're going to take a fifteen-minute recess."

I was taken aback—and a little embarrassed. All I could do was say, "I'm sorry," as she walked off the bench in a huff. (Out of an abundance of caution, McNamara also apologized, although the judge's comments were directed at me.)

I understood the judge's point about the proffer. It certainly didn't hurt for us to do it her way and ask Austin questions out of the jury's presence instead of summarizing his testimony. What I didn't understand was Judge Minaldi's sudden anger at me and the sharp, personal tone of her remarks. The fact was, she had *not* been "in the middle of a sentence," and I had *not* walked off before she had finished speaking. Beyond that, I had no idea why she had decided to single me out.

It was a bizarre exchange, to say the least. Unfortunately, it wouldn't be the last.

17

While I was upset, I didn't have time to fret about what had happened. Austin Arabie was probably our most important witness, and I needed to complete my redirect examination in an effective way.

I spent the short recess reviewing what I had left to cover. Austin had been on the stand a long time, and I didn't want to drag things out any longer. The jury had heard a lot, and I suspected that we were at the point of diminishing returns. I trimmed my questions down to some bare essentials.

I did have a couple of "smoking guns" I wanted to bring out, though. When we resumed, I showed Austin a three-page exhibit that I had described for the jury in my opening statement. After he reviewed it, I said, "Now, do you remember being asked whether you had seen any evidence of Ferdinand Heyd having any problems with Shell?"

He nodded agreeably. "Yes, I recall that."

Pointing to the exhibit, I said, "This is a Shell Oil Company document dated May 10, 1945, that refers to a ten-year accepted practice in the operation of the field to run lines and place structures, et cetera, on any of the four larger Shell leases in the field without obtaining rights-of-way or surface leases from the landowners, does it not?"

Austin replied calmly, "That's what it says, yes."

Continuing, I said, "And . . . it says 'our policy of not obtaining rights-of-way or surface leases on the larger area leases in the field . . . we believe it a good business risk to defer the acquisition of rights-of-way and surfaces leases for our new salt water plant and facilities on the Ardoin lease at least until several years hence. . . . In summary, therefore, we plan to defer as a legitimate business risk the acquisition of surface leases and rights-of-way on the Ardoin lease for the operation of our new salt water disposal plant,' correct?"

Austin responded quickly. "That's right."

I then turned to the response from management to this proposal from the field staff. "And the reply to that is: 'We concur with your recommendation that since no surface leases have been secured in the past for similar facilities on other leases in the Iowa Field, it would not be advisable to break with precedent. . . . At the same time, however, we believe it would be inconsistent to secure a surface lease around the disposal well while assuming none were needed for the pits, lines, and plant. Hence, we suggest that no attempt be made to obtain a surface lease around the well unless specifically requested by the lessor.'"

I paused, so that the jury could digest what I had just read. Here was Shell's field staff reporting to management that it had never obtained proper rights-of-way and leases from the Heyds and other families in the field for many of its activities—and of course had never compensated them for them, either. Their attitude was "let sleeping dogs lie," or "what the Heyds don't know won't hurt them."

That was remarkable enough. But what astounded me was the response from Shell's managers. They not only approved this lawless behavior, but went a step further and discouraged the field personnel even from getting the one lease they had been willing to pay the landowners for. It revealed Shell's utter contempt for the property rights of the landowners whose land was producing massive amounts of oil—and massive amounts of money—for Shell's treasury.

Turning back to Austin, I said, "Now, when this refers to a ten-year practice of doing things without notifying the landowner. Ferdinand Heyd couldn't know he had a problem if no one approached him about retaining rights-of-way, correct?"

Austin answered, "That's right."

I glanced over at the jury. They were quite attentive. I then said, "It appears this is a ten-year policy of keeping landowners in the dark, correct?"

Austin nodded. "Yes."

After having Austin explain a few details about his proposal to recover, treat, and dispose of the contaminated groundwater, I concluded my redirect examination. At that point, the judge declared a ten-minute recess.

As our team gathered out in the hall, I was pleased to see them all grinning from ear-to-ear. Austin's testimony had clearly gone well in their estimation. He was our first witness, and we had put our best foot forward. We all congratulated him on a job well done.

Our original plan was to call Bill Griffin, our petroleum engineering expert, as our second witness. However, Austin's testimony had lasted several hours, and we expected Bill's to be just as long and just as technical. Someone in our group suggested that we go with a less complicated witness to keep the jury's attention. In particular, since Shell had raised an issue about whether the landowners would use any recovery to cleanup the property, Tammy Garbarino suggested that we call Billy Corbello as our next witness. He could speak on behalf of the entire family and assure the jury that it was committed to ridding the property of Shell's contamination.

It was a good idea. For one thing, I was confident that the jury would like Billy. He was quiet, soft-spoken, and thoughtful. Although his language could be colorful, he knew how to keep it clean for the jury. He was also well prepared for any questions about whether the family would use any money they received from the lawsuit to cleanup the property.

Moving away from our group, I approached Billy. Grabbing him by the elbow, I said, "How do you feel about going on the stand next?"

He raised his eyebrows. I knew he didn't relish the prospect of testifying. "Well," he said slowly, "I guess I'd just as soon get it over with."

When court was in session again, we announced that Billy Corbello was our next witness. Upon hearing his name called, Billy approached the clerk and raised his right hand, taking the oath given all witnesses to tell the truth. He then settled into the chair reserved for those who come to testify.

Aside from the merits of a case, one of the most powerful influences on a jury is its perception of the parties. The jury had thus far been given reason to dislike Shell, but it had not met any of the Heyd family. We didn't plan to call any other members of the family, so Billy was our only representative. If the jury liked him, it would be much more inclined to award damages. If, however, the group was persuaded by Shell that the Heyds were a bunch of greedy landowners trying to take advantage of the situation, it could reject all of our claims.

For that reason, I needed to introduce Billy and the rest of the family to the jury in a personal way. To that end, I had him identify his wife Sheila and his three daughters, who were all sitting directly behind us in the courtroom. I had him mention his son Jeff, who was out of town at the time and couldn't be with us. I then asked him questions about his grandfather, Ferdinand Heyd, and the other members of the family. As he described them, I had him point out those who were present in the courtroom. I even put up a diagram on the Elmo showing the family tree, which I had Billy explain. The jury now understood who the Heyds were and that they owned this property.

One way to answer Shell's suggestion that the landowners might not spend an award cleaning up the property was to make the jury aware of the Heyds' lifelong presence in the area.

"Your mother was a daughter of Ferdinand Heyd, Sr.?"

Billy nodded. "That's correct."

"And what was her name?"

"Rosa Heyd Corbello." Billy spoke so softly that Judge Minaldi had to ask him to speak up. She reminded him that the microphone in front of him recorded but did not amplify.

Turning to the jury and then back to Billy, I said, "Were you born and raised in the Iowa area?"

He smiled. "I'm fifty-one years old, and I've been in the same place all my life."

"All right," I said. "Do you own a farm out there?"

"Yes, sir."

"Is that what you have done all your life?"

He nodded again. "Yes."

"Now, are you familiar with the property that is covered by that 1929 mineral lease?"

He glanced over at the map that had been on display. "It's . . . about a mile and a half east of me."

Billy then explained that he drove by the property on a daily basis and had been familiar with it since he was a boy. He also described the land lease and where it was located. In the process, he explained that Ferdinand Heyd had died before the land lease was signed in 1961 and that the four signatures on the lease were those of Ferdinand's four children.

Billy also explained that another cousin, Lawrence Heyd, Sr., also lived close by. In fact, he said, most of the remaining family members lived on farms within a few miles of the property. My mother, he explained, lived in Lake Charles, no more than fifteen miles away. The farthest relative, my aunt Bernice, lived in Orange, Texas, just across the state line and within forty miles or so of the property. This piece of land, Billy explained, had been in the family since around 1915, when Grandpa Heyd bought it as a farm, and most of the family had been raised there. It should have been clear to the jury that the Heyds had deep roots in the area.

Having completed the introductions, it was time for Billy to explain how the lawsuit came about. I asked him when he first became aware of the problems with Shell's activities on the property. He said it was in early 1991, when the surface lease was about to expire. That's when, he said, he approached me about it. I showed him the letter we sent to Shell dated May 9, 1991—our original demand letter.

I put the letter on the Elmo for the jury to see. Billy had been sitting in my office when I dictated the letter. It reminded Shell that the 1961 surface lease was due to expire the very next day, May 10, 1991.

I turned to Billy. "Did Shell vacate the property on May 10th?"

He shook his head. "No."

"How long did Shell stay on the property?"

He said, "Until the spring of '93."

"Do you happen to remember when we were forced to file this lawsuit?"

He thought for a moment. "I think it was in '92."

"So Shell stayed on the property even after the lawsuit was filed?"

He nodded. "Yes."

I then asked Billy about our meetings with Shell. "Did you repeat your desire to have the property cleaned up when you met with Paul Lair and Mr. Smith?"

Billy nodded. "I would say that I made that point every time I've met with them."

"Has the property been cleaned up?"

He shook his head. "Not to this day."

"All right," I said. "Did you also express concerns about what kind of salt water had been disposed of on the property?"

He nodded. "Yes, I did."

"Did you also express concerns about the fact that Shell had not moved from the property?"

He nodded again. "Yes."

It was time to address Shell's suggestion that the Heyds wouldn't cleanup the property if they won the lawsuit. "Now, there were some questions asked of Mr. Arabie about the family's intentions if the jury was to award money for cleaning up this property. Tell the jury if it awards any money to cleanup the property what you intend to do."

McNamara objected to the question as leading. Judge Minaldi overruled him. Not to be denied, McNamara then asked me to repeat the question. I was glad he did, because it allowed me to frame it better. Turning to the jury, I asked Billy, "Would you tell the jury what you intend to do if the jury awards money to cleanup the property?"

McNamara had made such a big deal out of the question that the jury was now more anxious than ever to hear the answer. Billy took my cue and likewise faced the jury. Pointing to his daughters seated several rows behind us, he said, "I would clean the property so that I don't pass on the liability to these kids back there."

"Do you know of anyone in the family who feels any differently than you do?"

Billy smiled as if the question was humorous. "If they have, I haven't heard it."

I wasn't through. "When you say the liability, what are your fears or concerns about the contamination on the property?"

He became serious again. "Well, my fears are in a number of years to come that someone will make them try to clean the property up and it will—I mean, you know what it would do to a family, that we just can't do it. We want to do it. That's my fear."

I could tell that the jury liked Billy and—more importantly—believed him. We were scoring points, but I wasn't through. We had a few more to score.

"Now, you heard Shell's lawyers stand up in front of this jury in opening statement and say that Shell is ready to cleanup the property. Have you ever prevented Shell in any way from taking steps to cleanup this property?"

Billy shook his head. "No, sir. In fact, we have done just the opposite. I've asked them repeatedly to clean it up, and it kind of surprised me when I understood in his opening statement that they were going to clean it up. I thought maybe we might be making progress."

I then asked Billy about our meetings with Lloyd Deuel. In response to my questions, he explained why Deuel's proposal to cleanup the property was unsatisfactory. First, he said, Deuel only proposed to cleanup the pits on the property and ignore the widespread contamination elsewhere. Beyond that, Deuel's plan only addressed the top three feet in the pits, even though everyone agreed that there was extensive contamination far below that. Even so, Shell never even attempted to do what Deuel proposed, much less to restore the property to its 1961 condition.

I then wanted to let the jury know more about Billy and his family. "So that the jury knows generally what your interests are and what kinds of activities you engage in, what has been the biggest activity in your children's lives?"

"Well," he said as he leaned forward, "all my children rodeo. That's why my son is not here today."

"He's on the professional circuit, is he not?"

Billy nodded. "Correct."

"And you were the Louisiana state champion steer wrestler, were you not?"

He seemed embarrassed. "Yes, sir."

Referring to the highest high school rodeo award for girls, I said, "And two of your daughters were 'All-Around Cowgirls' for the state of Louisiana?"

"Yes, sir."

I looked at him. "And I think each for three years?"

"Yes."

"And your other daughter was very active in rodeo as well, was she not?"

He nodded. "Yes."

"And you have facilities on your farm where they engage in those activities?"

He nodded again. "Yes."

I then had Billy testify about his many years of service as treasurer of the Louisiana High School Rodeo Association and how he helped put on the annual high school state championship rodeo.

By the time he was through, I was pretty sure there wasn't much about Billy Corbello that the jury didn't like. And my timing was very good; when I finished my direct examination, it was just about quitting time. Judge Minaldi declared court adjourned and sent the jury home. Shell's cross would have to wait until the morning.

She did not dismiss the lawyers, however. It turned out that she had another surprise for us.

18

When a plaintiff seeks damages because of a defendant's wrongdoing, the law says that he's entitled to be "made whole." That is the cardinal rule of compensation under Louisiana law. In other words, the object of a damage award is to restore the injured plaintiff to the position he would be in if the defendant had acted properly.

The rub comes when a defendant gains more from his wrongdoing than the innocent plaintiff loses. In that case, if making the plaintiff whole means that his damages are limited to what he lost, it allows the defendant to keep most, if not all, of his ill-gotten gains. When that happens, it rewards bad behavior and provides an incentive for future bad acts. That flies in the face of another well-known legal principle, which is that an individual should never profit from his own wrongdoing.

We were faced with that problem on our claim for illegal salt water disposal. The surface lease allowed Shell to inject salt water into the Heyd property only if it was produced from a lease operated by Shell in the Iowa Field. We had undisputed proof that Shell had ignored this restriction not only by injecting salt water it produced from leases outside of the Iowa Field, but also by injecting salt water produced by other operators in the field.

It wasn't that hard to figure out why Shell had ignored the contract. As with everything else with Shell, it had come down to money. It cost the company nothing to inject salt water into the Heyds' property. By injecting salt water from other leases it was operating outside of the Iowa Field into the Heyds' property, Shell didn't have to pay for costly commercial disposal or obtain permits to operate disposal wells on the leases that produced the salt water. Second, as part of the deal for taking and disposing of salt water from other operators in the area, Shell required them to send their produced gas to its nearby gas processing plant. That plant "dried out" the gas by removing the valuable gas liquids (primarily gasoline). The "dried" gas now met the specifications of pipelines and could be transported to customers. In return for "free" salt water disposal, the operators let Shell keep (and sell) the gas liquids.

From the company's perspective, it was a helluva deal both ways. Shell paid nothing to get rid of salt water from its other leases while selling the oil and gas from those leases at an increased profit. And it made even more profit off the liquid gas produced from other operators' costly drilling operations while, again, disposing of their salt water at no cost to itself. For these reasons, Shell's managers had concluded that doing these things without the landowners' permission was an "acceptable business risk."

We had done some calculations indicating that the present value of the profits Shell made at the Heyds' expense was over $100 million. Shell had filed a motion for summary judgment several months before trial, asking the court to rule that we could not recover these profits. Shell argued that the money it made had nothing to do with what the Heyds had lost because of the illegal use of their property. Thus, the company's lawyers said that we should be limited to presenting evidence of what we had lost.

The problem there, of course, was that what we had lost was intangible: the right to limit salt water disposal in accordance with the agreement that Shell had signed. There was no way to prove that the additional salt water injected below the surface of the Heyds' property had caused additional physical damage. Even if it had, there was no known way to calculate that damage. So, we argued that the best indicator of the value of the right that Shell improperly took was the amount of money they made using it—i.e., their profits. This argument had an equitable appeal, because it also prevented Shell from keeping its ill-gotten gains and profiting from its wrongdoing.

Louisiana law declared that, in awarding damages, the judge or jury was vested with "much discretion." At the pretrial hearing on Shell's motion, we argued that the jury was entitled to know what Shell made from its illegal activities, if nothing else than as a factor to assist it in arriving at a damage award. Shell's lawyers persisted in arguing that we were limited to showing what Shell's transgressions had cost *us,* not how much they profited Shell. I countered that Shell was free to argue that point to the jury, and the jury was free to consider that as a factor in assessing damages, just like it was free to consider our evidence of Shell's profits.

I was delighted when Judge Minaldi denied Shell's motion. It was now "the law of the case." We would be allowed to present evidence that Shell had made more than $100 million off its illegal disposal of salt water in the Heyds' property. To that end, we asked each prospective juror in *voir dire* if he or she could return a verdict in excess of $100 million if the evidence supported it. And, in opening statement, I reminded the jury that we would present evidence that Shell's profits from its disregard of the surface lease exceeded $100 million.

No jury is going to forget such a promise of proof. Judge Minaldi heard us make those promises during *voir dire* and opening statements. She never suggested (or even hinted) that our statements were not entirely proper. In fact, Shell didn't even object to our statements, because they were clearly consistent with the court's earlier ruling.

Nor would I have expected Judge Minaldi to have found anything wrong with what we were saying. Judges know and understand that pretrial rulings allow lawyers to fashion their cases by clarifying issues. She had clearly ruled that evidence of Shell's profits from illegal salt water disposal could not be excluded as a matter of law and that the jury was entitled to consider them in arriving at a damage award. She had to know that we would, in reliance on her ruling, talk to the jury about it.

My dad once told me that, while judges can't always be right, they should be consistent. Once a judge makes a ruling that the lawyers rely on in speaking with the jury, he (or she) shouldn't change it. If he does, it makes the lawyer out to be a liar with the jury, and a lawyer's credibility with the jury is a precious commodity.

But that's exactly what Judge Minaldi did.

After the jury left the courtroom, she addressed us. "All right. I had deferred ruling the defendant's motion to exclude evidence of Shell's profits. . . . I am going to grant the motion . . . to exclude evidence of Shell's profits. . . ."

I was stunned. First of all, the court had *not*, as she put it, "deferred ruling" on the earlier motion. She had ruled, and we had all relied on that ruling. She certainly didn't warn us after we began referring to the lost profits in front of the jury that she hadn't made up her mind. I wondered just how much thought the judge had given her ruling.

All that aside, the judge had just caused a major sea change in the case. What was the jury going to think when I didn't produce any evidence of lost profits after promising everyone that I would?

The tone of the judge's ruling was peculiar. Referring to the cases we had cited as authority for our side of the argument, she said, "those cases were *spectacularly* unconvincing as far as I was concerned." It was an unusual word for a judge to use, particularly because the cases were directly on point. I could understand her saying they were distinguishable, but to say they were "spectacularly" unpersuasive bordered on insulting. I had never heard a judge use that kind of hyperbole in giving reasons for ruling. It was as if she was trying to persuade us (or herself) that she was right, rather than simply making her ruling.

In any event, it didn't matter now. The jury had left the courtroom, and we put Austin Arabie back on the stand to make our proffer of the testimony she had earlier excluded. The proffer simply consisted of our asking the questions we weren't permitted to ask, with Austin's answers being taken down by the official court reporter. Now, his testimony was in the record for appeal.

That only took five minutes. It was time to go home. While the testimony had gone well for us, it was a tough way to end the third day of trial.

19

One of the things that occupied our postmortem of the day's events was the butt-chewing that Judge Minaldi had given me during our discussion of Shell's document shuffling. Everyone on our side was as mystified as I was. Apparently, what set the judge off was that I had turned away from her in reaction to my paralegal tapping me on the shoulder during our discussion at the bench. In Tammy's typical efficiency, she had located our Bates-numbered copies of the documents we were discussing, which showed that they had been furnished in a different order than the way Shell had arranged them. She had brought them to the bench so that I could show the judge their correct order. That was when the judge erupted with her "Mr. Veron, I know not everyone thinks what I say is important . . ." tirade.

Although it wasn't her fault, Tammy kept apologizing to me for causing the brouhaha. She said that she knew what we were discussing and assumed that having the actual documents would be helpful to the judge. Of course, she was right, and most any other judge would have recognized that. No one could have anticipated Judge Minaldi's reaction, and no one in our camp understood it. What was particularly puzzling was that, according to Tammy, the judge could plainly see that she had approached me and tapped me on the shoulder. It wasn't as if she could have believed I had turned away as an insult of some kind.

We had a long way to go in this trial, and the last thing our clients needed was for their lawyer to spark a running feud with the judge. The first thing I did when we resumed court in the morning was to approach the bench and apologize.

It wasn't the first time I had apologized to a judge, and I'm confident it won't be the last. Even the best lawyers say and do a lot of things in the heat of battle that, on reflection, call for an act of contrition. But what I'll never forget is the way Judge Minaldi reacted when I offered my apologies. Most every other judge would have said "Forget it" or "Thank you" and moved on. But Judge Minaldi clearly enjoyed watching me deliver my "mea culpas"—to the point of grinning broadly as I did so. It was as if she felt vindicated in some way. Her behavior was puzzling. In any event, I had done my duty, and it was on the record so that the court of appeal could read my explanation for our little contretemps (and hopefully be more convinced by it than Judge Minaldi apparently was).

I then shared with the court our dilemma over how to proceed now that she had ruled that evidence of Shell's profits from illegal salt water disposal was not admissible. We didn't want the jury to think we hadn't proven those profits because there wasn't any proof. That would damage our credibility, perhaps fatally. I suggested to Judge Minaldi that she consider explaining to the jury that, because of a ruling she had made, we wouldn't be submitting that evidence but would instead show our damages in another way. She put me off, suggesting that we discuss it during a break.

It was time to get back to work. Billy took the stand again. Tom McNamara stood and approached the podium to begin his cross-examination.

He went on for thirty minutes or so, but I didn't think the cross produced any memorable moments to speak of. First, McNamara asked Billy to repeat his testimony about who was on our family tree. Then, he asked

Billy about his land holdings. In response to questions, Billy indicated that he owned several pieces of land totaling about 2,000 acres. McNamara's apparent objective was to show the jury that Billy was sophisticated and therefore not some poor, dumb dirt farmer. Conceding that point, I wasn't sure how it excused Shell's bad behavior toward Grandpa Heyd and his children.

McNamara then showed Billy numerous pictures of the property that we had taken, asking him to identify the damage they showed. Since the pictures were taken in 1994, I supposed that McNamara was trying to suggest that the damage took place *after* Shell had left the property and had therefore been caused by one of the later mineral lessees. Of course, the pictures didn't show when the damage was done, just that it was still visible in 1994.

The most telling thing about the cross was that McNamara didn't impeach Billy's testimony with his deposition a single time. Nor did he ask leading questions designed to produce short "sound bite" admissions. It was as if he had a casual conversation with Billy rather than an interrogation.

As a result, my redirect was very brief. Billy's testimony was quickly over, and he had exceeded our already high expectations. Billy was the "face" of our family to the jury, and I was confident they liked what they saw.

After Billy stepped down, Judge Minaldi looked at me and said, "Call your next witness, please."

It was time to call Bill Griffin.

I remember thinking, "So far, so good." Austin Arabie had shown the jury where the contamination was and what it would cost to clean it up. Billy had hopefully persuaded them that the family would use any recovery to execute Austin's cleanup plan. Those were important parts of the puzzle, but Bill Griffin's part was as big, if not bigger. As our petroleum engineering expert, he would not only address how the contamination came about, but he would also teach the jury how to understand the salt water disposal and trespass claims.

The witnesses had been placed "under the rule of sequestration," which meant they had been required to stay outside the courtroom while other witnesses were testifying. However, the rule of sequestration didn't apply to expert witnesses. As an expert, Bill had been allowed to sit in the courtroom while Austin and Billy testified. Thus, he was familiar with

Shell's cross-examination tactics, as well as with Judge Minaldi's attitude about our case. It meant that he was less likely to be surprised by anything that happened during his turn on the stand.

Bill was a good witness to follow Billy Corbello for another reason. If the jury liked Billy because he was "country," they were going to like Bill Griffin just as much. The two were much alike, which probably explained why they had hit it off so well from the moment they met. They both talked slowly and with a drawl (Bill's was a little more pronounced) and enjoyed a good laugh. Both of them also had keen intellects and communicated well with each other and (I expected) with the jury.

When his name was called, Bill stood from his seat in the last pew in the courtroom and walked forward. The burly, sandy-haired West Texan had worn a suit and tie and looked very comfortable in business attire. Looks were deceiving in this instance; I knew that Bill would have preferred wearing his usual uniform, which consisted of a polo shirt and jeans.

The first order of business was to introduce him to the jury. In response to my questions, Bill recited his name, where he lived, what he did for a living, his education, and his work history (which included twenty-seven and a half years with Amoco). I had Bill explain his professional credentials, including his registration as a professional engineer in Louisiana and Texas. As Bill described his career, I made certain that he explained his experience in calculating the economics involved in every potential oil or gas well, as well as his expertise in protecting the environment by making certain that Amoco's oilfield practices were carried out safely. One of the things that distinguished Amoco from other oil companies was its extensive land holdings, which in Louisiana included several hundred thousand acres. This inevitably made its employees more "green," or environmentally conscious, than other oil companies.

The main objective in reviewing Bill's credentials was, of course, to persuade the court to accept him as an expert. Beyond that, however, I wanted the jury to appreciate that, having spent his entire career working in the oil industry, Bill wasn't some "Greenpeace" radical. In other words, Bill's wasn't bringing a point of view to the case that was inherently hostile to Shell's side. I hoped it gave him added credibility when he was critical of Shell.

At the conclusion of my questions, we tendered Griffin to the court as an expert in petroleum engineering. As part of the tender, I specifically stated that it included "expertise in drilling for oil and gas, production and marketing of oil and gas, evaluating the economics thereof, and safe practices in connection therewith." Judge Minaldi nodded and turned to Shell's lawyers. "Traversal?"

Pat Gray stood and said, "A few questions, Your Honor."

Tall and handsome, Gray was raised in the small South Louisiana coastal town of Morgan City. It was, as they say, "a good place to be *from*." There wasn't much reason for Morgan City's existence except to serve the offshore oil and gas industry. If your career plans didn't include working on a drilling platform in the Gulf of Mexico (or in a courtroom representing workers who were injured there), there wasn't much point in hanging around the area after high school.

Like most of South Louisiana, Morgan City was heavily populated with descendants of French refugees from Nova Scotia. It was easy to see that Gray had all the best features of his Cajun ancestors. He was dark-complected, lean, and athletic, and had long wavy hair of which he was obviously proud. Unfortunately for him, he was also the only lawyer in the courtroom with an ego bigger than mine.

Gray's questioning style contrasted with McNamara's. Where McNamara was warm and fuzzy, Gray was cool and pointed. It was closer to the style of cross-examination that I used, which is neither a compliment nor an insult, just a fact.

Gray wasted no time in marking out the limits of Bill's expertise. In short order, he had Bill concede that he was not a "land man" at Amoco and therefore was not responsible for negotiating oil and gas leases. In response to additional questions, Bill admitted that he was not an "environmental engineer" *per se*, although he pointed out that, as a petroleum engineer, his job "entail[ed] protecting the environment." Bill also conceded that he had never negotiated a contract for the sale of oil, gas, or gas liquids. He further admitted that he had not "totally" designed a gas processing plant, although he explained that he had designed some of the "components" for one. Gray continued on this tack for some time, essentially asking Bill to admit the various things he had not done, as opposed to what he had been responsible for as a petroleum engineer at Amoco. It was an effective tactic, I thought, to persuade the judge to place limits on the scope of Bill's expertise—and therefore on his testimony.

In the end, Judge Minaldi recognized Bill as an expert in the field in which we tendered him, which she said included "reservoir production, marketing with economic evaluation." However, in a bench conference, she warned me that she was concerned about the extent to which he was qualified to testify about the economics of oilfield production because she believed from his testimony that others on the "teams" in which he participated at Amoco had primary responsibility for that area.

We began the substance of Bill's direct examination by discussing how long he had been involved in the case and what he had done during that time. This would continue to provide a marked contrast with Shell's experts, who were essentially new to the case and had done little compared to the amount of work Bill and Austin had done. In particular, Bill described how he had visited the Heyd family property "about" fifty times. He had also visited other gas processing plants like the one that Shell had operated next to the Heyd property in order to gain a better understanding of how they worked. He also reviewed approximately ten boxes full of documents pertinent to the case. At the end of it all, he said, he concluded that Shell had improperly disposed of salt water on the Heyd property and that Shell had continued to operate "a rather large oil terminal on the property for a little over a year or so after the lease expired."

Bill testified that much of his investigation consisted of obtaining and reviewing salt water disposal records from the Louisiana Office of Conservation. As he explained to the jury, every operator that disposed of salt water into any injection well in Louisiana was required to file monthly reports stating the amount (in barrels) of water injected and where it came from. These reports were matters of public record, he said, and were available to anyone who wished to view them. Bill pulled all of the reports pertaining to the disposal wells on the Heyds' property and determined how much salt water was injected into those wells that was not permitted by the 1961 lease, i.e., that was not from a well operated by Shell in the Iowa Field. This included salt water from wells in the Iowa Field operated by other companies as well as wells outside of the field operated by Shell and others. Bill also explained how Shell took the salt water from other operators in return for their sending their gas to Shell's nearby gas plant for processing and kept the gas liquids as a processing fee. Thus, he said, Shell unlawfully used the disposal wells on the Heyds' property to make profits from its gas processing plant next door.

Bill had constructed a model of a typical oilfield operation, with a well, field separator, salt water disposal system, and pipelines. He used the model to explain how the oil, gas, gas liquids, and salt water were separated out of the wellstream. He further explained how the oil was marketed and how the gas and gas liquids were sent to a gas processing plant for further separation. He then showed the jury how the gas plant removed additional water from the gas feed and how all salt water that was separated from the well flow was sent to a disposal well for injection below ground.

Bill's visual aid was an obvious hit with the jury. Virtually every member of the jury leaned forward in their chairs as he walked them through the various stages of oil and gas production. It helped that Bill had an obvious knack for teaching. He kept things simple, and he avoided using big words and technical language.

As part of this tutorial, Bill explained the function of oil terminals like the one that Shell operated on the Heyds' property. As he showed the jury, the oil terminal took heavy and light oils and mixed them so that they achieved the most valuable middle weight. In that way, he explained, the whole became greater than the sum of its parts. Simply put, Shell could sell the middle-weighted oil for a lot more than it could sell the same amount of either the heavy or the light oil.

Shell was entitled to operate this system on the Heyds' land because of the 1961 surface lease. That was why, Bill testified, Shell didn't sell the 1961 surface lease when it sold the 1929 mineral lease in 1985. It stayed on the property operating the oil terminal long after it had sold the mineral lease—until 1993, to be exact, even after the surface lease expired in 1991. In fact, Bill said, Shell's own records showed that the company made a profit of nearly a million dollars (actually $927,000) from operating the oil terminal after the lease expired.

We then returned to the salt water disposal claims. Bill explained how he reviewed information about commercial salt water disposal in the area and determined that, over the years in question, the average cost of disposing of the salt water that Shell unlawfully injected beneath the Heyds' property amounted to $1 per barrel. This was the amount of money Shell saved by doing it for nothing as opposed to doing it at a commercial disposal well.

At this point, Shell's lawyers were interrupting virtually every question I asked with an objection of some kind. One of Shell's objections was that I had not furnished them with a copy of Griffin's calculations about salt water disposal cost savings beforehand. That prompted still another conference at the bench, and this occasioned another confrontation with Judge Minaldi.

After Pat Gray protested that he had not seen any of the documents that Griffin was testifying from, Judge Minaldi asked him: "You have never seen this before, is that what you are saying?"

Gray didn't answer directly. "This is the year 2000, and he is—"

I broke in. "The question is: Have you seen it before?"

Gray answered, "I have not seen it before."

At that point, I said, "Let me find out. I thought it had been produced."

The judge and Gray continued with their discussion, with the judge commenting that Gray should bring up his complaints about Griffin's calculations during his cross-examination rather than through an objection. When Gray finally admitted that he had no legal objection to make, the judge said, "All right. Thank you. Now everybody can sit down."

In the meantime, I had moved away to confer with my paralegal about whether our file showed that the documents containing Griffin's calculations had been furnished to Shell in discovery. Tammy confirmed that they had; in other words, Gray had been wrong in complaining to the court that he hadn't ever seen the documents before.

I turned back to the court to convey this information. Addressing both of them, I said, "Your Honor, Pat?"

At that point, Minaldi exploded again. "Mr. Veron, if you walk away again when we're discussing something, I'm going to have a severe problem with you, because we just resolved this issue but you weren't here to hear it."

I was flabbergasted. Answering quickly, I said, "I'm sorry. I was asking to see if that was produced, that's all."

Minaldi wasn't through. "This is two times now, Mr. Veron. I'm getting to the point where I'm losing my patience with it, so I'm warning you about that. Nobody else is doing that except for you. So, so—the issue has been resolved. He has no objection to this, other than something he is going to handle on cross-examination."

I knew all of this was on the record, and I was concerned that the court of appeal might think I had been rude to the trial judge. I had to say something to explain. I also had to do it without further offending the judge.

"I'm sorry, Your Honor. I thought you were through. I thought you had ruled and told him that's for cross-examination [which she had]. I thought that ended it and she [meaning Tammy] was walking up. If we hadn't produced it [meaning the document in question], I was going to withdraw it. I apologize. We were told we hadn't produced it, and I found out we had. That's all I was trying to do."

None of that mattered to Minaldi. She glared at me before she said icily, "You can sit down now."

There was nothing else to do but continue with Bill Griffin's direct examination.

Under further questioning, Bill described how various documents showed that Shell had granted another operator in the Iowa Field a "permit" to send its gas through a line across the Heyds' land to the Shell gas processing plant. As Bill explained, there was no such thing as a third party giving someone a private "permit" to cross another person's land. Shell apparently came up with the "permit" idea to avoid having the operator approach the Heyds for a right-of-way. That might have alerted the family that Shell should have been getting rights-of-way over the years for all of its lines as well. The documents also showed that Shell's personnel knew that the practice was probably illegal, but preferred to take the "risk" rather than do things the right way.

At that point, we had reached the end of the day. The fourth day of trial was over, and Judge Minaldi recessed court until nine o'clock the next morning.

Although the evidence had gone well, it had been a trying day. I had endured one more strange confrontation with the judge, and it was even more peculiar than the previous one. I was obviously getting on her nerves, but neither I nor anyone on our side could figure out what we were doing that offended her.

Tammy, my paralegal, was almost beside herself. For the second time, she had been in the middle of it, showing me a document that was clearly at the heart of what we were discussing at the bench. But what really alarmed me was a story she told me after we got back to the office.

"I didn't want to distract you before," she said as we stood in the lobby of our office, "but I need to tell you about my conversation with the judge." Tammy had known Judge Minaldi for a long time. So, when she saw the judge in the hall at some point, she apparently had taken it upon herself to apologize for getting me in trouble.

Describing what happened, she told me, "I said, 'Patty, I'm so upset about what happened. I didn't mean to get Mike in trouble. I was bringing him the documents that you all were talking about. He turned away because I tapped him on the shoulder.'" Tammy shook her head and opened her eyes wide. "Mike, she looked at me and said, 'Oh, Tammy, you don't have anything to apologize for; I saw what you were doing.'"

I raised my eyebrows. "If you didn't have anything to apologize for, why did I?"

Tammy just shrugged. "Beats me."

Trying any lawsuit is stressful. Trying one for this kind of money was even more so. Throw in psychological warfare with the judge, and you've got enough stress to give even the most jaded courtroom veteran heartburn.

In any event, I tried to comfort myself with the thought that, over the years, I had probably dodged a number of ass-eatings I deserved, so getting a couple I didn't was just a way of evening things out. Besides, I figured, it would make winning the case that much sweeter.

20

I finished my direct examination of Bill Griffin the next morning. It took less than a half-hour. In that time, Bill described how he calculated the amount of salt water that was unlawfully injected into the disposal system on the Heyds' property. The grand total, he said, came to 1,629,723 barrels. Based on his estimate that it would cost approximately one dollar per barrel to dispose of this salt water at a commercial disposal site, that meant that Shell had saved $1,629,723 at the time by injecting this water into the Heyds' property for nothing.

Of course, from our perspective, that was only the tip of the iceberg. With respect to the salt water that came from wells operated by others, Shell had actually charged other operators a few pennies a barrel to dispose of that salt water. Of course, it had never shared any of that money with the Heyd family. On top of that, in return for this cheap disposal, Shell had forced the other operators to send their gas to Shell's gas processing plant and had kept the valuable gas liquids it extracted from the gas as a processing fee. But Judge Minaldi had changed her mind about letting us submit any evidence of these profits to the jury. Under her ruling, Shell was allowed to keep most of its ill-gotten gains.

The difference was significant, especially after the dollar amounts were adjusted to their present value. As our economist would show, the cost savings that Shell realized from its unlawful use of the Heyds' property over the years was worth a little over $25 million in today's dollars. But Shell's profits from this illegal scheme, adjusted to present value, came to more than $100 million. That's the gaudy number I had told the jury we would prove as our damages.

To make matters worse, Judge Minaldi wouldn't let me offer any explanation to the jury about my failure to introduce evidence of Shell's unlawful profits, as I had promised before she changed her ruling. Toward the very end of my direct examination, I asked Griffin, "Now, Mr. Griffin, to be fair, you came here this week prepared to give testimony about how much money Shell made as a result of these activities, correct?"

Bill nodded. "That's correct."

"And you became aware on Wednesday that the court had ruled that you could not present those calculations, correct?"

At that point, Pat Gray stood and started to object. Before he could say anything more than "Your Honor," Judge Minaldi looked at me and said, "Mr. Veron, let's not go into that."

I then asked for a bench conference. After we approached, I explained that I didn't intend to present any evidence of lost profits, just explain why we hadn't done so. Again, this was critical because I had promised the jury that we would show the extent to which Shell profited from its unlawful use of the Heyds' land. As I reminded the court, I had made those promises both during jury selection and in opening statements, before she had changed her ruling.

I also advised the court that I had cleared things with Tom McNamara beforehand and was surprised that Gray had objected. McNamara lamely acknowledged that I had, but then backed off of that admission by saying that this witness was Gray's responsibility. McNamara wasn't going to throw himself on the grenade for anybody. (In Louisiana, we refer to this as "crawfishing," because crawfish crawl backwards, much in the same fashion as McNamara was backing off his word.) Despite McNamara's admission, Judge Minaldi told me Gray's objection was sustained.

There was little left to say. I tendered Bill Griffin to Pat Gray for cross-examination.

I like to think that cheap shots don't win lawsuits, and the early part of Gray's questioning proved that. Bill had great difficulty pronouncing the French name Ardoin (in Louisiana, it's "ard-wan"), which was the surname of one of the landowners in the Iowa Field. Bill even had me say the name over and over on a cassette tape that he would play in his truck as he drove to and from his home in Katy, Texas to Lake Charles. However, try as he might, he just couldn't get it right, and the facial contortions he made as he tried to pronounce the name were a great source of inside humor in our group.

Gray had discovered this inadvertently when he took Bill's deposition. I guess he thought it would score points for his side if he showed the jury that Bill was such an outsider that he couldn't pronounce one of our native French names. So he made a point of bringing up the Ardoin name right away in his cross-examination.

"This document contains a discussion between Shell personnel about whether special arrangements should be made to obtain a surface lease on the Ardoin property?"

Bill nodded. "That's correct."

Pat smiled, almost malevolently. Turning to the jury, he said, "Can you say Ardoin?"

Bill shook his head. Staring back as if embarrassed, he said evenly, "You know I have a speech impediment."

Griffin's answer slammed Gray so hard I half-expected to see snot bubbles come out of his nose. Shell's lawyer blinked a couple of times as he digested the certain realization that he had committed a major *faux pas*. He looked around the courtroom, as if to regain his bearings, and when he did he could see that the jury was glaring at him for belittling Bill's "handicap." Gray's mean-spirited attempt to make light of Bill's inability to pronounce French names had backfired in a big way.

After an awkward pause, Gray tried to change the subject with a few meaningless questions. He then felt compelled to revisit the "Ardoin" imbroglio. Gray asked Bill to read a line from a document he had highlighted, and Bill again stumbled when he came to the name "Ardoin."

Gray seemed almost frantic to redeem himself with the jury, so he said, "Okay. Just so the jury won't think I was being mean to you, you have trouble with that word?"

Bill nodded. "Well, I had trouble with another word earlier, also. Sometimes I have trouble with words."

"Okay. Ardoin, if you're not Cajun, is a hard word to pronounce."

Bill shrugged. "Okay."

"That was my only point."

Gray wasn't asking questions; he was just making statements. But I wasn't about to object, because he was just digging himself in deeper. However, Judge Minaldi apparently felt the need to intervene on Gray's behalf. As if to explain away his gaffe, she commented to the jury, "It's just a Texas thing. That's all it is."

Even after getting help from the judge, Gray refused to let go. Apparently needing to have the last word, he said, "Those of us that grew up in Morgan City know how to say it. It rolls off."

I was amused by this little exchange, because it only served to make things worse. Throughout it all, I noticed—and I suspected the jury did, too—that Gray never apologized. Instead, he acted as if he had been making a joke, and Bill had just misunderstood. The entire display was consistent with Shell's attitude about the case in general—belittling and unapologetic.

The remainder of Gray's cross-examination was lengthy. Much of that was inevitable. The legal rules required him to lay foundations to show the relevance of his questions. For that reason, real-life courtroom interrogation rarely if ever matches the courtroom drama seen on television and in the movies. The challenge in real life is to get the necessary work done quickly and without boring the jury so that, when you do get to the punch line, it carries the desired impact with the audience. None of us ever gets it quite right, and you won't find an experienced trial lawyer who doesn't cringe at times when later reading a transcript of his own interrogation.

One sure way to lose impact is to bury the good points inside a long series of dull questions or to use technical language that isn't understood by the jury. That's why it's important to make any concessions by the witness crystal clear. The time to nail down those kinds of admissions is in the deposition of the witness, before the trial. Once that's done, the cross-examiner uses the transcript to ask the same questions at trial. Gray apparently eschewed that approach. His cross-examination didn't follow what he had done in the deposition, but seemed to wander over different parts of the case at random. He only used Bill's deposition once during the entire cross-examination to contradict one of Bill's answers.

Instead of the short, pointed questions he had asked during his traversal of Bill's qualifications, Gray insisted on showing Bill numerous documents from the past, including various surface leases that Grandpa Heyd and his children had given Shell before the 1961 lease. All of these leases had expired or had been superseded by the 1961 agreement, so none of them was relevant to the case. Despite this, all of my objections to the relevance of these questions were overruled.

Gray then challenged Griffin's estimate that it would have cost Shell a dollar a barrel over the years to dispose of the unlawful salt water at a commercial site. Bill felt that estimate would be valid for disposal before 1970 as well.

Gray hammered on this. He appeared insistent on getting Bill to admit that he had no direct knowledge that the disposal rates before 1970 were essentially the same as thereafter. Bill did so, but not to Gray's satisfaction, and so Gray pressed on. It is axiomatic that lawyers must know when to stop on cross-examination, and this became an example of that.

As Gray continued to pound on Bill about what information he could have relied on, Bill recalled that one of Shell's own experts, John Berghammer, had testified in his deposition that such expenses had remained constant over the years. It was a powerful refutation of Gray's point, and it would never have come out if Gray had left well enough alone.

Now, Gray was embarrassed, and he became visibly agitated. Making a statement rather than asking a question, the Shell lawyer literally bellowed: "Mr. Berghammer conducted an extrapolation in order to demonstrate that your method of extrapolation to come up with these costs was absurd."

I was pretty sure his statement contained at least one too many "extrapolations" for the jury to follow, but I let it go. Bill must have understood. He just shook his head and said, "That's not the way it was represented to me."

Without thinking, Gray challenged this answer by asking, "Were you there at his deposition?"

Bill nodded. "Yes, sir."

Gray must have forgotten that Bill had been sitting next to me during the entire time that we took Berghammer's deposition. He had walked right into a haymaker. Instead of stopping, though, he forged ahead. "Didn't he take your number and extrapolate from it in order to demonstrate that you had used completely improper methodology in arriving at your number?"

Bill leaned forward. His demeanor, which had remained as pleasant as could be throughout Gray's questioning, now turned serious. Narrowing his eyes, he looked directly at Gray. "That's a totally false statement."

Gray was now beside himself. He was getting answer after answer that he didn't like, and his frustration was evident. In an irritated and raised voice, he asked Bill, "Well, why won't we just wait and ask Mr. Berghammer what he did with your dollar?"

I was having too much fun to interrupt Gray's fuming with an objection. However, Judge Minaldi apparently felt compelled to rescue Gray again, so she interjected, "That would be a good idea, but I don't think this witness can answer that query."

Gray's remarks surprised me for more than one reason. Berghammer had been sitting in the courtroom throughout this exchange. I knew that, if he testified, I was going to score a lot of points on cross-examination, taking admissions right out of his deposition testimony. I had assumed that Shell's lawyers understood this as well and might be having second thoughts about putting him on the stand. Now, however, Gray had declared on the record that Berghammer would be testifying. Not only that, but he had promised that Berghammer would say that Bill's calculation of the cost of salt water disposal was "completely improper." I knew he wouldn't be able to deliver on such a promise, and I wondered why he had made it. One thing was clear: Shell was now obligated to call Berghammer as a witness.

The same thing happened when Gray attacked Bill's testimony that field separation did not eliminate all of the salt water from the stream of fluids coming out of a well. More specifically, he stated in passing that it was able to remove at most 98 percent of the water, and the remaining 2 percent went on to further processing with the oil and gas.

Gray kept asking Griffin about his 98 percent figure. Bill talked about various sources for the figure, including manufacturers' specifications for oilfield separators. When Gray persisted, Bill finally recalled that he had heard another one of Shell's experts, Richard Jones, give that figure in his deposition testimony. Once again, Gray had failed to stop and leave well enough alone, and Griffin had made him pay for it by telling the jury that Shell's own experts agreed with his testimony.

I no longer objected to Gray's repetitious questions. I couldn't see how any of this really mattered; the evidence was clear that Shell had injected salt water into the Heyds' property that was not authorized by the 1961 lease. Thus, I was content to let Gray ask these same questions over and over. As a good measure of how tedious this became, however, Judge Minaldi interrupted Gray twice on her own with suggestions to "wrap it up."

Even after the second warning, Gray felt compelled to ask Bill several more times where he got his information that field separation didn't extract all salt water from a well. This enabled Bill to recall that Thomas Brashear, another Shell witness, had also testified in his deposition that field separation did not remove all salt water from the oil and gas. It also allowed Bill to repeat his opinion over and over, further imprinting it in the jury's collective mind.

Gray then spent twenty minutes or so arguing with Griffin about technical aspects of field separation and processing plant separation of water from gas. In my judgment, none of this had any real impact on the jury, except to show that Bill could hold his own when discussing complicated aspects of oilfield production. It was never apparent how these technical questions related to the issues that the jury would have to decide.

At one point, Gray himself recognized that he was making little headway. He looked up at the judge and pleaded, "Can we take a break? I will organize and try to get done with this." With that, Judge Minaldi ordered an early break for lunch.

As we left the courthouse, my paralegal Tammy grabbed my sleeve. "I don't think they'll be too long with Bill when we get back."

I looked at her. "Why not?"

She laughed. Referring to Shell's entourage, she said, "I walked by them in the hall just a minute ago, and they were all telling Pat Gray that he was getting nowhere with Bill and that he needed to wrap it up and get him off the stand."

When we returned, Gray asked questions for perhaps another five or ten minutes and then sat down. It was my turn to redirect. I knew the jury had heard enough, so I just asked a few questions that allowed Bill to clarify issues that I thought might have become confused and then sat down, too.

21

We had called our three most important witnesses right off the bat, and they had all done well. In reality, we were more than halfway home on our side of the case. Our remaining witnesses would all be testifying about smaller slices of the pie and were unlikely to produce any real drama (or so we thought). The real fireworks from our side would come when Shell began its case, and we cross-examined its witnesses.

Our next witness was J.W. Perry, a former land man who had actually negotiated the 1961 surface lease on Shell's behalf with the four Heyd children. We had learned that Mr. Perry was still living after all these years, and we were able to take his deposition several months before trial. He was now retired in Florida and unavailable for trial, so we submitted the deposition transcript in lieu of his live testimony. This meant that we had to read the transcript out loud to the jury, with each lawyer playing himself. Since my partner Pat Gallaugher had taken the deposition, Pat read his part, and one of Shell's lawyers read his part. I agreed to play Mr. Perry and read his answers to the lawyers' questions. The main reason we wanted to put Mr. Perry's testimony in evidence was his recollection that the provision about cleaning up the property was inserted in the 1961 agreement at the Heyds' insistence.

The jury must have been thrilled at how quickly Perry's deposition was read. It was over in twenty minutes. We didn't expect Walter Moss, our next witness, to be as short, but he definitely wouldn't take as long as Arabie or Griffin.

Walter Moss worked on the property as a gauger for Dean Enterprises, who was hired by the present leaseholder to operate the lease. (A gauger checked readings on the various gauges on the production equipment and recorded them for the operator.) More importantly, Moss had worked on the property since 1985, the year that Shell sold the lease. In fact, he started work about two months before the lease was transferred to Rosewood Resources, Matt Randazzo's client.

Moss's testimony was particularly helpful to dispute Shell's claim that no salt water came to the Heyd property from its gas plant next door. Moss testified that there was a six-inch salt water line that ran from the gas plant to the salt water disposal plant on the Heyd property. While the Shell gas plant had closed shortly before Moss came to work, the line was still intact and connected to the disposal system on the Heyd property. Moss also testified that Mobil had opened a gas plant in partnership with Shell to replace the old Shell gas plant, and this new plant sent approximately 350 barrels of salt water a month to the Heyds' property. This further contradicted Shell's claim that gas-processing plants did not produce salt water and, therefore, Shell's gas plant could not have sent salt water for disposal on the Heyds' property.

We knew that part of Shell's defense was to blame Rosewood and Kreuger, who owned the lease in succession after Shell, for the contamination on the property. Moss firmly testified that the contamination shown in the numerous photographs we had put into evidence existed when he first came to work in 1985—before Shell ever transferred the lease. He further stated that both Rosewood and Kreuger ran clean operations and promptly cleaned up any incidental spills that occurred on their respective watches. Finally, he emphatically testified that neither Rosewood nor Kreuger ever buried sludge, rotting asbestos pipe, old Shell gas dispensers, or the other materials we had located in the deep trenches on the property.

Pat Gray handled Moss's cross. As before, he covered a number of technical details. He also had Walter admit that the lines on the property leaked. It was a small point; Moss had already said that Rosewood and Kreuger prompted repaired any spills. Besides, the leaky lines were Shell's to begin with. If they leaked, it was because Shell never replaced them as they aged.

Nonetheless, Tom McNamara was so pleased to hear a decent line of testimony in Shell's favor that he reverted to a very old lawyer's trick. Pretending not to have heard Moss say that some of the lines had leaked on Rosewood's and Kreuger's watches, he stood quickly and said, "What was the answer, please?" The object, of course, was to make sure the jury heard it twice. It was a fairly obvious ploy, because Gray, not McNamara, was questioning the witness, and he had not pretended to have any difficulty hearing Moss testify.

Judge Minaldi either didn't recognize the trick or, if she did, decided to play along. She turned to Moss. "Can you repeat your answer, Mr. Moss?" Which, of course, he did.

I couldn't suppress a small chuckle at these antics. If Shell's lawyers were desperate enough to resort to this, I figured that we must be in pretty good shape.

As he did with Bill Griffin, Gray got away from asking pointed, specific questions that could only be answered "yes" or "no" and started asking open-ended questions, as if he didn't know what answer to expect. And he was getting pretty much the same mixed results that he got with Bill Griffin. At one point, I wondered why Shell had bothered to take the man's deposition, because Gray never referred to it during his entire cross-examination.

My redirect lasted less than five minutes. Judge Minaldi then excused Moss and, noting that it was late afternoon on Friday, adjourned court for the weekend.

It was a sign of our preparation that we didn't work much over the weekend. Our case was, as they say, "in the can." I had completed my trial notebook a week before the trial began. There was a tab in it for every witness, both ours and Shell's, with carefully scripted questions. In the cross-examinations I had planned for Shell's witnesses, each question had a number next to it, indicating the page in the deposition transcript where the witness gave me the desired answer to that question. If the witness didn't know his lines, I would bring out his deposition and show him what he had said earlier under oath.

Of course, there was always something to tweak. I spent a few hours on Saturday reviewing the list of witnesses we planned to call during the remainder of our case. If any could be eliminated, I did so. If questions for others could be trimmed, I did that as well. We had been at it for a week, and I didn't want to tax the jury's patience by prolonging the agony any more than necessary.

Our first witness Monday morning was Jody Miller, who was Walter Moss's boss. The two men had worked together on the Heyds' property for the various lease operators for fifteen years or so. Like Moss, Miller had personal knowledge about working conditions during that time. Jody was also a native of the area. He knew several of the men in the Heyd family, including Billy Corbello, Lawrence Heyd, and Gene Fontenot, and he came across just like Billy, as a "good old boy" who had no ax to grind.

Jody's main function was to corroborate Bill Griffin's description of how the Iowa Field was operated and to verify Walter Moss's testimony about conditions on the Heyd property over the years. He did both admirably. The direct examination came off without a hitch.

Pat Gray did the honors for Shell in cross-examining Jody. Again, his questions lacked emphasis. Not one of them began in the classic form of a leading question on cross-examination: "Isn't it true that . . ." or "Isn't it fair to say that . . ." or some variation. He did a workmanlike job of covering the issues, but he still didn't "close the loop" so that it was apparent to the jury what he had accomplished. As a result, my redirect was again less than five minutes long.

Neither Walter Moss nor Jody Miller had been exciting witnesses, but they had accomplished everything we had hoped for. They came across as honest, hardworking men who were there to speak the truth rather than take sides. When they corroborated Bill Griffin's testimony, they gave our case a real boost. Shell wouldn't be able to dismiss Bill as a "hired gun" whose testimony had been bought and paid for, because all of the facts that Bill relied upon had been corroborated by two independent witnesses.

While Jody and Walter's appearances had produced little excitement, the jury was about to see some fireworks. Joe Standridge was our next witness. He had been identified by Shell in discovery as among its former employees who had worked on the Heyd property in the Iowa Field. When we took Standridge's deposition, he proved to be a talkative witness. He had held a number of positions during a thirty-five-year career with Shell and prided himself on his knowledge of oilfield operations. During his deposition, his garrulous nature got the better of him, and he volunteered damaging testimony that made Shell's lawyers cringe. Standridge so thoroughly enjoyed telling us about what he did—and what he knew—that he didn't realize he was spilling Shell's beans in the process.

I knew that we wanted to call Standridge as a witness. As a longtime employee, any damaging testimony he gave against Shell would be powerful. However, Standridge lived and worked over in St. Martinville, Louisiana, which was barely inside the subpoena powers of our local district court. Fortunately, we were able to get him served. Once we did, I was confident that he would honor his subpoena; he was working as a courtroom bailiff after retiring from Shell and couldn't afford to ignore any court's process. Mr. Standridge appeared on schedule to testify. When he came forward and took the stand, I took notice of his appearance again. He was a fairly tall man, and he held himself erect, exuding an air of authority. After he was sworn and identified, I established right away that he had worked for Shell from 1955 until 1990 and that he had worked on the Heyd property for Shell in the mid- to late 1970s.

One of Standridge's responsibilities during the time he worked for Shell was to decide what had to be done to restore property when a Shell lease expired. After surveying the property, Standridge would prepare an "AFE" (authorization for expenditure) and submit it to upper management for approval. Typically, he testified, the scope of the cleanup work included removing old pipelines and cleaning up any contamination on the property—two things that had not been done on the Heyd land.

It soon became clear that Standridge no longer had the same enthusiasm for my questions that he had during his deposition. I began having to repeat questions in order to get him to answer them. Soon, I was forced to ask leading questions. Shell's lawyers pounced on this, objecting to my leading one of "our" witnesses. I reminded the court that because Standridge was a former Shell employee and not cooperative, I was allowed to ask leading questions. It was a familiar exception to the rule against asking leading questions on direct examination. Nonetheless, Judge Minaldi sustained Shell's objection.

Not only that, but she also sustained Shell's objections that there was no foundation to ask Standridge certain questions about how Shell went about cleaning up leased property. That surprised me too; after a thirty-five-year career in which he did just that, I couldn't understand why he shouldn't be allowed to state what Shell's customs and practices were. It was obvious to me that Shell was afraid of what he might say and was making frequent objections in a frantic effort to disrupt and limit Standridge's testimony. Although Judge Minaldi was unwittingly supporting McNamara's efforts to keep the jury from hearing what Standridge had to say, I knew it was important to keep cool and plow ahead.

After a number of fits and starts, I was able to get Standridge to admit that one of his responsibilities at the Heyd property was to close old pits. I asked him, "What was the first thing that you had to do when you went about the process of closing pits?"

He didn't hesitate. "Well, the main thing was to see what kind of contamination was in the pit."

Standridge explained that, in order to determine what needed to be done with a pit, he would pull samples from the pit and send them off for analysis. Based on the contents of the sample, Shell's environmentalists in New Orleans would provide him with a "prognosis," which he explained was a "step-by-step [of] what has to be done to close the pit." If the soil wasn't badly contaminated, the prognosis would spell out what "bugs" or chemicals were to be added to treat the soil in place. However, if the soil was too badly polluted to be treated in place, the prognosis would call for the contaminated soil to be removed and replaced with clean, virgin soil. The removed soil was then sent to a state-approved disposal facility.

At that point, Standridge balked when I asked him if soil removal and replacement was more expensive than treatment in place. This was important, because Shell had obtained a $1.1 million bid from Campbell Well Service in 1984 to remove just a part of one of the old pits on the Heyd property. After soliciting the bid, Shell had done nothing, presumably because it didn't want to spend the money. Based on what Standridge had said under oath, this meant that Shell had first determined that the pit was too contaminated to be treated in place but apparently didn't care once it learned that removing the contamination would be expensive. Not only that, but the size of the bid for such a small area to be cleaned also helped support Austin's Arabie testimony that the total cleanup of the Heyds' property would be expensive. Simply put, if just closing one pit alone cost $1.1 million, then Austin's "worst case" estimate of $34 million for the entire 120 acres seemed much more credible.

For these reasons, Standridge now tried to say that treatment in place was often more expensive. Of course, that wasn't what he told us in his deposition, and so I read his deposition testimony back to him. He admitted that was his earlier testimony and didn't attempt to explain the contradiction. After that, I expected Judge Minaldi to let me use leading questions, because Standridge was clearly an uncooperative witness. However, she refused to cut me any slack and continued to sustain Shell's objections whenever I asked him a leading question.

It was clear that Standridge wasn't going to help me, either. Shell's lawyers had really worked him over before trial. When I asked him to go over the sequence for obtaining an outside bid on the cost of removing soil, he flatly contradicted his deposition testimony by saying that he obtained the cost estimate before, not after, he received the prognosis from Shell's environmental department.

"Well," I said, "the prognosis is what told you [whether] you needed to remove the soil or you could treat it in place, correct?"

He shook his head, both in denial and in confusion.

"Well, all I can remember is that we would do what we had to do to get the cost estimate and then later on down the road I would get an AFE from management saying you have got this number of dollars to do this using these steps and we would go do it. That was based on what we sent them for the original cost estimate, you see."

It was my turn to shake my head. "Well, Mr. Standridge, isn't it true that during the time you were with Shell, you didn't get a cost estimate until *after* you had a pit prognosis that told you . . ."

He interrupted. "Right, right."

". . . what you were going to have to do?"

At that point, McNamara was again on his feet. Confidently, he said, "Objection to leading, Your Honor."

For the first time, Minaldi disagreed with him. "I'm going to overrule the objection." Maybe, I thought to myself, she finally understands where I'm going with this.

Pressing forward, I said more than asked, "That's the way it was done when you were at Shell?"

Standridge was becoming noticeably subdued. He reluctantly agreed. "Right. Uh-huh. Right."

"Okay," I said. "And that procedure never changed during the time you were with Shell, correct?"

He shook his head. "It hadn't changed."

In the next breath, however, Standridge said that he didn't "necessarily" obtain a cost estimate before the pit prognosis.

I leaned in on him. "Didn't you tell us there's no way to write up a cost estimate until you have a prognosis on what's there and what has to be done?"

He jabbered on a bit, trying to explain, but what he said didn't make much sense.

I leaned forward again. "Didn't you tell us that a cost estimate without a prognosis wouldn't be worth anything?"

Standridge again mumbled something that was unresponsive.

I asked him if he remembered what he told us in his deposition. He said lamely, "You people caught me by surprise on that deposition, and I'm no spring chicken, you know. It was hard to remember at the time, and in fact it's hard to remember now, but I'm doing the best I can."

I wasn't buying his alibi, and I didn't want to jury to buy it, either.

"Before the deposition you met with Shell's lawyers, didn't you?"

He nodded. "Yeah."

"They spent time preparing you for your deposition, didn't they?"

He nodded again. "They did."

I looked over at the jury. I was about to give them the obvious explanation for Standridge's turnabout in his deposition testimony. You're never supposed to ask a question that you don't already know the answer to, but I was confident about this one. Looking at the jury and back at him, I said, "Since your deposition, you have talked with Shell's lawyers, again, haven't you?"

"Yes," he said simply.

"Did they discuss with you the testimony you gave here when you said you don't get a cost estimate unless you already have a pit prognosis?"

"Yes. Yes."

"So now your testimony is different from what it was in the deposition?"

Standridge was now visibly uncomfortable. "It's not really different," he said unconvincingly. "I'm trying to get my words together here. A prognosis describes to you what to do step-by-step to close that pit. If I'm—am I saying this right in your book? Because it's been a long time since I did this."

I nodded. I did not want to appear to be unsympathetic, but I had to remain firm. "Yes, sir." After pausing, I added, "I don't have a book. All I have is your deposition that was taken."

He shrugged "Well, okay."

I couldn't resist reminding him (and the jury), "When you were sworn under oath."

He raised his eyebrows, showing his embarrassment. "Right."

I then showed him his deposition and read where he testified, "There's no way you can write up a cost estimate on closing a pit until you have a prognosis on what's there and what has to be done."

His shoulders slumped. All of the starch was now gone from his once-proud demeanor. Speaking more softly now, he admitted, "Well, yeah, that's absolutely true."

As I hammered Standridge with more questions, McNamara stood to object again to the leading nature of the questions. After hearing that Shell's lawyers had tried to coach Standridge into changing his testimony, however, Minaldi had had enough. She looked at McNamara sternly and said, "I'm not going to consider those objections anymore at this time, Mr. McNamara." The squat Irishman sat down. For the remainder of my direct examination, he only voiced one more objection, and it was quickly overruled.

McNamara's cross consisted of serving leading questions to a friendly witness who now understood that his testimony had hurt the company and was eager to repair the damage by agreeing with whatever Shell's lawyers asked him. Remarkably, just when I thought the judge was fed up with Shell's tactics, she overruled my objection to Shell leading a man who was, in effect, its own witness. In any event, Standridge's performance on cross was brief and unconvincing.

An example was McNamara's last question: "Mr. Standridge, have you done your best today to tell the truth as best as you can recall these events from long ago?"

Standridge jumped on the question like a hungry dog that had just been offered a scrap of food. "Yes. Yes."

I stood quickly on redirect. "Mr. Standridge, just so the record is clear: We never met with you before or after your deposition to discuss your testimony, did we?"

He answered just as quickly. "No."

It was my way of reminding the jury that Standridge's damaging testimony had come despite Shell's best efforts both before and after his deposition to have him testify otherwise.

After a couple more questions, we were done with Joe Standridge. Judge Minaldi announced it was time to break for lunch.

22

Our first witness in the afternoon was Dan Cliffe, a CPA from New Orleans. Dan frequently appeared in court as an expert witness who calculated economic losses. Ordinarily, Dan testified in personal injury cases, where his testimony consisted of determining the present value of future earnings that an injured worker presumably lost because of injuries he received in an accident.

I had known Dan a long time. Although he was older than I was, we had been Sigma Nu fraternity brothers at Tulane. He had gone on to earn an M.B.A. from Tulane's Business School and had spent time on the faculty there. At some point, Dan began working with another "B-school" faculty member, Dr. Ken Boudreaux, assisting lawyers with courtroom testimony that presented calculations of economic losses. This part-time consulting apparently became too lucrative to remain a "side job," and Dan eventually left the Tulane faculty to work as a forensic economist on a full-time basis.

It was a good time in the trial to put Dan on the stand. He was a very straightforward, business-like witness, which would be a contrast to what the jury had just heard from Joe Standridge. Although we didn't plan it that way, calling Dan Cliffe at this point would provide a change of pace, as it were, and allow the jury to catch its breath after witnessing the fireworks and controversy that had taken place before lunch.

Dan's original scope of work in the case was to convert the profits that Shell had made over the years from illegal salt water disposal to their present value. However, all of that suddenly changed when Judge Minaldi had made her "turnabout" ruling on the third day of trial that the Heyds could not recover the profits that Shell had illegally made. Bill Griffin had testified that Shell had illegally disposed of approximately 1.6 million barrels of salt water into the Heyd property. He also had determined that the average disposal cost at the time was about $1 a barrel, meaning that Shell had saved itself roughly $1.6 million in disposal fees in the process. Some of this illegal salt water disposal took place as far back as 1956, and it continued until Shell sold the mineral lease in 1985.

Obviously, the value of a dollar received in 1956 was far greater than one received in 2000. Awarding the Heyds $1.6 million in the year 2000 would not make them "whole" for the $1.6 million they theoretically should have received during the years 1956 to 1985. Dan Cliffe's new scope of work, therefore, was to calculate the present value of these past losses, so that we could present the jury with the amount of dollars in the year 2000 that would roughly equal the $1.6 million that had been lost from 1956 to 1985.

This was the mirror image of what he usually did, which was to project what an injured plaintiff would have earned *in the future*. His approach was to assume that, if the plaintiffs had received the money when they should have received it, they would have been able to invest it in a reasonably prudent manner. The principal plus interest to date would be the proper amount of lump-sum damages. To that end, Dan performed several calculations using different rates of return. One calculation simply used the Consumer Price Index, or CPI, which just adjusted the value of the dollar to account for inflation. Another calculation used the annual investment return of the Standard & Poor's 500, which he believed was a representative average for the stock market as a whole. Finally, Dan also calculated present value by using the returns on equity that Shell had realized from 1956 to the present. The CPI yielded the smallest number, the S&P 500 produced a much more sizeable increase, and Shell's return on equity made the number jump to a very high level.

Shell's lawyers hit the roof, objecting to Cliffe's testimony on numerous grounds. First, they claimed that we were limited by law to recovering legal interest on all past due sums. Thus, they argued, there was no need for Cliffe to testify at all. Once the jury determined what amount, if any, should be awarded for the illegal salt water disposal, the judge could just apply the legal interest calculation to it. Next, they argued that Cliffe's approach was based on speculation rather than facts, even though Dan said it was actually *less* speculative than what he usually was permitted to do in court on a routine basis, which was to predict future income for an injured worker and discount that to present value. Finally, Shell argued that none of Dan's methods of computing interest was customary or accepted in the economics profession and therefore wasn't sufficiently reliable to be admissible.

Judge Minaldi had already sliced our damage claim by nearly 75 percent when she changed her mind and disallowed any evidence of Shell's profits, we hoped that she would not further eviscerate our claim by excluding Dan's testimony. After a lengthy and somewhat heated bench conference the judge opted to split the baby. She took out another chunk of our damages by ruling that we could not present any calculations based on Shell's return on equity over the years, but held that we would be allowed to show our two other methods of bringing those past losses to present value. This meant that we could present evidence of what the $1.6 million would be worth today if adjusted by the Consumer Price Index or invested over time in the S&P 500.

It was another victory for Shell in that they had knocked out our next biggest number. Still, we managed to save something. As Cliffe would testify, adjusting the $1.6 million to present value using the S&P 500 increased it substantially. For that reason, Shell still wasn't entirely satisfied. After my younger partner Todd Fontenot had presented Dan's qualifications and the court had recognized him as an expert in calculating economic loss, Pat

Gray convened still another bench conference (we were having more of them than in any case I'd ever seen) to complain that Shell had not been able to conduct discovery on Dan's calculation of the present value of Shell's past cost savings.

This was a remarkable complaint. It took a lot of gall to complain about Cliffe's new calculations, because they came about only because Judge Minaldi had ruled that we couldn't show Shell's profits from illegal salt water disposal. Essentially, Gray was now bitching about a ruling that benefited Shell by about $80 million.

That wasn't lost on the judge. She looked at him and said, "Well, the rulings that have caused the change were to your benefit. Therefore, I find that there is no prejudice in this regard."

I couldn't resist adding, "If they will withdraw their objections, Your Honor, we will be happy to revert to the original analysis."

We then moved forward with Dan's testimony. Using the Consumer Price Index, he told the jury that the present value of Shell's cost savings from illegal salt water disposal was $6.9 million. However, if the past savings were adjusted to present value by assuming the money would have grown in accordance with the S&P 500 (which was the majority of stocks in the market over the relevant period of time), the number grew to $28 million. It was a large number, but still a whole lot less than the $100 million or more number we would have presented based on Shell's profits.

Shell's cross-examination focused almost entirely on Bill Griffin's testimony, not Dan Cliffe's calculations. Under the guise of asking Cliffe questions, Shell's lawyer (George Arceneaux, another member of the Liskow & Lewis firm) argued about whether Griffin's testimony was correct.

"Are you aware that Shell's witnesses have said that no salt water came from the gas plant to the Heyd property?" he asked Cliffe.

Cliffe, of course, said repeatedly that his expertise was limited to his economic calculations and that he had no basis to pass judgment on anyone else's testimony. The questions, therefore, were clearly irrelevant. Remarkably, Judge Minaldi refused to sustain a single one of our objections, saying that it was up to the jury to decide whether to believe that there was a proper factual basis for Cliffe's calculations.

It was ironic that this same judge had taken such a different view when the shoe was on the other foot. When we were asking Bill Griffin about the economics of oilfield operations, Judge Minaldi repeatedly made us establish Griffin's experience and knowledge about such things. Here, despite Dan Cliffe's statements that he was an economics expert and knew nothing about oilfield operations, including salt water disposal, Minaldi continually ruled that Shell could question Cliffe about something he admittedly didn't know anything about.

Even with the judge's clear support, Shell didn't make much headway with Dan on cross-examination, other than to remind the jury that his calculations were based on Bill Griffin's testimony about Shell's illegal salt water disposal. However, Griffin's estimate of the number of barrels of salt water that were improperly injected into the Heyds' property had mainly come from monthly reports that Shell itself had filed with the Office of Conservation, so it was difficult to see how Shell could dispute those numbers.

Todd Fontenot asked just a few questions on redirect, and Cliffe was dismissed. The most important thing we had gained was that he had put $28 million in front of the jury as a proper award for Shell's illegal salt water disposal.

Next, we intended to call Dr. Everett Dillman, an expert witness who would provide testimony about Shell's earnings and net worth. In addition to our other claims, we had asserted a claim for punitive damages (i.e., damages that don't compensate the victim for his losses but rather punish the wrong-doer) because Shell's activities in burying sludge and other toxic substances and in ignoring the advice of its own experts to cleanup the contamination constituted "gross and wanton reckless behavior in the handling, storage, and transportation of toxic substances." Although the statute authorizing punitive damages under these circumstances had been repealed several years earlier, it was in effect during the times when Shell was misbehaving. The purpose of Dr. Dillman's testimony was to enable the jury to understand the impact of any award it made for punitive damages in the case. He would compare Shell's net worth to that of an average family of four and then show what amount of money would affect Shell the same as the loss of, say, $1,000 to a family of four. In short, if we were going to argue that the jury should award sufficient punitive damages to "send Shell a message," we wanted to have Dr. Dillman show them how much it would take to get Shell's attention.

While the concept of punitive damages was common in other states, including our next-door neighbor Texas, it was rare under Louisiana law. So, when we announced that we wanted to call Dr. Dillman as our next witness, Judge Minaldi let it be known that she wasn't sure his testimony should be allowed.

I couldn't see how the issue was still on the table. Shell had filed a motion before trial to exclude punitive damages, and the judge had denied it. But Minaldi stated that she believed the motion hadn't been decided and therefore had to be addressed.

"That's not my recollection," I said.

The judge wasn't impressed. She let me know that she was thinking of granting Shell's motion to dismiss our punitive damages claim. With that, we adjourned for the day so that we could spend the rest of the afternoon putting the excluded testimony of Bill Griffin and Dan Cliffe, relating to Shell's profits from illegal salt water disposal, on the record as a proffer.

After the jury was excused and the judge left, we put Bill on the stand and had him state for the record his calculation of Shell's profits from its illegal salt water disposal. In all, Bill estimated that Shell had made $70,438,828 in profits over the years. We then put Dan Cliffe back on the stand so that he could furnish his estimate of the present value of Shell's past cost savings, based on Shell's return on its invested equity over the years. Using Shell's historical rates of return, Dan testified that the present value of the costs that Shell saved by illegally using the Heyds' property for salt water disposal came to $41,295,384.

From our perspective, those were both terrific numbers, of course, and judging by how the trial was going we would have had a good chance of getting the jury to include them in its verdict. Unfortunately, Judge Minaldi's rulings meant the jury would never hear either number. With the completion of the two proffers, we were through with court for the day. Of course, we had to hurry back to the office to research and draft a brief that we hoped would convince the judge not to dismiss our punitive damages claim.

As so often happened in trials, we were in for a long night.

23

Before court convened the next morning, we managed to submit a short brief that we hoped would persuade Judge Minaldi to reject Shell's attempts to dismiss our punitive damages claim. Our biggest problem was that the judge was uncomfortable with our side of the issue. First, we were seeking millions of dollars in damages. There hadn't been another case of this magnitude in the history of this court, much less anything in the judge's experience. Second, adding punitive damages to the case probably didn't sit well with Judge Minaldi's conservative nature, either. Third, it didn't help that the judge had very little experience in civil cases to begin with, having been a career criminal prosecutor. All of this combined to put our claims considerably outside the judge's "comfort zone."

People tend to believe what they want to believe. There was no reason to believe that Judge Minaldi was immune to that fact of life. The judge no doubt preferred to believe that we weren't entitled to get punitive damages on top of our other damages, and that didn't bode well for us where the issue was a close call, as this one was. True enough, when court opened the next morning, she wasted little time in granting Shell's motion to dismiss our claim for punitive damages. As she had first done with our claim for Shell's profits and then with our adjustment of Shell's cost savings to present value, the judge had once again sliced another huge part out of our case.

I smiled, pretended not to be disappointed, and thanked the court for its efforts in reviewing our brief. We then made a proffer of the video of Dr. Dillman's testimony in order to preserve our right to argue on appeal that our claim for punitive damages should have gone to the jury.

The jury was then brought into the courtroom, and it was time to put on our next (and final) witness. We called Benny Miller to the stand. Benny was Jody Miller's brother and operated a land clearing and restoration business. As further proof that it was a small world, his son Scott was married to Shelley, Billy Corbello's middle daughter. At our request, Benny had inspected the Heyd property and prepared an estimate of what it would cost to return the surface of the land to the same condition as it was in 1961. He calculated that clearing away the trees that had grown on the property during the last thirty years (the land was a pasture in 1961) and restoring and regrading the surface would cost $523,875. This cost was in addition to the costs estimated by Austin Arabie to cleanup the contamination in the soil, subsurface, and groundwater. The largest part of Miller's estimated cost involved the removal of abandoned flow lines that crisscrossed throughout the property.

Pat Gray stood to cross-examine Benny. Besides reminding the jury that Benny's son was married to Billy Corbello's daughter, Gray's main objective appeared to be to show that Miller couldn't identify the flow lines he intended to remove on Shell's maps of the property.

Miller conceded that he couldn't show them on the maps, but added in a counterpunch, "I know where they go if we're out there [at the property]. If you want to go out there, we'll go." After Gray ignored the challenge, Miller explained that he had toured the property with his brother Jody and had identified each abandoned flow line with his brother's assistance.

When Miller's testimony was over, we informed the court that he had been our last witness and that, after we introduced a few additional exhibits, we intended to rest.

Tom McNamara immediately reargued Shell's assertion that certain aspects of our case should be barred by the statute of limitations. This same exception had been rejected by the court in a separate hearing before trial. That should have made it "the law of the case," meaning that the issue was settled and could not be visited again. It was a measure of the judge's sympathy for Shell, however, that she continually let them reargue their defenses. I had never been before a judge so willing to re-plow old ground and reconsider her rulings—at least where Shell was concerned. Fortunately, after allowing McNamara to expound once again on Shell's theories about why some of our claims were filed too late, Judge Minaldi again denied his exception.

Curiously, Shell did not move for a directed verdict dismissing our case. Like most states, Louisiana law provided that, if a plaintiff failed to present sufficient evidence in support of its case to warrant consideration by the jury (sometimes called a "prima facie case"), the judge could direct a verdict in favor of the defendant. Although directed verdicts were rare, Shell knew the judge was sympathetic to its case, and I would have expected McNamara and Gray at least to give it a try.

Counting Mr. Perry's deposition, we had called a total of nine witnesses. It was now Shell's turn to respond. I expected its lawyers to produce an equal, if not greater, number of witnesses. For one thing, they had more than nine expert witnesses alone. After a brief recess, Judge Minaldi gestured to Shell's lawyers to present their first witness. Tom McNamara stood and announced that Shell was calling Bill Hise to the stand.

I had never met Mr. Hise. When we deposed Shell's experts, my partner Richard Gerard had taken Hise's deposition. I knew from reviewing the deposition that Hise was a petroleum engineer who frequently testified as an expert witness on behalf of the oil industry. In short, he was Shell's intended antidote for Bill Griffin.

I noticed immediately that Hise passed the "looks" test, in that he had a pleasant and professional demeanor. He also appeared to be quite comfortable as he settled into the witness chair, evidence of his considerable experience in courtroom testimony. This no doubt explained why Tom McNamara approached him so confidently.

Hise began his testimony by explaining that he had received his petroleum engineering degree from the University of Oklahoma and worked for Shell during the early part of his career before joining the faculty at Louisiana State University to teach petroleum engineering on a full-time basis. After a number of years at LSU, he formed his own consulting firm. After eliciting this testimony, McNamara tendered Hise as an expert in petroleum engineering.

My traversal was brief. I asked Hise to confirm that he had been retained "essentially . . . to re-create the history of salt water disposal in the Iowa Field." "That is a fair characterization," he replied.

"Do you know why no one from Shell who was responsible for salt water disposal in the Iowa Field would have been asked to have done that?" I asked.

He seemed puzzled and replied, "I don't know the answer to that."

My point (which I would make more than once) was that Shell had carefully avoided bringing anyone into the courtroom from inside the company who might have firsthand knowledge about its illegal practices and therefore could be cross-examined about them. Instead, the company's lawyers hired "outside experts," who could fend off the tough questions with a shrug of the shoulders and "I don't know." That ended my traversal, and Judge Minaldi recognized Hise as an expert in petroleum engineering.

Hise began his direct examination by describing the Iowa Field as a "giant field." Under further questions, he presented the total number of barrels of oil that had been produced from the field. No doubt, Hise had been prepped by Shell's lawyers to remind the jury that the landowners had received substantial royalties from the mineral production. Shell's hope, obviously, was that the jury would ultimately say to one another, "Look, they already got a lot of money, so why give them any more?"

Much of Hise's testimony consisted of his interpreting the Shell documents that we had introduced. Of course, he put an entirely different spin on them, giving benign explanations for Shell's apparent indifference to the

Heyds' property rights. In addition, McNamara tried to justify Shell's behavior on the ground that it was consistent with the "custom and practice"
in the industry at the time. We objected, because Shell's breach of the surface lease could not be excused by "custom and practice." Simply put, if
Shell agreed by contract that it would not inject salt water from other leases
into the Heyds' property, that agreement became the law between the parties. Shell couldn't later excuse its breach of the contract by claiming that
what it did was "customary." Although I thought this was an easy call,
Judge Minaldi overruled our objection.

McNamara then had Hise testify about "adjacency clauses" in mineral
leases. These were clauses that permitted the oil company to inject salt
water into the leased property that was produced from "adjacent" leases as
well as from the leased property. This, of course, suggested that it was permissible for Shell to inject salt water from other leases into the Heyd property if the salt water came from "adjacent" land.

There was only one problem with this theory: There was no "adjacency
clause" in any agreement between the Heyds and Shell. For this reason, all
of this testimony was irrelevant, and we objected to it on that basis.

Judge Minaldi again overruled our objection.

I was becoming frustrated. It seemed to me that Shell's strategy was to
confuse the jury rather than to address the issues. Minaldi's rulings were
giving McNamara clear license to talk about all kinds of things that had
nothing to do with our claims. The case was complicated enough, I
thought, without this kind of unnecessary distraction.

We adjourned for lunch. When we returned, the judge apparently had
been having second thoughts about her earlier rulings—not enough to re-
verse herself, but enough to explain them further on the record to make
them look better for the court of appeal. She said, in essence, that she was
permitting Hise to discuss the documents in question (concerning the
"adjacency" clause) because she felt that Bill Griffin's earlier interpretation
of other documents in the case was "unfair and inaccurate." She said that
Hise's additional testimony was "necessary to put P-19 [the document that
she believed Griffin had interpreted "unfairly"] into context."

It was an interesting comment. First of all, the fact that the judge thought her earlier rulings needed further explanation betrayed her misgivings about them. Beyond that, it seemed to me that she was confusing her role with that of the jury. As judge, she had to decide as a threshold issue whether evidence was relevant and therefore admissible. Once she let the evidence in (as she did with Griffin's testimony), it was up to the jury to decide whether they believed it or not. Simply put, it was the jury's call as to whether Griffin's testimony about any exhibit (including P-19) was "unfair and inaccurate." By taking it upon herself to decide whether Griffin's testimony should be believed, the judge had invaded the province of the jury.

McNamara continued with questions that allowed Hise to say that Shell had behaved "reasonably" in everything it did in the Iowa Field. Over our objection, Judge Minaldi even allowed McNamara to ask Hise "whether it was reasonable for Shell to have relied on all of these leases [including ones that had expired or were terminated by the parties] to handle the water that it handled on the Heyd property." And, of course, Hise said it was.

After having Hise repeat the historical production numbers for the field and for the Heyd lease—presumably to remind the jury that the Heyds received substantial production royalties—McNamara then asked Hise about the conclusions he had reached regarding Shell's conduct in operating the Iowa Field. Hise replied, "I think that Shell . . . met or exceeded industry standards in their conduct of operations, including their salt water disposal operation."

McNamara then smiled and asked, "What conclusion did you reach with regard to whether Shell's operations were conducted in a reasonable and prudent manner?"

Hise's answer did not surprise anyone. "I thought they were."

After additional questions, Hise even expressed the legal opinion (again, over our objection) that Shell had always obtained "the agreements to cover the operations they conducted." With that, McNamara triumphantly tendered Hise for cross-examination.

I began my questions by having Hise confirm that he had reviewed records showing that Shell had injected salt water into the Heyd property that did not come from Shell wells in the Iowa Field, contrary to the terms of the

1961 lease. I then said, "We talked a lot about reasonable and prudent operators. Does a reasonable and prudent operator pay attention to its contracts?"

He nodded. "Yes." He then tried to add that it was "clear" to him that Shell was paying attention to "what they needed to do to get the rights to do what they were doing."

I pressed him on that, because the 1961 lease was clear. Hise tried to argue that the lease permitted non-Shell water. This, of course, was contrary to the plain meaning of the surface lease—as verified by one of the court's pretrial rulings. When I referred to the ruling, he admitted that Shell's lawyers had never shown him the ruling, even though it had been issued before he was ever retained in the case.

Even as I cross-examined him, I found Hise to be likeable. At one point, after I had impeached him by showing that his earlier deposition testimony contradicted an answer he had just given, he smiled and said, "You know my deposition better than I do, I'll bet."

That was right before I reminded him that he had testified in his deposition that he had looked at the 1961 surface lease but "had no legal understanding of it." Right after that, I also reminded Hise that he had also found that many of Shell's earlier leases did not contain rights-of-way, a fact that he admitted was "hard to understand."

I wanted to dispose of the Shell defense that what it did was okay because it was "industry custom and practice." Leaning toward the witness, I said, "Is it fair to say, Mr. Hise, that it is not a typical custom or practice in the oil industry to do things that you don't have the right to do?"

He nodded. "I think that's fair. That's not customary practice."

I looked at the jury and then back at him. "Would you agree with me that you can't justify an illegal act by saying it's part of industry custom and practice?"

He nodded again. "I would agree with you."

"You would never say it's industry custom and practice to violate the law, would you?"

Hise shook his head. "No."

"And you would never say it's industry custom and practice to breach a contract, would you?"

Again, he shook his head. "No. It's not good practice."

I bore in on him. "And it shouldn't be industry custom and practice, should it?"

He agreed. "No, it shouldn't be."

"Okay," I said. "Fair enough. You would never say it's industry custom and practice to lay a pipeline across someone's property without a right-of-way to do so, would you?"

He nodded agreeably. "That's correct."

Those questions had gotten good answers, but then I stumbled into a *really* good answer. On direct examination, Shell had made a big point out of the fact that Hise was in charge of the Pennington properties, which were part of the Tuscaloosa Trend, perhaps the biggest gas find that Louisiana had ever seen. In an effort to draw an analogy, I asked Hise, "Let's suppose you had a surface lease on one of the Pennington estates. Do you have surface leases on that land?"

He thought for a moment. "I can't think of a single Pennington-operated property that has a surface lease on top of the mineral lease."

I was surprised, since he had testified so extensively on direct examination about what the surface lease meant. I then asked him, "Do you have any other situations where you're responsible for land and someone, an oil operator, has a surface lease on that property at the current time?"

He shook his head. "No."

"Okay," I said. "Have you ever had a situation in which you were responsible for land and someone had a surface lease, an oil operator had a surface lease similar to this one?"

He shook his head again. "Not similar to this one, no."

Now I was really surprised, but regained my composure quickly enough to seize the opportunity that had just been handed to me. "So, do I understand you have been brought here to talk about all of this, and you have *never* experienced the same thing that we're talking about here?"

Hise became noticeably uncomfortable for the first time. "Our companies had leases for disposal of salt water on other lands, but we didn't take a surface lease to do it."

That wasn't a good enough explanation. "So all of your testimony about industry custom and practice and all the things that were reasonable and prudent and you've never actually been in the shoes of the Heyd family or Shell Oil Company in working on property under a surface lease *like the one this case is all about?*"

Hise shook his head slowly. "Not like the one this case is about, no."

I stepped back, pretending to be thinking about my next question. What I was doing, though, was letting Hise's answer sink in with the jury.

After a suitable pause, I asked him, "Would you ever bury material on someone else's land without their permission?"

He shook his head, more quickly this time, almost as if he was relieved that I had changed the subject. "No."

"You think any reasonable and prudent operator would bury barrels of sludge on somebody else's land without their permission?"

Hise answered, "Well, they might in the course of business, but when it came time to clean up the lease at the end of production, they would remove it."

After quoting the language in the surface lease obligating Shell to restore the property when the lease expired, I asked him, "Do you think nine years is a reasonable time to allow an operator to fulfill its obligations under the contract?"

Hise replied, "I can't imagine that you couldn't do something in nine years." Since Shell had done *nothing* in the nine years since the lease had expired, that line had to have made Shell's lawyers cringe.

I believed that we were scoring points with the jury with every one of these answers, and I wanted to maintain that momentum. I asked Hise, "Do you think there's anything wrong with a landowner expecting an oil company to keep its promises?"

He shook his head. "No."

When Bill Griffin had testified, he was not allowed to discuss a document he found in the Office of Conservation files that severely criticized Shell's behavior in the Iowa Field. Even though the document had been written by an official with the agency, Judge Minaldi made it plain that the harsh wording of the letter offended her and therefore she considered it to be inadmissible hearsay.

The rule against hearsay (short for "I heard him say") prohibits the admission of evidence of what someone besides the witness says they saw, rather than what the witness who is testifying in court says *he* saw. Ordinarily, a letter from someone is considered to be hearsay evidence.

There are numerous exceptions that allow the introduction of hearsay evidence. The exceptions are based on circumstances that make the out-of-court statements sufficiently reliable to overcome the considerations against admitting the evidence. One of the most common exceptions to the hearsay rule relates to records of government agencies. The idea is that these documents are routinely relied upon to make decisions and therefore are sufficiently reliable to be admitted into evidence.

I couldn't for the life of me understand what the supposedly harsh tone of the letter from the Office of Conservation had to do with whether the document was hearsay. We had pointed out that, under textbook evidence rules, official agency records were admissible under a well-established exception to the hearsay rule. Despite this, the judge wouldn't budge.

During Hise's direct examination, however, Tom McNamara had shown the witness a letter from the Office of Conservation files that had commended Shell on some of its activities in the Iowa Field. Over our objection (what was good for the goose should have been good for the gander), Judge Minaldi had allowed Hise to comment on it for the jury. Because Shell had now "opened the door" on this issue during Hise's direct examination, I again brought up the critical letter from the same Office of Conservation files that Griffin had not been allowed to talk about. The idea, of course, was to show that Hise had ignored evidence of Shell's bad behavior. Shell objected. Minaldi surprised us all by sustaining the objection.

In a bench conference, I argued that the judge was applying a double standard. "The problem I have," I told her, "is [that], over our objection, they were allowed to put that [letter of commendation] in, which paints them in a positive light. Just because this, a very similar document, paints them in a negative light should not make it inadmissible."

Even though both documents came from the Office of Conservation files, the judge said "that doesn't make it part of the regularly conducted business." I was dumbfounded. If a document authored by an official of the Office of Conservation criticizing Shell wasn't part of "regularly conducted business," what was it? And if *our* file letter wasn't part of "regularly conducted business," how could *theirs* be? The judge offered no further explanation for her application of the hearsay rule and, despite my best efforts to persuade her otherwise, held fast to her ruling.

At that point, Minaldi noted the late hour and adjourned court for the day. It was not the way I wanted to end things, but I reminded myself that we didn't have to win every battle in order to win the war.

And I felt like we *had* to be winning the war.

24

When court resumed the next morning, Hise returned to the stand for the remainder of his cross-examination. I'd like to say I brought him to his knees with some carefully planned questions, but in the end our most effective cross-examination came about quite by accident.

I wanted to show that a particular well south of the field had been sending water to Shell's gas plant. This would be another breach of the surface lease, which restricted Shell to disposing of water produced from its leases in the field. I didn't want Hise to know where I was headed, so I began by asking him to give the jury the boundaries of the Iowa Field. He surprised me with his answer. "I'm not sure I can [identify] the total boundaries of the Iowa Field. . . . I couldn't give you the exact area without consulting or doing some work. I couldn't actually draw an outer limit around it."

I immediately forgot about my earlier strategy and pounced on this admission. "Well, Mr. Hise," I said, "am I correct you testified yesterday that the reason you came here was to talk about Shell's practices in the Iowa Field . . . ?"

He nodded. "That's correct."

I shook my head. "And to tell the jury all about salt water disposal in the Iowa Field, correct?"

Again, he said, "That's correct."

Turning in the jury's direction, I asked him, "Are you telling us now you can't even tell us what the boundaries of the Iowa Field are?"

He shook his head. "Not the official boundaries." He went on to say he could tell us how many wells were drilled and all kinds of other information, but I could tell from the jury's reaction that we had dealt a major blow to Hise's credibility.

Shell's redirect was brief and uneventful. Hise was then excused, and McNamara announced that Shell's second witness would be Paul Lair.

We were very familiar with Paul Lair. He had been a "land man" with SWEPI, Shell's subsidiary, for twelve years. The Iowa Field was one of his responsibilities, and so he had been one of the first people we dealt with when the 1961 lease expired. Under questioning by Pat Gray, Lair essentially described his involvement in the case. When he began to discuss "negotiations" with Billy and me, however, I objected. We had already had a lengthy bench conference about this when Billy testified, and Judge Minaldi had properly ruled that evidence of settlement negotiations was inadmissible. The commonsense reason for this rule is that parties wouldn't ever discuss settlement if what they said could be repeated in court. In other words, a defendant would never make an offer to pay money to a plaintiff if it could later be construed as an admission of liability.

We thus had to approach the bench for another unnecessary conference, again re-plowing the same ground as before. Our discussion lasted fifteen minutes or more, as both Gray and McNamara talked endlessly about why they needed to bring this out to rebut Billy's testimony that Shell had never offered to cleanup the property. As the judge already knew, the only offers Shell had made to cleanup the Heyd land were conditioned on the Heyds' signing a release and waiving all of their claims. As Judge Minaldi had ruled, these "strings-attached" offers were inadmissible because they were made in furtherance of settlement. Even so, Gray and McNamara went through a laundry list of suggested questions to find out what they could ask Lair. In the end, the judge let them establish that Lair had visited the field, had met Billy, had discussed the family's complaints, had conducted some tests, and had sent "some" of the information that we requested.

On cross-examination, I pressed Lair on the fact that Shell had not vacated the property when the surface lease expired. It was a win-win question, because there was no answer that would justify Shell's trespass. It turned out better than I expected.

First, I asked Lair, "During all of the discussions that you've described, you know June, July, August [1991], whenever they were, was there ever any doubt in your mind that Shell no longer had the right to be on the Heyd family property?"

Lair squirmed to avoid the obvious answer. "The lease had expired. We were negotiating for a new terminal lease during those times."

The answer was unresponsive. I knew better than to let him off the hook. "But that isn't my question. My question is: Was there ever any doubt in your mind that Shell was occupying that property when it did not have the right to do so?"

Lair was clearly becoming defensive, and his demeanor communicated more than his words. "We were occupying the property after the lease expired."

The longer he tried to avoid answering my question, the better it got for us. "And that meant you did not have the right to do so, correct?"

That's when the pressure forced Lair into saying something that I'm sure Shell's lawyers wished he hadn't. "That is correct." Then, as if explaining why Shell didn't leave, he added, "You could have locked the gate. *The sheriff could have come out and locked the gate.* He did not."

Immediately, I said in an incredulous tone, "So, Shell wasn't going to leave unless we went and got the sheriff and made Shell leave?"

"No, sir," he said weakly.

Lair had also testified that the Heyds had not made him aware of any complaints about unlawful salt water disposal, as if they had only recently manufactured that claim. However, we impeached that testimony by showing him where he admitted in his deposition that he knew from the outset that the Heyds had complained about salt water disposal on their land. (For one thing, we said so in the very first letter we wrote to Shell dated May 9, 1991—the day *before* the surface lease expired. Lair had admitted receiving that letter just four days later.)

Later, Lair again tried to justify Shell's failure to be forthright in giving the Heyds information about salt water disposal, saying he really didn't understand that they were complaining about that. I brought out his deposition once again and showed him where he had testified to the contrary under oath. I then asked him to explain why his testimony changed. Unfortunately, Judge Minaldi apparently saw that Lair was in trouble and declared a recess for lunch while my question about his earlier testimony was still pending. Once again, she had bailed a Shell witness out of a tight spot by recessing court before he was forced to answer a tough question.

After lunch, neither the remainder of my cross nor Pat Gray's redirect produced any memorable moments. Lair was off the stand in less than fifteen minutes.

Shell's next witness was Thomas "Buster" Brashear. Born and raised in the area, Brashear knew Billy Corbello and virtually everyone else in the Heyd family. He also knew Shell, having worked for the company in various capacities beginning in 1962, including a stint in the Iowa Field during the 1970s. Brashear's main function, it seemed, was to testify that the gas and gas liquids going to Shell's gas plant contained no water and therefore the gas plant could not have sent water to the Heyd salt water disposal plant. However, Brashear appeared to contradict himself when he testified that between fifty and 150 barrels of water and condensate were sent from the successor Mobil gas plant (in which Shell owned an interest) to the Heyd property each day. Interestingly, Brashear also acknowledged that, sometime after the surface lease expired, he toured the property with Billy Corbello and Jody Miller so that Billy could explain the various problems that needed cleaning up. Brashear even made a written list of the things that Billy pointed out.

Although Brashear appeared to toe the company line, every once in a while he gave answers that surprised Pat Gray. For instance, when discussing the inspection he made with Billy and Jody Miller, Gray asked him, "What was the condition of the field at that time when you did your inspection in 1991?"

Brashear shrugged his shoulders and said, "It didn't look too good." He went on to say that there were "oily spots" and lots of barrels and "junk" lying around.

On cross, Brashear acknowledged that, despite his extensive testimony that Shell's gas plant didn't send water to the Heyds' property, he had never worked in the gas plant. He also admitted that he had no reason to believe that Shell's plant generated any different amount of water than Mobil's plant, which he had said sent up to 150 barrels a day to the Heyd property.

Next, I showed Brashear a copy of his old handwritten list from 1991 and went through all of the problems listed on it. The list showed things like old abandoned flow lines, old cement slabs, oily soil, old well pads, shell and gravel roads, and other conditions that needed to be removed or cleaned up. Brashear said he passed the list along to his superiors at Shell, but admitted that none of the work was ever done.

Brashear also blew a hole in Shell's theory that field separation extracted all of the water from the wellstream. I asked him, "You can't separate 100 percent of the oil and gas from the water in the field separators, can you?"

He shook his head. "No. No."

"Some water gets past the field separators every time, doesn't it?"

He nodded. "I would say some."

With that, he was essentially done.

Shell then announced that its next witness would be its environmental expert, Michael Pisani. When we took Pisani's deposition just two months before trial, he had not conducted any tests on the Heyd property when he visited it. In fact, he indicated that he had been instructed by Shell's lawyers *not* to conduct any tests before his deposition. As a result, Pisani's deposition was largely meaningless, because he had nothing of substance to tell us. Shortly after the deposition, Shell's lawyers had Pisani revisit the property. That's when he ran tests and gathered data about contamination on the property—so that, presumably, he could surprise us with this new information at trial.

Before Pisani was questioned, I asked for a bench conference. Somewhat naively, I assumed that Judge Minaldi, like virtually every other judge I'd ever appeared before, would be offended by Shell's obvious "sandbagging" and would exclude any after-the-deposition testimony. Besides, Shell's lawyers hadn't complied with Judge Minaldi's pretrial order, which required them to divulge this kind of information well in advance of trial.

It turned out I was wrong. For reasons I still don't fathom, Judge Minaldi didn't seem concerned in the least that Shell's lawyers had ignored her pretrial deadlines. Moreover, she didn't seem to understand why it bothered us that Pisani had done his work *after* we deposed him, rather than before. When I objected to Shell's sandbagging, Minaldi chastised me instead of Shell, saying that I should have taken another deposition of Pisani over the weekend. I knew that the judge had never taken a deposition when she was an assistant DA, but I assumed that she had learned since taking the bench how indispensable they were to lawyers in civil litigation—and how unreasonable it was to expect any lawyer, over a weekend during the middle of a jury trial, to depose an important expert witness, get the deposition transcribed, review it, and prepare to cross-examine the witness with it. However, nothing I said could change her mind. Like so many other bench conferences during the trial, I came in second when it was over.

Michael Pisani was an environmental engineer. There was no questioning his pedigree. He had two degrees from reputable universities and a work history that gave him experience in charting and cleaning up various forms of pollution, including oilfield contamination. He was very familiar with Calcasieu Parish, having worked as a consultant for a number of the chemical plants that had installations west of Lake Charles. As McNamara's questions made clear, Pisani was Shell's counterpart to Austin Arabie, at least as to groundwater and subsurface soil conditions.

When Pisani was tendered for traversal as an expert, I knew there wasn't a chance that Judge Minaldi would reject him as unqualified. Rather than roll over, though, I took the opportunity to score a few points before McNamara got to direct him. I established that Shell had many environmental engineers like him, but that Shell's lawyers chose not to use any of them, but instead to hire him. I also established that Pisani had first been contacted about the case only three or four months earlier, even though the litigation was nine years old. The idea was to let the jury know that Pisani, like Bill Hise, was not a regular Shell employee but rather was a hired gun called in by Shell's lawyers. When I was through, Judge Minaldi formally recognized Pisani as an expert in his field.

Much of McNamara's presentation with Pisani was very technical and, in my opinion at least, less persuasive as a result. Pisani criticized Austin Arabie's sampling of the property as "biased," in that Austin took soil and ground-water samples from the areas that showed the greatest contamination. Next, he theorized that the high levels of salt that Austin documented in the ground-water beneath the Heyd property may have come from an underground "river" of sorts that flowed from the north through the property and then on to the south of it, as opposed to oilfield operations. The remainder of Pisani's direct examination largely consisted of his explaining numerous charts and graphs that either he or McNamara had prepared. In the end, Pisani calculated that the cost of cleaning up metal debris on the property was $133,200—considerably less than the millions that Austin Arabie had projected. Nothing else needed to be done because, in his opinion, the groundwater contamination was an "anomaly" that was not attributable to Shell's oilfield operations.

I began my cross-examination by having Pisani admit that, while Austin had taken eighteen borings on the property and analyzed the groundwater in each boring, he had only taken two borings on the entire 120 acres. Pisani also conceded that Austin had installed monitor wells in every one of his borings, whereas he had not installed a well in either of his two borings.

Next, I questioned Pisani about why he didn't take any borings or conduct any tests on his first visit to the property, before his deposition. That produced an interesting exchange.

"You were out on the property on March 3rd, but you didn't take any borings at that time, did you?"

He shook his head. "No."

"And you wanted to wait and see Mr. Arabie's borings first, didn't you?"

Pisani nodded. "I prefer to, yes."

I got to the point. "Because you certainly didn't want to find any trouble that Mr. Arabie didn't find, correct?"

Pisani smiled in a cocky way. "Well, that wasn't my purpose, but . . . ."

I broke in. "That served that purpose, though, didn't it?"

He nodded. "From your view, it did, but it was not what I had in mind."

At this point, Shell's lawyers objected to my going into what Shell's experts failed to do before their depositions. In a bench conference, I explained our position to Judge Minaldi as clearly as I could. "It's a credibility question, and I'm entitled on cross-examination to go into it. . . . I think I'm entitled to show what he did, how he did it, and I'm entitled to present my side that what he did was sneaky. And if the jury believes that, they're entitled to believe it. If they don't, they can choose to reject it. They [Shell's lawyers] have had their go. They presented what he did, and I want to put it in context, and that's awfully important."

Minaldi was curt. "Well, I disagree with you. The objection is sustained."

I was again disappointed at what I perceived to be the judge's "one-sidedness." But things have a way of evening out. Before I was finished with cross, Pisani made several key admissions.

Most importantly, I asked Shell's environmental expert, "Do you have any reason to believe that Mr. Arabie's measurements are wrong?"

He hemmed and hawed before finally saying, "They are indicative of what the real situation is." As I questioned him further, Pisani also characterized Austin's investigation of the property as "a very thorough site evaluation."

No doubt, Shell wasn't pleased to hear its environmental expert give such a ringing endorsement of his adversary's work.

Pisani had also testified that, in his opinion, his proposed cleanup was easy to accomplish. I wanted to follow up on that.

"Now, do you think that what you have proposed is easy—I think you said straightforward?"

He nodded. "Yes."

"Something that's very easily done?"

Again, he nodded. "Yes."

"Kind of hard to figure out why it hadn't been done after nine years, huh?"

Pisani's cocky nature came through again. "Well, I don't know about that," he said . . . and then laughed.

I suspected that his cavalier attitude wouldn't go over well with the jury, and I hoped to bring more of it out. I established that Pisani had drilled his two borings down to 70 feet, that this was close to the Chicot Aquifer, and that he nonetheless had not tested the water he pulled to see if it was contaminated. Again, this showed that, like his failure to conduct any tests before his deposition, he was interested only in protecting Shell, not in finding the truth.

The best line we got, though, came after I asked Pisani if anyone who drills into the ground should be careful not to contaminate the Chicot Aquifer. Pisani gave me that cocky smile again and said, "I don't know what being 'careful' is, but it's a consideration." I raised my eyebrows in disapproval and turned to look at the jury. They were showing the same reaction.

Judge Minaldi knew we had scored points on cross, and it apparently bothered her. She went so far as to make her own objection when I impeached Pisani's testimony with contrary statements from his deposition, even without Shell's lawyers voicing any complaint. At other times, when I asked a question she didn't like, she would stare intently at Gray and McNamara as if seeking an objection so that she could again interrupt my progress with the witness.

McNamara spent nearly an hour on redirect, trying to repair the extensive damage that had been done. I didn't even listen to much of what he asked Pisani at that point and made no objections to any of his questions. I did rise and object to McNamara's pronouncing in front of the jury that he "thought [Pisani] gave an honest answer" to one of my questions—the kind of editorial "puffing" of his own witness that wouldn't be tolerated by most judges. I was disappointed but not surprised when Judge Minaldi overruled my objection.

There are several factors that cause jurors to believe or reject the testimony of an expert witness. A lot depends, of course, on whether the witness seems to know what he's talking about and can support his opinions with facts. Beyond that, however, there is the human element. Simply put, a jury that likes a witness wants to believe him, and a jury that doesn't like a witness is easily persuaded to reject his testimony.

I had a hunch that the jury didn't like Michael Pisani.

25

After Pisani, the case began to move more quickly, as Shell put on a number of witnesses in quick succession. The first witness testified by deposition. Austin Stutzman was an elderly gentleman who had worked at the Shell gas plant many years before. Sadly, he passed away after we deposed him, and so the transcript of his deposition had to be read to the jury. Essentially, Mr. Stutzman testified that very little salt water entered or left the Shell gas plant. This tended to support Shell's theory that the gas plant did not send salt water to the Heyd property for injection into the salt water disposal system.

After we finished reading Mr. Stutzman's deposition, Shell called another former employee, Nol Broussard, to the stand. Under initial questioning by Tom McNamara, Broussard described himself as a longtime Shell employee (he was about to reach his thirtieth anniversary with the company) who was a construction foreman on offshore platforms. One of his previous assignments with the company had been in the Iowa Field from 1976 to 1980. During that time, he testified that he was involved in closing the "big pit" on the Heyd property. However, he moved on before the job was completed.

The apparent purpose in calling Broussard was to have him suggest to the jury that Shell "spared no expense" in closing pits. However, I wasn't sure that message came through as clearly as Shell would have liked, because Broussard had been in the Iowa Field such a short time. Beyond that, it seemed that Shell's plan was to have Broussard corroborate Joe Standridge's now-discredited testimony that getting a $1.1 million bid from Campbell Well Service to cleanup part of a pit didn't mean that the work was necessary. If anything, however, Broussard did the opposite by testifying that Shell's environmental department, working with Lloyd Deuel, determined what needed to be done before any cost estimates were formulated.

During his direct with Broussard, McNamara spent a great deal of time going over two documents pertaining to the operation. When I had a chance to ask on cross-examination what those documents meant, Broussard did no favors for Shell.

"I have no idea," he replied.

Shell's next witness was a toxicologist from Baton Rouge named Bradley Droy. Droy described himself as an "environmental consultant" who specialized in "using the science of risk assessment." He said that his work involved determining the potential adverse effects on human health presented by a contaminated site. In doing his work, Droy followed RECAP, which he said was an acronym for the "risk evaluation and corrective action program" developed by the Louisiana Department of Environmental Quality. That program established standards for identifying, measuring, and cleaning up hazardous materials that presented a health risk if left in place. After having Droy describe his professional credentials, McNamara tendered him as an expert in toxicology.

On traversal, Droy admitted that he was not a medical doctor and had never treated anyone for illness or disease caused by exposure to harmful substances. He also admitted that he wasn't called upon in his work to make a medical connection between someone's symptoms and any toxic substance that may have caused them. He also agreed that, not being an agronomist, he wasn't in a position to describe what effects a toxic substance might have on plant life, either. Under further questioning, Droy also admitted that he had never before been asked to work on a case in which the defendant was obliged to restore property "as near as possible" to its earlier condition, rather than according to RECAP standards. He also conceded that there was a difference between what a contract might require and what a regulation might require, meaning that a contract may call for something not required by any rule or regulation. Finally, I brought out that, like Shell's other "hired guns," Droy had been contacted about this case by Shell's lawyers only a month or so earlier.

Notwithstanding these limitations, Judge Minaldi recognized Droy as an expert in toxicology.

On direct examination, Droy testified that his assignment in the case was to review the available information concerning what substances had been found on the Heyd property and determine whether the site was safe or "needed to be cleaned up." When asked what he meant by "safe," he explained that the substances did not present any "risk to humans and the environment." He further explained that this kind of risk assessment was at the heart of his field, the science of toxicology.

At that point, the judge noted that it was nearly five o'clock and adjourned court until the next morning. She also informed us that, because of the upcoming Memorial Day weekend, we would adjourn on Friday (the next day) at three o'clock and reconvene on Tuesday at nine o'clock.

Trials are driven by schedules, and lawyers know the importance of tailoring their presentations of proof to that schedule. Shell's lawyers knew that, with a three-day weekend coming up, they needed to leave the jury with a good impression when things wrapped up the next day, and so I fully expected them to time their presentation so that they finished with a strong witness just as court adjourned.

Droy returned to the witness stand when court reconvened the next morning. He wasted little time in explaining that, in his view, the groundwater at the site did not violate the environmental standards set forth in RECAP and therefore did not need to be cleaned up. As evidence of Shell's desire to move things along, McNamara tendered Droy for cross after just fifteen minutes of questions.

On cross, Droy admitted that he had made no borings and that a formal RECAP evaluation required "a full delineation of all contaminants including the construction of plumes." He conceded that hadn't been done, mainly because no one at Shell had asked him to do it. In fact, he had only been to the Heyd property once, less than a month before trial. No one at Shell had performed a formal RECAP evaluation, either.

Since Droy hadn't performed any independent tests, I knew he wasn't in a position to dispute what Austin Arabie had found. For that reason, I asked him, "You don't doubt the accuracy of Mr. Arabie's tables, do you?"

He shrugged. "I don't."

Later, Droy also said that he had no reason to question Austin's expertise and volunteered that he "did a pretty good job" investigating the property. As we had done with Michael Pisani, we had obtained an endorsement of Austin Arabie and his work from still another Shell expert.

What troubled me was that Droy's opinion about whether the property should be cleaned up was based on RECAP rather than our contract. As I tried to make clear during my traversal of his qualifications, it was irrelevant whether RECAP required the property to be cleaned up; Shell had signed a contract that said it would restore the property as near as possible to its original condition when the lease expired. For that reason, Droy's entire testimony should have been excluded. Since Judge Minaldi had not done that, I needed to bring the point out again during my cross.

"You're not here to suggest that RECAP should be substituted for the contract between the parties, are you?"

Droy shook his head. "No, I'm here to say that RECAP is a reasonable way to cleanup the site."

I then asked him. "If you and I enter an agreement to cleanup a site, we're free to make an agreement that we both consent to, are we not?"

He nodded in agreement. "I think that would be reasonable."

"Did anyone ever tell you that this agreement refers to RECAP anywhere?"
He shook his head. "No."

I knew that RECAP was fairly new law, having only come into existence in 1998. "Was RECAP part of the law in 1961 when the parties signed this agreement?"

Droy seemed almost annoyed by my question. "No."

"Do you think that the parties in this case in 1961 were thinking about RECAP being passed in 1998 when they made this agreement?"

Droy shrugged. "I can't comment. . . ."

Before he could finish, McNamara apparently couldn't take it any longer. Jumping to his feet, he said, "Objection, Your Honor." He didn't state any legal ground, probably because there was none to support the objection.

Judge Minaldi didn't ask McNamara to explain the basis for his objection. Without blinking, she said, "Sustained."

Even though Droy hadn't answered my question, I thought I had made my point with the jury. I looked at them, said, "I have no further questions," and sat down.

The next witness, Thomas Bateman, was a principal with Iowa Production Company. He lived in Texas and was beyond the subpoena power of the court, so his deposition was submitted into evidence and read to the jury. I never did figure out why Shell's lawyers wanted it in evidence, because it didn't contain anything that seemed to help one side or the other.

Shell then announced that it was calling Gene Cope, a real estate appraiser from Lafayette, as its next witness. Cope had made an appraisal of the Heyds' property. As raw farmland, he estimated the 120 acres to be worth $108,000. Shell wanted this testimony in evidence because it had argued in pretrial motions that the Heyds were not entitled to recover more than the value of their property. According to Shell, the Heyds' property should be treated like a car wrecked so badly that the cost of repairs exceeded the value of the car before the accident. In other words, Shell contended that the Heyds' land should be "totaled," and the Heyds should be limited to recovering $108,000.

Of course, contaminated land is not like a wrecked car. Contaminated land can't be hauled away to a junkyard. The landowner is stuck with the contaminated land. He can't sell it, because no one wants to buy contaminated land. Even if they did, banks won't finance the purchase of contaminated land. Still worse, if the contamination spreads to other land, the landowner will be liable for the damage it causes to his neighbors.

Despite all this, Shell continued to argue that its liability should be limited to the value of the land. I countered that this would mean leaving innocent landowners like the Heyds holding the bag with a multimillion dollar cleanup bill. By now, Judge Minaldi was fully aware of our respective positions. If she agreed with Shell, then Cope's testimony was relevant and Shell's liability was limited to the value of the land, regardless of Arabie's cleanup estimate. If she agreed with us, then Cope's testimony was irrelevant to what it would cost to cleanup the property and therefore should be excluded. It had to be one or the other. At a bench conference, however, the judge answered the question with a definite "maybe," overruling my objection to Cope's testimony but maintaining our right to seek the full cost of cleaning up the property.

Cope then proceeded, under questioning by Pat Gray, to give his opinion about the value of the land, based on the assumption that it was in "pristine" condition. On cross, I brought out that Gray had purged Cope's file of notes he had made from conversations with people as he was gathering information for his appraisal. It was safe to assume that Gray pulled the notes because they contained information that was adverse to his side of the case. Still, it was standard procedure for an expert to produce his file and for the deposing lawyer to review that file in order to ask effective questions about the basis for the expert's opinion.

When I brought up in front of the jury that Gray had removed notes from Cope's file, he immediately objected and asked for a bench conference. I reported to the judge what happened and showed her the deposition transcript where Cope reported that Gray had pulled notes from his file before the deposition. Gray defended this with the self-serving statement that the notes he pulled contained "nothing" that Cope had relied on in forming his opinion.

Of course, the purpose of discovery and cross-examination is to test those kinds of self-serving assertions. Neither side is required to take the other's word for anything. That's when I said, "Why would [Cope] take notes of conversations that meant nothing to him? It's got to be assumed that those were things that were adverse to the opinion he's rendering. We're defenseless if this kind of thing is done."

Remarkably, however, Judge Minaldi accepted Gray's explanation and ruled in essence that allowing me to ask questions about this in front of the jury would be too prejudicial to Shell.

I was dumbfounded. Shell's lawyer had admittedly hidden evidence from us, and the judge had condoned it. I wasn't sure what questions I now could ask, so I said, "Your Honor, does that mean that we are . . ."

Before I could say another word, the judge ripped into me. "Do not argue with me anymore about the ruling. It's clear. Do not argue with me, Mr. Veron. I've been patient with listening to your arguments, but you have a habit of always wanting to continue after I rule and frankly I'm at the point I'm just not going to tolerate it anymore."

I momentarily considered telling the judge that I wouldn't have to argue as much if she would get things right, but decided against it because I didn't want to go to jail. Instead, I managed to respond with, "I'm simply trying to find out what the court has ruled."

She cut me off again and went off on a tangent about various things I had done during the trial that offended her, including the way I impeached Shell's witnesses, calling it a "waste of time and inappropriate." (That would prove to be a particularly interesting comment, as both the court of appeal and state supreme court later recognized that making an issue of Shell's credibility had been an important—and altogether appropriate— part of our case.) Minaldi even went so far as to threaten not to allow me to use depositions anymore in the trial.

When she said that, I was no longer puzzled. I was pissed. Looking her squarely in the eye, I said coolly, "Thank you, Your Honor. For the record, we believe it's for the jury to determine the value of the impeachment, and we have a jury trial. Secondly, with respect to my arguing with you, I don't believe the record will show that. But I do note that my opposition has re- visited every one of your rulings repeatedly throughout the case." I wondered briefly if I needed to remind her of how often she had reconsidered—and changed—her rulings in the case at Shell's request.

I knew she would have the last word, but this time her remarks carried less conviction. "Well, Mr. Veron, if you didn't in my opinion continue to do things outside what is proper, you wouldn't be called down such as, once again, just now having an argument about my ruling." Then, suddenly, she said, "I'm going to take a ten-minute recess."

As these confrontations continued to mount, I repeatedly asked everyone on our side if they observed something in my behavior that was causing the judge to be so outdone with me. No one could explain her reaction. As one of my senior partners said, "I don't see how you can stand it." I knew, however, that we had to maintain our focus on presenting the case for the jury and avoid being distracted either by Shell or the judge.

After the break, I asked Cope, "Is the value of property diminished by contamination?"

He agreed by saying, "Generally, yes."

"Have you ever encountered a situation where property actually had a negative value because of liability for environmental problems?"

He agreed again. "Yes, I have."

"Explain to the jury what that means."

Cope turned to the jury. "Well, a negative value would occur when the value of the property after it has been recovered is substantially less than the cost of recovery of that property. If you spend a million dollars and make a place worth $500,000, you have negative value because you spent more money than it's worth—than you can sell it for after you have recovered it."

While it was a technical explanation (I didn't quite get his use of the word "recover," but I didn't want to press the point and have him retract any of his testimony), I think the jury understood how it applied to the Heyd property. Cope also admitted that it was becoming customary for buyers to require that land pass an environmental audit before they bought it. He also agreed that buyers tended to shy away from land that had potential environmental liabilities.

We must have done some damage on cross, because Pat Gray took as long on his redirect examination as he did with his direct, backtracking over every issue as he tried to rehabilitate his witness. In fact, by the time Cope was finally dismissed as a witness, we had reached quitting time and were done for the weekend.

26

I knew one thing for sure: I was going to have a better weekend than Gray and McNamara. The member-guest tournament at the Lake Charles Country Club was held each year on Memorial Day weekend, and a dear friend of mine from California had arrived in town that day to play as my guest. Thus, while I expected Gray and McNamara to be holed up all weekend working on the case, I intended to be playing golf with my buddy for three straight days.

Frankly, I had never done something like that in the middle of a trial before. But this had been planned for a long time, and I couldn't bring myself to cancel it. Besides, we were as prepared for the rest of the trial as we could be. If anything, I figured that the break would refresh me and recharge my batteries.

It did. By the time I put my friend on his plane back to San Francisco late Monday afternoon, my head had cleared, I had regained some needed perspective about the case, and I was ready to get back into action.

One thing was clear from our different approaches to the weekend: Shell hadn't matched our preparation for trial. While we had our case "in the can," Gray and McNamara continued to spring surprises on us by submitting new or revised expert reports and evidence even as the trial progressed. I had never seen anything like it; they were making a mockery out of the deadlines set in Judge Minaldi's pretrial order. Still, part of me couldn't blame them for doing it; the judge had yet to enforce the deadlines against them.

When court reconvened on Tuesday morning, Gray announced that Shell was calling Calvin Barnhill, a petroleum engineer from Lafayette, as its next witness. I requested a bench conference, at which I informed Judge Minaldi that Shell had sent us a packet of materials relating to Barnhill's testimony as late as Friday evening. They included a "market study" that Barnhill had allegedly done regarding the cost of salt water disposal, supposedly to counter Bill Griffin's testimony that it would have cost Shell a dollar a barrel to dispose of the salt water.

This constituted new information that Barnhill had "never disclosed in his deposition," I told the judge, "and it was furnished too late for us to verify or otherwise check."

In addition, Shell also sent us a revised expert report from its farming expert, Donald Sagrera, over the weekend. Shell's lawyers originally had given us a four-page report from him on the night before trial began. That report, of course, was furnished well past Judge Minaldi's pretrial deadlines. As if that were not enough, however, Shell then had Sagrera prepare a new, sixteen-page report that dramatically changed the nature and scope of his expected testimony. That report was given to us Monday night.

Minaldi could tell I was agitated. For once, she seemed to have some sympathy for our being ambushed like this. She said, "Let's talk about Mr. Barnhill now. Why was [the new information] delivered on Friday?"

Pat Gray hemmed and hawed for a bit. Minaldi pressed him again, "Pat," she said (although the judge continually called me by my last name, she always addressed my opponent in a more familiar way), "do the [new exhibits] relate to his earlier testimony?"

Again, Gray was evasive. This forced Minaldi to ask again if the new exhibits related to anything that Barnhill had already testified to in his deposition. Impatient with Gray's refusal to answer, I broke in and said emphatically, "No." Although Gray then rambled for several minutes, he never denied that it was new information. Eventually, he tried to justify the changes by saying that the information came about because of rulings the judge had made during the trial. It was hard to feel much sympathy for Shell. We all knew that the judge's rulings on salt water disposal had come about at Shell's insistence and had greatly benefited Shell.

Finally, the judge said, "I'm not going to allow testimony or exhibits that come in two weeks after the trial has started regardless of rulings that are made during the trial."

Although the judge had ruled, Gray continued to argue. "We've got to be able to use the [new information] because the ruling was in the middle of trial."

I waited to see if Minaldi would rip into Gray for arguing after she ruled, as she had done to me on Friday. She didn't. Instead, she allowed him to argue for another five or ten minutes that she should change her ruling. In the end, however, she held fast to her original ruling and excluded the new submissions and any testimony from Barnhill about them.

After Barnhill was qualified and accepted as an expert in petroleum engineering, Gray questioned him at length about salt water disposal. It didn't surprise me that he eventually steered Barnhill into the very areas that Minaldi had said they could not discuss, and it also didn't surprise me that Minaldi overruled my objections despite her earlier ruling. Barnhill ultimately testified that, in his opinion, the value of the unlawful salt water that had been injected into the Heyd property was only $900, which was a far cry from the $1.6 million that Griffin had calculated (and that Dan Cliffe said was now worth as much as $28 million). He reached that number by dividing the $4,000 annual rental the Heyds received for the surface lease by the total barrels of salt water that Shell legally injected into their property to reach a per-barrel cost, which was minuscule. He then multiplied that by the number of illegal barrels that Shell had injected into the Heyd property to get his total.

On cross, Barnhill conceded that his method of calculating salt water disposal damages had not been approved by the American Petroleum

Institute, which was the leading organization of the oil and gas industry. He also admitted that the methods he used were not recognized in any professional literature of which he was aware. Under normal circumstances, this would have raised a serious question about whether Barnhill's opinion was sufficiently reliable to be admissible, under what is called the *Daubert* rule (based on a U.S. Supreme Court opinion of the same name). I knew better, however, than to expect the judge to exclude any of Barnhill's testimony.

Barnhill also conceded that he had not considered whether there was any other consideration besides the annual rental for the Heyds' agreement to allow salt water disposal—specifically, Shell's promise to cleanup the property. The point, of course, was that the annual rental wasn't the only thing of value that the Heyds received in exchange for the salt water disposal agreement, so it shouldn't be the only value used to compute the damages for illegal salt water disposal.

Barnhill also admitted that, under his analysis, the damages for Shell's unlawful salt water disposal were the same whether the Heyd family had allowed Shell beforehand to do what it did or said "no" and later discovered that Shell went ahead and did it anyway.

Throughout my cross Pat Gray made frequent objections that interrupted me. Most of them were sustained. Sometimes McNamara objected as well. Often, neither Shell lawyer even bothered to state a ground for the objection. On one occasion McNamara just said, "We're going to object to any further (sic) along this line of questioning, Your Honor." Minaldi replied, "And it will be sustained."

It was curious to me that Minaldi continually allowed both of Shell's lawyers to object and argue on every witness. In virtually every other case I had ever had, the standard procedure was that only one lawyer could speak for each side on a given witness. In other words, whoever questioned the witness for each side was the only lawyer entitled to object when the other side asked questions. Minaldi imposed no such restraints on Shell's lawyers.

As I continued to score points with my questions to Barnhill, the judge's patience with me again grew short. At one point, I showed Barnhill a Shell document in which company officials complained that surface leases with salt water disposal rights were "hard to acquire and costly" in the Iowa Field. This directly contradicted Barnhill's opinion that salt water disposal was a trivial thing that wasn't worth much of anything. As I continued to ask Barnhill about Shell's attitude toward surface leases, Gray complained that we had been through this line of testimony "witness after witness." I responded, "It goes to the heart, Your Honor, I believe, of his theory that he is offering. I'm trying to find what . . ."

She interrupted me. "I disagree. It's sustained."

I responded. "I can't show him any documents? I mean, they objected before I finished my question."

Minaldi frowned. "I know where you're going, Mr. Veron. And I don't think it's relevant with this witness. I think it's clear to the jury what your point is. I don't think it's relevant to this witness's testimony."

Despite these obstacles, we continued to bring out weaknesses in Barnhill's testimony. For instance, even though the purpose of his appearance was to give his version of the Heyds' salt water disposal damages, he reluctantly admitted that he knew nothing about what it would have cost Shell to dispose of the salt water legally.

"You didn't investigate how much it would cost to dispose of salt water by the barrel in this area at that time?"

He shook his head. "I did not."

"And you don't know where the nearest commercial disposal facility to the Heyd property was at the time?"

Again, he replied, "At this time I do not."

"You don't know in the '60s [the relevant time period for most of the illegal disposal]?"

He shook his head again. "That's correct."

It later turned out that Barnhill didn't even know how much it cost to dispose of salt water at the present time, either.

"Do you know what the cost per barrel of injected salt water is at a commercial facility?"

He tried to avoid answering. "I would think it would depend on your facility, what kind of volumes they deal with, those type things, the more volume they have, probably the cost per barrel. . . ."

I broke in. "My question is: Do you know?"

He shook his head. "No, I have not done a study on that."

I hoped the jury would find it as odd as I did that a petroleum engineer whose entire testimony was directed to this issue couldn't answer that question.

Our biggest break, however, came a few minutes later. During direct examination, Barnhill had said that we were wrong to claim that tanks at the Shell gas plant were used to hold water extracted from the gas that ran through the plant. It was an important point, because it contradicted our claim that the plant removed water from the gas stream and sent it to the Heyds' property.

To support Shell's position, Barnhill had testified that the tanks held propane, not water. That prompted Bill Griffin (who was still in the courtroom observing the rest of the trial) to pass a picture to me through my paralegal Tammy. It was a photograph of the tanks that he had taken on one of his visits to the gas plant. The picture was taken at close range and showed both tanks in great detail. Attached to the photo was a note from Bill. I immediately understood its importance and decided to end my cross-examination with it.

Directing Barnhill's attention to the subject, I asked him, "Is propane maintained under pressure?" As I asked the question, I glanced over at two gentlemen on the jury who were sitting in the first row. Both had disclosed during jury selection that they had worked for many years in local chemical plants. I knew they would be familiar with pressure vessels. They each nodded.

Barnhill tried to be coy. "What do you mean by maintained under pressure?"

"Is propane," I said, "maintained under pressure when it's in a vessel, a tank?"

He was clearly wary of where this was headed. "It depends."

"Isn't [propane] customarily, for instance, at a gas plant maintained under pressure?"

Barnhill nodded. "Yes."

"What pressure is typical, do you know?"

He shook his head. "I do not know."

"You don't know that?"

Again, he shook his head. "No."

I wanted to make sure I pinned him down. "But you do use pressure vessels when you maintain liquids under pressure, correct?"

He said, "Yes."

I looked over at the two jurors again. They were again nodding in agreement. They would know that water cannot be compressed and therefore is not stored under pressure. Thus, there is no need to weld the seams of water tanks. If, however, the tanks had been used to store propane under pressure, the seams would have been welded to contain the pressure.

Turning back to Barnhill, I asked, "And pressure vessels are generally welded tanks, are they not?"

He nodded. "Typically . . . ."

I looked at the jury again. "Explain to the jury why pressure vessels are welded rather than bolted or riveted."

Barnhill turned to face them and said, "Well, you want to have pressure and integrity for your tank. What happens when you insert pressure into a vessel, the forces applied against that vessel are basically the pressure across the cross-sectional area, so you want to make sure it's good and sturdy."

The two local plant workers again nodded, showing that they understood the point.

I then put the picture from Griffin on the "Elmo" so that it showed on the television monitors across the courtroom, including the big screen that was directly in front of the jury. "I'm going to show you something that we represent to be Corbello 30546 [referring to the Bates number]. Do you see rivets or bolts on the tanks in that picture?"

He looked at the picture. His shoulders slumped. "I do."

"Do you remember testifying that the slop tanks next to the gas plant were used for propane storage?"

Barnhill now sounded almost apologetic. "That was my understanding. That's what I was told." We all knew who had told him that: Pat Gray.

"Those are rivets all around these tanks, are they not?"

He nodded slowly, clearly embarrassed. "They are."

I didn't need to explain further. The seams of the tanks were held together by rivets, and it was apparent that the tanks had not been used to store propane, as Barnhill had said, but rather had stored water, as we had claimed.

I marked the picture and offered it into evidence. As I did, I glanced again at the jury. Several of them were smiling. Turning back to the judge, I said, "I've got no further questions. Thank you."

In his first question on redirect, Gray asked Barnhill, "Does anything about rivets or bolts on the tank affect your opinion one way or the other?"

Even though the rivets had unquestionably proved that Barnhill's opinion about the tanks was wrong, he quickly answered, "No."

You don't have to try many cases to learn that, when you take a punch, you shouldn't show the jury how much it hurt. But that's exactly what Gray did. First, asking Barnhill right out of the box if our obvious impeachment "affected" his opinion merely called the jury's attention to it again. Moreover, having Barnhill deny that it mattered—when it plainly did—hurt Shell's credibility with the jury even more. After a few minutes more, Gray indicated he had no further questions, and Barnhill was excused.

Shell then announced that its next witness was an economics expert from Baton Rouge named James Richardson.

27

Richardson was a tall and slender man who was obviously comfortable in a courtroom. After he came forward and took the oath, George Arceneaux (who apparently was Shell's designated hitter on economic issues in the case) began to ask questions to establish Richardson's credentials as an expert witness. Richardson disclosed in a soft voice that he was a professor of economics at LSU and, in addition, served on the revenue estimating conference of the state legislature providing economic forecasts to those planning the state budget. He was also an experienced expert witness, having testified on economic issues in litigation on many occasions. Richardson's mission, obviously, was to provide the counterpoint to Dan Cliffe's testimony adjusting the past losses from Shell's unlawful salt water disposal to their present value.

I had no questions about Richardson's qualifications, and Judge Minaldi recognized him as an expert in the field of economics.

On direct examination, Richardson testified that he had been contacted by Shell's lawyers just two months earlier and asked to calculate the present value of the damages claimed by the Heyds for improper salt water disposal. Using information given to him, Richardson determined that the present value of those damages was only $3,426. He was able to keep his number low by minimizing the amount of unlawful salt water (for instance, he didn't allow for any salt water from the Shell gas plant "since witnesses have testified that no water came from that facility"), excluding any cost of transporting the water from the field to a disposal site (a major cost), using Barnhill's method to determine a per-barrel disposal cost, and adjusting to present value only for inflation. In the alternative, Richardson said that using the historical interest rates for short-term securities, such as Treasury Bills, increased his number to $6,473.

These numbers were ridiculously low. If Shell was hoping to give the jury something besides Dan Cliffe's numbers as a possible award, these figures were probably too extreme for the jury to consider as a viable alternative. I suspect that Shell's lawyers realized as much, because they also had Richardson calculate the disposal cost at the five cents a barrel rate that the State of Louisiana paid under its contracts. Using that number, Richardson's present value calculation increased to $280,386. After having Richardson explain why he disagreed with Dan Cliffe's method of determining our damages, Arceneaux tendered him for cross-examination.

I began my cross by asking Richardson if he knew of anyone besides the State of Louisiana that had a contract allowing them to pay only five cents a barrel for disposal of salt water. He replied, "I did not do any research on that." It was obvious that, like Shell's other expert witnesses, he only considered what Shell's lawyers told him to consider.

I then showed Richardson Shell documents showing that the company was paying forty cents a barrel for disposal back in East Texas in 1981 and asked him to calculate what the cost for disposing of the same amount of unlawful salt water would be at the present time, some nineteen years later, adjusted for inflation. He said it came to $1.96 million. He also acknowledged that this number did not include transportation costs, which could run more than the disposal costs and therefore more than double the total.

To show that Richardson knew nothing about transportation costs, I asked him if he had any idea how much it had cost Shell to truck salt water from its King's Bayou field to the Heyd property, which was a distance of fifty-three miles. He lamely admitted that he had not "investigated" that, either.

Richardson had criticized Dan Cliffe's use of stock market growth averages as a way to adjust the costs Shell had saved in the past from illegal salt water disposal to their present value. Richardson said few people invested in the stock market, so it wasn't a valid way to bring past sums of money to present value. Explaining further, he said that, if Shell had paid the Heyds for the salt water disposal in question, they probably wouldn't have invested the money in the stock market and therefore would not have experienced that amount of growth in their investment over the years. (It was an interesting assumption, given that Richardson had never laid eyes on any of the Heyds. It also ignored the fact that getting that money might have freed up other money for investments.) The better way to adjust for present value, he said, was to use something more conservative, like bond rates or the CPI.

On cross, I asked Richardson if he was aware that millions of Americans were routinely invested in the stock market through their retirement plans, particularly 401(k)s. He reluctantly conceded that more and more people now owned stocks because of retirement plans.

"Do you think the average person buys bonds on a regular basis," I asked.

"Most people don't own bonds," he said.

In the end, Richardson's criticism of Dan Cliffe missed the point. The purpose of adjusting past or future losses to present value was to make the victim whole with a present-day sum of money that was closest in value to the actual loss. It didn't matter if the victim would actually have invested the money or not.

Richardson's testimony didn't last very long. As soon as he was excused, Tom McNamara announced that Shell was calling Don Sagrera as its next witness.

Sagrera was another one of Shell's experts. Specifically, his assignment was to testify about the condition of the soil on the Heyds' property and what it would cost to clean it up. In response to questions by McNamara, Sagrera described himself as a longtime rice and crawfish farmer (he looked the part) who also taught various courses in agronomy and agriculture at the University of Southwestern Louisiana in Lafayette. He also disclosed that he was a principal in a consulting firm that assessed damage to soil and made recommendations on restoring damaged soil to a "productive condition." He estimated that approximately half of his firm's work involved assessing damage to soil caused by salt water intrusion. In connection with that work, he said that he had often testified in court as an expert witness. With that, McNamara tendered Sagrera as an expert in the fields of agronomy and soil assessment and restoration.

I began my traversal by asking Sagrera whether he had ever testified on behalf of a landowner in all of his court appearances. Of course, I knew the answer to the question, because I had asked him about it in his deposition. He said, "No, sir."

"Every one of your appearances has been on behalf of some industry that was opposed to a landowner, correct?"

He nodded. "That's correct."

In further testimony, Sagrera admitted that Shell had first contacted him just a couple of months before trial. He was only asked to give courtroom testimony. He had never been consulted by Shell over the previous nine years about the proper way to cleanup the Heyd family property. Having made those points, I was finished with my traversal.

Minaldi then recognized Sagrera as an expert in his tendered fields.

On direct examination, Sagrera described how he took numerous soil samples from the Heyd property to determine what needed to be done to restore the soil to a condition in which it would again be productive for farming. Of course, he had done most of this work after we had deposed him. In fact, he had done most of it after the trial had begun. There was little we could do about it, however, since Judge Minaldi refused to exclude his testimony. In the end, Sagrera said that the land could be restored to farming at a cost of $270,692. He even boasted that, with his program, the land would be "better than it was in 1961," when the surface lease was signed.

I began my cross-examination by asking Sagrera if his "program" removed any of the oil or grease from the property. He said that wasn't necessary, because plowing the ground would cause the oil and grease to disintegrate. I knew he couldn't substantiate that claim.

"Now, you're suggesting that, if you just plow stuff up then all this stuff goes away; is that what you're saying to the jury?"

Sagrera began to equivocate. "It helps it to go away," he said.

Pointing to pictures of the extensive surface damage to the property, I said, "Plowing is not going to make that go away, is it?"

He shifted in his seat. "If it's on the surface. . . ." He then realized that he was on shaky ground. Then, he volunteered, "I'm not even sure of what it is."

Putting another photograph on the "Elmo," I said, "Or this? No one has ever told you about any of this?"

Sagrera shook his head in an uncertain manner. "I'm not sure what you're referring to in the photograph. Is it . . ." His voice trailed away. After an awkward pause, he admitted, "That material in the photograph I've not seen it before."

After he weakly asserted again that plowing would make oil and grease "go away," I said, "For the record, I'm showing photographs. The last one is Corbello 4130. You believe that just plowing would make that go away?"

Again, Sagrera said, "I'm not sure what it is, what that is."

Referring to more photos, I said, "That's 4151. Or this . . . this is 4149. Do you know what that is?"

Once again, Sagrera was forced to admit, "I don't know what it is."

Here was an expert who had spent the better part of an hour on direct examination telling the jury that he knew how to cleanup this property for a fraction of what Austin Arabie said it would cost. But on cross he couldn't identify what was in any of the photographs taken of the surface of the property.

When Sagrera finally gave a decent answer for Shell, saying that none of the deep subsurface damage that Austin had documented would affect crop growth on the property, McNamara was so thrilled he reverted to the old trick of pretending not to hear the answer. Leaning forward and holding his hand to his ear, he called out, "I didn't hear the answer. Could you repeat the answer, please, Don?"

Several members of the jury smirked at the obvious ploy.

It had to hurt Shell's cause that Sagrera had completed his calculations just the day before. I asked him, "Now, this plan that you presented was actually completed just yesterday, is that correct?"

He squirmed slightly. "Well, the . . . values to carry it out were just completed yesterday."

I shook my head. "But in this nine-year-old case, you finally put this plan together on the day before you testified?"

He more or less shrugged apologetically. "Well, the value of the final figure for tree removal I put together yesterday."

There was good reason to question a plan so hastily thrown together. Continuing with my cross, I asked Sagrera, "You mention in [your] report that it would take some time for the grass to become completely established, and you suggested considering [crop] yield reductions over the next five years, correct?"

He nodded. "On some areas." After a pause, he added, "Some areas longer than that."

I followed up on that. "You have been involved in cases in which you have had to monitor property, particularly some land near Crowley, for eight or nine years?"

He nodded. "Yes."

It was obvious that, even with Sagrera's plan, restoring the property was no quick fix. Remarkably, even while admitting that his plan could take years to restore the property, Sagrera had not included anything in his "budget" for monitoring his plan's progress.

In reviewing documents in the case, we had discovered a 1986 report in which Sagrera had inspected the Heyd property for Rosewood, which had acquired the mineral lease from Shell the year before, and had tested the soil around one of the pits. I showed Sagrera his report from that inspection. Its conclusion was that Shell's pits had leaked salt water into the subsurface soil.

Holding up the report, I asked him, "You did not remember this when we took your deposition, did you?"

He shook his head. "No, sir. To be honest with you, I still don't remember going out there."

"So you have no independent recollection other than what that paper says?"

He nodded. "That's correct."

It also developed that, while Shell's lawyers had asked Sagrera to estimate the cost of restoring the surface, they never showed him the list of "to do" items for surface restoration that Buster Brashear had compiled while walking the property with Jody Miller and Billy Corbello. Thus, Sagrera hadn't included the cost of removing contaminated soil, abandoned lines, old junk, shell and gravel from abandoned roads on the property, and other items that Brashear had listed. Nor did he include the cost of hauling off the numerous trees that he had proposed cutting. Instead, Sagrera said, they would burn the trees on the property.

I was surprised by this and asked Sagrera, "He [the contractor] was going to burn fires on top of a producing oil field?"

Sagrera nodded. "That's correct."

I looked at the jury and back at Sagrera. "Do you consider that to be a safe practice?"

Sagrera squirmed again. "Well, I'm sure that he would not have them piled up in an area that he would think would have been a place where there would have been a problem. I'm sure he would not have used an area where he was expecting it to spread or to get to any kind of oil or gas."

The news that day had prominently featured an oilfield fire in New Mexico. I leaned toward Sagrera. "Have you watched the news in New Mexico?"

Sagrera shrugged. "No, sir, I haven't had a chance."

Several members of the jury laughed.

I wanted to get to the real reason Sagrera's estimate assumed that the trees would be burned on site. "It is a considerable expense to haul off trees when you clear property, is it not?

Sagrera nodded. "I would think so."

"Do you know whether this contractor obtained the consent of the present operator of the field to light fires when you've got lines carrying hydrocarbons around this field?"

He shook his head. "I don't know whether he did or not."

McNamara spent a lot of time on redirect attempting to repair the damage done on cross. Much of it simply involved his asking Sagrera to repeat the reasons why he believed his plan should be adopted.

When he was through, McNamara informed the court that Sagrera was Shell's final witness. After introducing additional documents into evidence, Shell rested.

I was pleasantly surprised. Shell's lawyers had apparently decided not to call several expert witnesses, including Lloyd Deuel, John Berghammer, and Dick Jones. In addition, Shell had decided not to call Mike Maier, a Shell representative who refused to share information with Billy Corbello and me about the profits made by the company's oil terminal after the lease expired.

Judge Minaldi then ordered a recess and advised the jury that we would present rebuttal evidence after the break. However, when we returned, I informed the court that we waived rebuttal. With that, the judge sent the jury home for the day, ordering them to return the next morning for closing arguments.

After the jury left the courtroom, we asked for a directed verdict on our trespass claim. We argued that the evidence was undisputed that Shell continued to occupy the property after the 1961 surface lease expired and refused to leave even when we asked them to do so. Thus, no reasonable juror could conclude that Shell wasn't liable for trespass, and the only question should be what damages were due as a result of Shell's failure to vacate the property at the end of the lease.

We also asked for a directed verdict on our cleanup claim. The surface lease unquestionably required Shell to cleanup the property, and the undisputed evidence was that no cleanup had ever been done. There was no reasonable basis for any jury to conclude that the lease had not been breached as a result of Shell's failure to restore the property, and the only question for the jury should be what amount of money was owed to the Heyds as a result of Shell's failure to return the property at the end of the lease in good condition.

Minaldi granted our motion with respect to the trespass. My cynical side persuaded me that she did so only because it was our smallest claim. She then denied our motion with respect to the cleanup claim. My cynical side said that she did so because it was our largest claim. In any event, she didn't explain her reasons for either ruling.

With that, we were through for the day. The only things left for the next day were closing arguments, jury instructions, and the jury's verdict. Our long battle with Shell was almost over.

28

The closing argument is the lawyer's last opportunity to persuade the jury about what has been proved—or, from the defendant's perspective, what has *not* been proved. Unlike opening statements, when lawyers technically aren't permitted to argue, the gloves come off during closing arguments. Each lawyer is expected to do his best to close the deal for his client.

There are a few rules, however. You can't appeal to prejudice (verdicts must be based on facts, not prejudice). You can't argue outside of the record (verdicts must be based on the evidence). You can't invoke the "Golden Rule" (i.e., "how would you feel if you were in my client's shoes?") because it destroys the jury's third-party objectivity. And you can't express your personal opinion about the case (a lawyer's personal opinion is not evidence). Other than that, though, there are no holds barred.

It's easy to say that closing arguments are the most critical point of a trial. Certainly, books, movies, and television make it appear that way.

However, that's probably an overstatement. I suspect that, in many (if not most) cases, the jury has more or less made its mind up by the time the lawyers make their closing arguments.

There's no doubt that closing arguments can be the most dramatic moment in a trial, though. It's a time when good lawyers pull together all of the evidence into a compelling version of events—their "story"—that they believe will persuade the jury to rule in their favor. It's also an opportunity for each lawyer to express his righteous indignation over the injustice done his client by the other side. That's the tricky part, though. Good lawyers know that overplaying that card will turn the jury off. Simply put, you don't pretend your client's a victim if the evidence doesn't show that he's a victim.

As I prepared for closing arguments, I hoped that the evidence had gone so well for us that whatever I said wouldn't matter. It was a rationalization that helped relax me, and I was determined to enjoy the closing. It worked to some degree, but I knew that, as long as the decision was in the hands of someone other than me, I couldn't afford to take anything for granted.

So I spent several hours that night going over my notes and reviewing the important testimony in the case. I pulled together a few exhibits. I tried to construct an outline that I could commit to memory. Most of all, I wanted to deliver my closing argument without any notes.

I got a good night's sleep ("the sleep of the just"?) and felt refreshed and ready the next morning. My mind was clear, and I felt like I knew exactly what I wanted to say. When we got to court, Judge Minaldi asked to meet with all of the lawyers in her chambers to finalize the jury instructions and verdict form. I had asked a couple of my partners, John Pohorelsky and Rusty Stutes, to take care of that aspect of the case, and I stayed in the courtroom to hone my remarks.

It turned out that I had more time than I needed. As usual, Shell's lawyers wanted to argue about numerous things, so the conference lasted nearly an hour. When Judge Minaldi and the lawyers finally returned to the courtroom, we were ready to begin. Each side had been allotted forty-five minutes for closing arguments. As the plaintiff, we bore the burden of proof, so we were allowed to speak before and after Shell's closing argument. I informed Judge Minaldi that I was reserving twenty minutes for my rebuttal, and she nodded for me to begin.

I stood, faced the jury, and smiled. After telling them that this two-and-a-half week trial was the longest of my career, I complimented them on their attentiveness. Several of them, I commented, had taken copious notes during the trial. For that reason, I said, "I'm not going to spend a lot of time giving you a detailed recital [of the evidence]. I don't think you'd want me to at this point in the trial. You've heard it all, you've listened to it all, and if I need to show you right now what's been said, then we're really all in a lot of trouble, I suppose. So I don't intend to do that."

Not only that, I said, but, "I don't intend in my initial remarks to you to show you document after document. My goodness, they were on this [Elmo] screen, they were up, they were big. You know what was said. You heard both sides' witnesses tested by cross-examination, and so I hope by now you have decided, as I suggested in my opening statement, who's kept the faith with you, who's appealed to your logic, and who's appealed to your common sense; and so I hope that much is clear."

I also reminded them that I had promised in my opening statement that the case would be easy to decide. I said that, if the case seemed confusing at times, it was "Shell [that] made it confusing, and I think it had a reason to make it confusing. . . . Behind the barrage of technical detail and information that quite often we felt had nothing to do with what this case was all about but only was an attempt to hide things, it became very clear what this case was about."

Continuing, I said, "This has been a nine-year journey, and we have experienced everything imaginable; because when you go up against a company as big and as powerful as Shell, you can expect to be tested every step of the way." I looked at them and said, "Now, I'm not one of those who believes that big companies are bad. I'm not some vigilante, I'm not some Ralph Nader. I'm not radical about much of anything." Continuing to look at each one of the jurors, I opened my hands and said, "I represent big companies, but I do believe that even big companies can do bad things; and when they do, that's what this place is for. When they force the little man to come into this courtroom, that's what this place is for, because it is your only protection against the kind of wealth and power that a company like Shell Oil can bring to bear."

I turned and swept my left arm around the courtroom, taking in Shell's lawyers, entourage, and mounds of briefcases, charts, and exhibits. "And you saw how much wealth and power it brought to bear here. You saw how it assembled in the last month or two an amazing cast of characters, none of whom had anything to do with the events that gave rise to this litigation. We waited and waited and waited to hear from the people who made the decisions that caused this thing to come about, that forced the Heyd family into litigation." I paused. "They never showed."

It was the perfect segue to talk about missing witnesses.

Pointing to the back of the courtroom, I said, "Lloyd Deuel was here in the courtroom. They didn't put Lloyd Deuel on the stand. The man who tested the soil and said, 'You know, you got problems,' who to this day, sixteen years after they spent $220,000 cleaning up the skimming area still has problems, the man who said 'It's going to be expensive,' the man who said 'I wouldn't warn anybody about drinking water unless they complained first,' they didn't put him on the stand to face us—and to face you." I paused. "More importantly, to face you."

I let that sink in a moment before continuing. Then, I said, "Mike Maier, the oil terminal man—the one that Billy Corbello said 'If you want to stay on our property, I need to know what are y'all doing here, what are your profits, what's a fair rental, I can't arrive at that [without information on your profits].'" Gesturing toward the rear of the courtroom again, I quoted Maier. "No, you're not getting anything, any information on profits, and we're going to stay."

I paused. "They did bring Paul Lair who told us, 'Well, you know, you didn't send the sheriff for us, so we're entitled to stay.'" I have a bad habit of talking fast, so I was making a conscious effort to speak in an even and calm voice. "It was a kind of arrogance that was . . . in a way I was glad to see it. It always makes you sad when people have that kind of an attitude, but when it finally came out, at least it showed you what we have faced for nine long, long years."

It was time to talk about our witnesses, beginning with Bill Griffin. After reminding the jury that Griffin had spent his entire career working for a major oil company and that he still did consulting work for oil companies, I said, "If anything, he's speaking against his own interest by coming here, and he came here and you heard him say what was wrong. You heard him speak on behalf of the industry that this is wrong, it shouldn't have happened. And he gave his calculations, and they cross-examined him and never, never shook him. Never showed where he was wrong."

Then I talked about Austin Arabie. "Again, I didn't want some wild-eyed radical. I wanted somebody solid, and I was recommended to Austin Arabie. And I was told he did the very groundwork of this courthouse, the police jury [the parish governing body in Louisiana] uses him. He's got the kind of reputation everybody trusts. He works for the Cameron Parish School Board, he works for PPG, he works for BFI, and he works the industry side." I reminded the jury how Shell's own witnesses admitted that Arabie did a much more comprehensive investigation of the contamination on the property than they did. Not one of them had found an error in his measurements.

I then talked about how Shell's witnesses all seemed to unravel on cross-examination.

Nol Broussard had given what I called "very carefully rehearsed" testimony about documents that had been "reshuffled . . . to put a new version on" them. Then, I said, "First thing I asked him on cross about the documents: 'Well, how does this relate to that?' Quote, 'I have no idea.'"

I then reminded the jury that Bill Hise couldn't even identify the boundaries of the Iowa Field. "That astonishes me," I said shaking my head. Moreover, I pointed out that Hise claimed that the property was free of contamination in 1960, meaning that all of the contamination we documented occurred thereafter, during the term of the 1961 surface lease and was therefore subject to its "cleanup" provision.

I then talked about the claims, starting with the "cleanup" claim. I emphasized that Shell's talk about the mineral lease, and how it transferred that lease to Rosewood in 1985, was a "smoke screen." We were suing under the surface lease, and Shell never transferred any of the surface lease.

I also reminded the jury that there wasn't a single witness who attributed any of the contamination to anyone other than Shell. And, of course, it was undisputed that Shell had done *nothing* to cleanup its mess. Austin Arabie, I said, gave a range of $6 million to $26 million for groundwater contamination, but said he couldn't predict how long it would take to clean it up. No one, I reminded them, could foresee the future. Even Don Sagrera admitted that one of his cleanup projects had taken eight or nine years.

I continued to look up and down the two rows of jurors, making eye contact with each one of them. It was easy to do, because I didn't have to look down at any notes. I wasn't using notes.

"Shell comes here to tell you that it really doesn't cost much. You know, the thought I kept having over and over was, if it really doesn't cost much, why didn't they do it? The truth is, they had a $1.1 million bid in '84; they just went to cleanup part of the pit, and it cost them $220,000; they couldn't get it all. They said, 'This is going to cost too much money. We're walking.' And that's what happened. And they walked."

The jury was just watching me, without any obvious facial expressions. "And there's no dispute but that they never cleaned up the property when the lease ran out in 1991. Never. No one came here to say, 'We cleaned it up.' Billy Corbello's testimony is unrefuted, and Shell never brought anyone."

I paused and took a deep breath. "Mr. Pisani laughed at me when I said 'Why wasn't Mr. Deuel's plan implemented?' He thought that was funny. I didn't think it was funny. Mr. Pisani is somewhere in New Orleans right now. He doesn't have the liability. He doesn't have to worry about the Lake Charles drinking water. He doesn't have to worry about the drinking water wells in the area. He's not worried about that, just like the rest of Shell's witnesses, and just like Shell's lawyers and everybody here from Shell, tomorrow—they're not spending the night in Lake Charles—they're going to be out of here. Lake Charles will be in their rearview mirror, but this community is left with Shell's mess. We're left with it. And if we don't clean up all of it, we've got a big problem."

Shell, of course, was going to argue that our cleanup cost estimates were outrageously inflated. In anticipation of that, I said, "Shell wants to tell you, 'Well, you know, be conservative.'" I paused. "I think Shell has forfeited the right after nine years to come here and tell any of us how much that cleanup costs. And now they have the gall to come here and suggest to us that our estimate is high?"

My voice was rising with emotion. "We can't predict the future, but we can judge the past. And the past is very clear: Shell has done nothing. Shell has forfeited the right to tell us how much that cleanup would cost. Shell hasn't shown that Austin Arabie was anything but a rock-solid person who's concerned about the environment and who's got a reputation in this community that he earned from good, solid work. They've given us no reason to believe that the estimate couldn't go as high as $26 million."

I then turned to our second claim, for trespassing. As I reminded the jury, Shell's own financial records showed that the company made $927,000 at the oil terminal alone by staying some twenty months past the termination of the lease. "Shell wants you to let them keep that money. They want to profit from their own wrong. They want to be able to say, 'Hey, you, it's worth our while to stay on people's land.'" I then suggested that the truest measure of the value of Shell's trespass was the amount of money it made.

Before getting to the salt water disposal claim, I said, "It's been incredible to me. The documents, the testimony, the arrogance of the witnesses who come here putting together things the night before they're going to testify, who sit in the courtroom over there and get coached openly during breaks. Mr. Standridge gets coached before his deposition and then after his deposition to be told, 'Say it differently.'" I paused. "That's what I mean when I say you have to decide who's kept the faith with you, who's appealed to your logic and your common sense."

Commenting on Shell's calculation of damages for salt water disposal, I said, "Shell wants to say, 'Well, what would the Heyd family have agreed to if we had gone to them, and that's what they ought to have." I shook my head. "You know, it's like, I'm going to come and take your house, and if you catch me, I'm going to say, 'Well, if I had gone to you, you'd have sold it to me for this much anyway.' In other words, there's no downside to my illegal behavior. There's no downside to me doing the wrong thing, so it's in my best interest; because if I don't get caught, I walk away free and clear with your property. If I do get caught, I'm only going to pay what I should have paid up front." I then reminded them that Griffin and Cliffe's calculations of our salt water disposal damages came to $28,031,108.

Judge Minaldi signaled that my original twenty-five minutes were nearly up. It was time to get off my feet. I said, "In a case like this, I have to put my faith in you. You've listened. You've listened far beyond the call of duty. You've heard everything. And so when I address you again, I'm going to go through the verdict form and tell you the ways in which—if you believe as we believe and you believe that Shell needs to be made to accept responsibility for what it's done—that verdict form should be completed."

I smiled at each of them, said "Thank you," and sat down.

29

Tom McNamara stood, indicating that he would deliver Shell's closing argument. The first thing he did was to bring the podium back in front of the jury. (I had removed it because I wasn't using any notes and didn't want anything separating me from the jury.) He then placed his notes on the podium.

McNamara began with a question. "So why are we here? You would have thought the issues—the real issues that you've seen in this lawsuit—could have been worked out without coming to court. We certainly would have preferred to avoid all of this we've been going through for the last two weeks." It was an improper comment about settlement negotiations, but I let it pass without objection.

Looking up from his notes, McNamara sounded the theme for his closing argument when he said, "The real issues [in this case] are: What is the fair market rental value for the period of the holdover [Shell's euphemism for trespassing] on the oil terminal lease during the period that they were trying to renegotiate a new lease? And, secondly, what is the fair value for any salt water that exceeded the permissions granted by the 1961 surface lease? And, third, what is a fair and reasonable and practical way to restore the plaintiffs' property?"

Before answering these questions, McNamara returned to his theme of landowner greed. "So why did we have to come here to work it out? You've seen that from the evidence that the tensions between Shell and the Heyd family are relatively recent in origin. For sixty years they got along in a friendly and businesslike relationship, but from the moment the terminal lease expired this case evolved into what you have been hearing in the courtroom for the last two weeks."

It was an odd approach. The evidence was undisputed that Shell had done *nothing* in the nine years since the lease expired to cleanup the property. The evidence was undisputed that Shell had stayed on the Heyds' property without permission after the lease expired, making nearly a million dollars in profits from the oil terminal. The evidence was undisputed that Shell had over the years deliberately not obtained proper leases and rights-of-way as it used and abused the Heyds' land.

But here was McNamara, telling the jury with a straight face that all of this had been a "friendly and businesslike relationship" until recently. Friendly and businesslike for whom, I wondered. It didn't make sense for Shell to complain about the Heyds. The Heyds hadn't trespassed; the Heyds hadn't refused to cleanup the property despite their contract; the Heyds hadn't unlawfully disposed of salt water. Shell did all of that. I hoped the jury was asking itself, how was any of that the *Heyds'* fault?

Returning to the trespass, McNamara told the jury that the issue was the fair rental value of the "three-acre tract used for the oil terminal during the holdover period." I was amused. It was a typical example of Shell's over-reaching. They weren't even willing to concede that they "held over," or trespassed, on the entire 120-acre tract. They wanted to limit it to the three acres in the middle of the property where the oil terminal sat. Of course, they used the entire 120 acres. They couldn't have gotten to the oil terminal without driving on the roads that crossed the 120 acres. I whispered to Pat Gallaugher, who was next to me, "Do they expect us to believe that they *parachuted* in to the middle of the property?"

Still, McNamara insisted to the jury, "It's the rental value, not Shell's profits" that was at issue. "You must determine the actual loss or damage to the plaintiffs themselves. How much could they have rented that property for if Shell hadn't been there. What's the fair market value?" He then reminded them that Gene Cope, Shell's appraiser, said that the rental value of the three acres in the middle of the Heyds' land was $450 a year. Since Shell had trespassed (or "held over") for almost two years, McNamara suggested that the amount due was $900.

He then addressed salt water disposal. McNamara relentlessly attacked Bill Griffin's testimony, arguing that it was some of the most "tortured" testimony ever given. He suggested that the jury should disregard it entirely. Offering the jury an alternative number, he told them that the cost savings to Shell was about $35,000 all total. Even if you "ramp that number up on [the] stock market," he said, it only came to $280,000.

Now it was time to address the claim for cleanup costs. Cobbling together the estimates of Don Sagrera and Mike Pisani, McNamara told the jury that it would only cost a total of $403,892 to cleanup the property. He then suggested that the jury "take into consideration the value of the property, $900 an acre for property worth $108,000 for the whole area."

After being warned by the judge that his time was short, McNamara chose to bring up the buried materials in what he called the "junkyard." Remarkably, he called it "buried household trash." Given the undisputed evidence that the buried materials included sludge, rotted asbestos pipe, an old gasoline dispenser, benzene, and other toxic substances, I wondered what kind of "household" McNamara was referring to.

After a few additional remarks, McNamara's forty-five minutes were up. I still had about twenty minutes left for rebuttal, but I knew I wouldn't need all of that time. It was a gut feeling, but I just didn't sense that Shell's closing argument caused any serious damage to our case.

We had blown up the verdict form to poster size. Setting it on an easel, I began my rebuttal by telling the jury, "This is the form you'll be asked to fill out. It takes nine of the twelve of you to agree to answer each question. So when nine of you are in agreement in answering a particular question, you can enter it and you can move on."

I then pointed to the first question on the verdict form, which asked, "What damages are owed by Shell and SWEPI to the Heyd family for failing to vacate the property when the 1961 lease expired?" I told the jury that "the best measure of that is $927,000."

The second question on the verdict sheet was: "Was there a failure to reasonably restore the Heyd property?" Since Shell had admittedly done nothing, the obvious answer to this was "Yes." In truth, the judge should have granted a directed verdict on this issue. I looked at the various jurors and said, "Now I listened for the forty-five minutes that Shell and SWEPI talked to you, and I kept waiting to hear a reason to answer that 'No.' They never gave you a reason. You know, what I got out of it was, 'Hey, we're an oil company; and if we pollute, that's to be expected and we're out of here.'"

I probably didn't need to say any more than that, but I continued. "They didn't do anything. You know, for Shell to play the victim and say we were taking advantage of an opportunity. . . . Did you ever hear Shell say that they were ever prevented from going on the property to restore it for nine years? Who's taking advantage of whom? Did anybody say that the Heyd family ever did one thing wrong? Did anybody from that witness stand ever say Billy Corbello made an unreasonable request?"

I shook my head. "The witnesses who dealt with him all said, 'No, no, . . . he was courteous and he was polite and we walked the property and we went through and made a list.' Of course, Shell didn't give the list to Mr. Sagrera, you know. I mean, the list just disappeared. They would walk us through and patronize us and have us make lists, and then they'd walk away and the list would disappear and we'd never hear anything. And they're the victim? *We* took advantage of an opportunity?"

I could feel my passion rising again. "Time and time again Shell ignored the Heyd family, ignored every attempt to say, 'Would you please just cleanup the mess? Would you please do something?'" I paused, shaking my head in disgust. "And now they have the unmitigated gall to walk in here, come into town, hire a bunch of new people. . . . We just want to know why instead of the people who knew what was going on they went and assembled this cast of characters to come into town and put on this dog and pony show for everybody. Why didn't they bring the people who made the decisions?"

I talked about Mike Maier, whom they didn't put on the stand. I talked about the unidentified Shell supervisor to whom Buster Brashear gave his list, which then ended up in the "wastebasket." Shell didn't bring him to explain what he did with the list. Referring to Shell's controversial environmental expert, I said, "They had Mr. Deuel sitting in the back row of that courtroom. They didn't want to put him on the stand to explain why he said, 'We're not going to tell anybody if the drinking water's bad. We'll wait and see if they get sick and complain.'"

All of that, I said, was more than enough to justify finding that Shell had failed to restore the property. I then moved to the next question on the verdict form, which was "What damages are owed to the Heyd family for failing to restore the property?" It was time to respond to Shell's suggestion that the damages for contamination should be "capped" at the value of the Heyds' land, which Shell said was only $108,000.

"You don't have to accept this incredible reasoning to you that says, 'We're going to come in, we're going to trash the property, we're going to create harm worth many, many times more than the property's worth, that would cost many, many times more than the property's worth, and we're going to walk away and leave the Heyd family owning the property and owning the problem.'" I looked over at Shell's lawyers and then back to the jury. "That's what Shell's asking you to do. . . . I am incredulous that they would come here in open court and take that position." I then reminded the jury of Austin Arabie's estimates of what it would cost to cleanup the property.

The next question on the verdict form asked the jury to state by percentages whose fault contributed to the need to cleanup the property. The jury was asked to choose between Shell, Rosewood, and Kreuger. I reminded the jury of the testimony given by Jody Miller and others about how well Rosewood and Kreuger maintained the property compared to Shell. I suggested that Shell bore 100 percent of the responsibility for the contamination.

The next question was "Did Shell and SWEPI illegally dispose of salt water on the Heyd property?" As I looked at each juror, I said, "There's no dispute about that. I've never heard Shell really deny that."

After the jury answered "yes" to that question, I told them, they would come to the final question on the verdict sheet, which asked them to determine what damages were owed for the unlawful salt water disposal. I wrote on the form the $28 million number that Griffin and Cliffe had calculated.

Stepping back from the verdict form, which I had filled out as I spoke, I said, "Those are our suggestions as to what the evidence revealed in this case. It will send a message. It will send a message about corporate responsibility. It will send a message to Shell that when you do trample on people's rights and then walk away from it and try to bludgeon them through the court system, when you do use all of your power for the wrong reasons, when you do bad things and turn your back on this community, you will be required to make full and fair compensation for the damages that you do. Because, ladies and gentlemen, not everybody is perhaps as stubborn as I am or silly enough to go through this. And for all the people out there who are victims, who are the recipients . . ."

McNamara stood up. "That's improper argument, Your Honor."

Minaldi shook her head. "Overruled."

I was coming to the end. "Do they deserve the benefit of any doubt? You've heard their witnesses. Have they earned your trust? Have they earned the right to be believed? I think not."

I ticked off the various witnesses, both Shell's and ours, comparing their credibility. I even read my original letter of May 9, 1991, which McNamara had characterized as a "threat." It plainly was not. In fact, it never threatened anything. Instead, in courteous but firm language, it asked Shell to advise of its intentions about leaving the property and to provide information regarding salt water disposal and its plan to cleanup the property.

With five minutes still left in my time, I told the jury, "I don't really have anything more to say other than to tell you that I understand what a sacrifice you have made for this trial. I understand you have been pulled away from your families. I understand it's been disruptive, and I also understand how attentive you've been. . . . I've never been around a jury that was more attentive, more dedicated, more intent on doing the right thing. And for that, everyone in this courtroom is grateful to you. Thank you very much."

We were finished.

30

After one more conference in which several of my partners and Shell's lawyers argued over the court's jury instructions, we were finally set for the court to charge the jury. The instructions that were finally agreed upon were typical of what litigation produces: They were a hodgepodge of submissions from both sides. As in so many cases, the instructions had something for everyone. Of course, being a patchwork quilt, it was inevitable that some of it was inconsistent and contradictory.

I used to agonize over what the judge was going to tell the jury during the charge. But I eventually learned that the instructions carried far less influence than I originally believed. The truth is, most juries have a pretty good idea of how they want the case to come out long before the court delivers its charge at the end of the trial. By the time they hear what the judge says about the law, the jury has already heard the testimony, looked at all of the exhibits, and listened to the lawyers' closing arguments. What the judge has to say then is less important to them than what their basic sense of fairness tells them to do.

Given the numerous issues in the case, Judge Minaldi's charge was a good effort to guide the jury. She boiled things down as much as she could to understandable language, and she kept the charge to fifteen minutes. At the end, she gave the jury the verdict form, explained it briefly, and excused them to retire and deliberate.

It wasn't long before Judge Minaldi announced that the jury had sent out a note. They were asking for a copy of the 1961 surface lease, a copy of the court's instructions ("what Judge Minaldi read to us"), and "Austin Arabie's chart." No one was certain about what Arabie's "chart" was, so it was decided to send them the aerial photographs, Arabie's photographs, charts showing his borings and test results, and his cost estimate.

In less than an hour, however, we were summoned back into court. Judge Minaldi informed us that the jury had sent a second note. This one requested a calculator.

Every trial lawyer has a touch of paranoia in him, the result of years of distrusting the other side in court cases. Each side tends to read something negative into every jury request. We immediately became worried that the jury would use the calculator to reduce the damages. Shell's lawyers were worried that the jury wanted a calculator because they were considering an astronomical number for the damage award.

In any event, Judge Minaldi agreed with my partners that she should bring the jury back into the courtroom and instruct them not to reduce any damages by any fault they might attribute to other parties besides Shell. She explained that she would perform that calculation herself. With that instruction, she sent the jury back into deliberations.

A short time later, the jury sent out another request. This time, they asked for "Arabie's land chart displaying and outlining his sample borings." We were all confused by that; the chart had been one of the fifteen or twenty exhibits that had already been given them. Judge Minaldi sent a note back to that effect.

Things stayed quiet for about an hour before we received still another note. This one asked: "Are we confined to award, if we see fit, the amounts, or in between? Or can we go above or below the figure told to us?" Reading the note to us, Judge Minaldi said, "[T]he answer to that, of course, is 'yes.'" She sent back a note that read, "Yes, you may award as you see fit."

You can imagine what that note did to everyone involved. Each side saw bad news in it. Shell was scared to death that the jury would go above the figures I had given them, and despite the assurances of my group, I kept thinking that the jury might come back with an award that was even less than the meager amounts Shell had presented.

The jury sent out a fifth note sometime later. This one said, "We would like to see Griffin's chart on gallons of salt water on the property. Also Barnhill's chart on salt water disposal." We gathered together the two exhibits that had been introduced into evidence and sent them back to the jury.

It seemed like another half hour or so when we were told that the jury had reached a verdict. I remember thinking how hard it was to believe that this nine-year war was finally coming to an end.

As the jury filed in, I saw that Jimbo Guilbeaux, one of the jurors, was carrying the verdict in his hand. He looked at us and smiled. My heart leaped. Several of the other jurors gave us a friendly expression as well. I held my breath, trying not to let myself think about what that might mean.

After everyone was seated, Judge Minaldi said, "All right. Mr. Guilbeaux, I've gotten the impression since you've been sending all the notes and you have the paper there that you're the foreperson of the jury; am I correct?"

Guilbeaux smiled and nodded. "Yes, ma'am."

"And have you reached a verdict?"

He nodded again. "Yes, we have."

"And have nine out of the twelve of you—at least nine out of the twelve of you—agreed on each answer to every question?"

Guilbeaux answered, "Yes, we have."

She then asked him to hand the verdict form to Bill Day, the court bailiff. Day then walked over to the bench and gave it to Judge Minaldi. She read through the entire form. I suppose she couldn't help herself, but she frowned momentarily as she finished with the second page. Looking up, she said, "All right. The verdict is proper as to form. I'll ask the clerk to publish it."

The deputy clerk of court then read the verdict aloud. First was the trespass. The jury set damages for Shell's "holdover" at $927,000, the exact amount we had suggested.

The clerk then read the question about whether Shell had failed to reasonably restore the land to its proper condition. The jury said "yes." She then came to the next question, which asked the jury to set the amount of damages due for Shell's failure to restore the property. She paused as she looked at the number, before reading aloud "$33,000,000."

The next question asked the jury to allocate among Shell and others responsibility for the cleanup. Any percentage not attributed to Shell would reduce our recovery. I thought it would take forever for the clerk to read the question before she announced the jury's findings: "Shell . . . 100 percent." This meant that the jury had allocated zero percent to Rosewood and Kreuger, the parties who had operated the mineral lease after Shell. It also meant that the amount of money awarded for cleanup would be owed exclusively by Shell, because no one besides Shell had caused the contamination.

The next question on the verdict form asked whether Shell and SWEPI "illegally disposed of salt water on the Heyd property." The answer from the jury was "yes." The next question asked was what damages were owed by Shell and SWEPI for the illegal salt water disposal. The clerk read aloud: "$16,679,100."

I went limp. The total was nearly $51 million. Moreover, legal interest had been running on the verdict since suit was filed nine years earlier. I did some rough calculations in my head and realized that we were looking at approximately $100 million.

Shell's lawyers asked that the jury be polled to confirm that at least nine out of twelve jurors had agreed to each answer. So the clerk once again read each question and then asked each individual juror if he or she agreed with that answer.

The jury was unanimous on every question.

31

We were, to put it mildly, stunned by the verdict. After Judge Minaldi excused the jury and adjourned court, we packed up our gear and walked the block and a half from the courthouse back to our office.

Even then, I don't recall anyone saying much of anything as we walked, as if talking about what happened would break the spell.

When we got to the office, however, several members of the group let loose with whoops and high-fives. I was still numb from it all. I vaguely remember my mother hugging me and telling me that she was proud of me. I also seem to recall Billy shaking my hand and saying, "We did it, cuz."

After we stowed our boxes of files, we decided to go somewhere to celebrate. It was mid- to late afternoon by that time. Someone wondered if a bar was open. Pat Gallaugher, a veteran of many late nights from his band days, laughed and said, "This is Louisiana. The bars are *always* open."

We settled on the Pujo Street Café, a nice place just down the street from the office. When we got there, we began to toast our victory in earnest. We hadn't gotten to our second round of drinks when someone spotted Judge Minaldi over on the other side of the restaurant. I felt like I should go over and say hello, but I really didn't know what to say. After the way things had gone, I suspected that she wasn't dying to see me, either. We hadn't exactly been bosom buddies during the trial. So I decided to leave well enough alone and went back to celebrating in earnest.

A little later, I was surprised to see Jimbo Guilbeaux walk into the restaurant. We hailed him over, and he sat down with us and had a drink. That's the way things are in a small town, I thought. Several folks at the table asked Guilbeaux about his impressions of the trial. I couldn't hear everything he told them. I do recall him saying once, "We did what was right. It was obvious to us." Of course, we all expressed our great appreciation to him and his fellow jury members for what they did. He made his excuses and left shortly thereafter.

After an hour or two, someone came up with the idea of moving the party to the Holmwood Bar and Grill, which was owned and operated by Steve Natali, one of Billy's good friends. Holmwood is the name of the community southeast of Lake Charles where the bar is located. The name is something of a euphemism; the bar is a side room to Steve's grocery store. It is best described as rustic, meaning that the restrooms are outside of the building.

Billy called Steve and told him we were coming. Steve had opened the place up by the time we got there, and our gang streamed in. We were the only customers there. Steve started pouring beer, and a group gathered at the jukebox in the corner of the room. Pat Gallaugher looked up and yelled across the room, "They've got Patsy Cline! I can't believe it! They've got Patsy Cline!" Soon, we were listening to her country classic, "Crazy" (written, incidentally, by Willie Nelson).

It wasn't long before none of us was feeling any pain. Gallaugher, in particular, was well into his cups and had reached a transcendental state. At one point, he stood on a bar stool and began yelling, "I kicked their ass! I kicked their ass!" Looking over toward me, he said, "Oh, yeah, and Mike helped."

My wife Melinda, who had joined us, commented that I was being quiet and wanted to know how I felt. If the truth be told, I wasn't sure. I was damned happy about the verdict, of course, but the paranoid lawyer in me was already thinking about whether it would stand up on appeal. Too, I was just completely drained from the experience.

Billy came over and sat down at the bar next to me. Steve Natali had chopped up links of boudin and spread them on butcher paper on top of the bar. I was helping myself and washing it down with beer. Billy had had a few beers, too. Referring to our often-chuckling adversary, he smiled and said in the slow, easy drawl that I had grown to love, "Well, I wonder if Pat Gray thinks everything is so funny now."

&

Like any lawyer, I would like to think that the cases I handle mean something. That was certainly true with *Corbello v. Shell*. In fact, a representative of the foremost publisher of court decisions in the United States told me not long ago that our case against Shell was the biggest legal development he had witnessed in his career. He then asked me what I thought the case proved.

After a moment's reflection, I remembered a standard jury instruction given in virtually every trial. The charge states that our law is no respecter of persons and that all parties stand equal in the eyes of the law regardless of their personal circumstances and should be judged accordingly. If nothing else, I told him, our case against Shell proved that the American legal system is still a place where any man can obtain justice—no matter how powerful the other side may be.

That lesson alone makes *Corbello v. Shell* a victory for us all.

EPILOGUE

Shell fought our case to the bitter end. In fact, it took nearly three years before there was a final judgment.

First, Shell's lawyers filed a motion in the district court attacking the jury's awards on numerous grounds and asking Judge Minaldi to set the verdict aside. In a brief that ran over fifty pages, Shell reargued the facts of the case at length in an effort to persuade Judge Minaldi that the verdict was contrary to the evidence.

That much didn't surprise us. However, it did take us aback when Shell's brief also accused the judge of making numerous wrong rulings at the trial and argued that this furnished additional grounds to order a new trial. In fact, Shell's litany of complaints about the judge's rulings was so long that it bordered on accusing her of incompetence. That was a curious tactic, because to our way of thinking Judge Minaldi had bent over backwards for Shell, and the oil giant's intense attack against the way she had conducted the trial amounted to a slap in the face.

The tactic didn't work. The judge eventually denied Shell's motion, finding that the evidence was more than sufficient to support the verdict. Among other things, it no doubt disappointed our opposition that Judge Minaldi's apparent unhappiness with me during the trial wasn't sufficient to persuade her to set the verdict aside.

The appeal came next. In a frantic effort to get the verdict overturned by the Louisiana Third Circuit Court of Appeal, Shell hired the Houston megafirm of Vinson & Elkins to handle that part of the case. That's how I met Marie Yeates, the head of that firm's "appellate section." Yeates had reportedly graduated first in her class from LSU Law School and over the years had gained a reputation good enough to get her included in one magazine's list of the "Top Fifty Women Lawyers" in the country.

Shell's move to hire new counsel surprised me. I always believed that appeals should be handled by the lawyers who tried the case. For one thing, they've earned it, having gone through the fire of the trial. For another, no one else can ever hope to learn what the lawyers who tried the case already know.

That certainly proved to be true in the appeal of the *Corbello* verdict. Yeates and her cadré of Texas lawyers made several blunders in their appeal briefs about what had happened in the court below (complaining, for instance, about Judge Minaldi giving a jury instruction that *Shell* had requested), and we were only too happy to pounce on them and accuse Shell of reinventing what took place at trial just to get its way. To make things worse, Yeates inexplicably refused to yield the podium at the conclusion of her oral argument in the court of appeal, even after being warned more than once that her time was up. She finally sat down only when the judge chairing the panel turned away from her.

The court of appeal issued its opinion in the case on December 26, 2001. Notwithstanding Shell's assault on the trial judgment, the court's ruling not only maintained what we had won, but awarded us an additional $33 million in interest, an additional $3 million in attorney's fees, and a reinstatement of our claim for punitive damages, which the court of appeal remanded to the district court for a separate trial. Shell was now worse off than it had been before its appeal.

Of course, Shell wasn't about to give up. Its lawyers pressed on with a petition to the Supreme Court of Louisiana, asking the state's highest court to exercise its discretionary right to review the case. After several filings in which the parties argued back and forth about whether or not the case should be heard, the court's seven justices voted unanimously to take up the case.

We naturally took the court's action as a bad sign. The justices rarely went to the trouble of hearing cases they thought had been correctly decided.

The state supreme court's decision understandably breathed new life into Shell and its team of lawyers. They bombarded the court with numerous briefs, arguing every conceivable issue. Some of it seemed misguided. For instance, Shell devoted lots of space in its briefs to the trespass award (which Judge Minaldi had reduced to $32,500), but said virtually nothing about the $33 million in additional interest.

In our brief to the court, I tried to keep things simple, because simple is more persuasive than complicated. To that end, I inserted the following quote by itself on the first inside page:

"Clean up your own mess."
—Robert Fulghum, *All I Really Need to Know I Learned in Kindergarten*

This was important, because one of Shell's main arguments was that the award for cleaning up the property should have been limited to the value of the raw farmland, which was only $108,000. Shell apparently thought it could persuade the state's highest court that it should be free to pollute land and walk away for a mere pittance, leaving the innocent landowner holding the bag for a multimillion dollar cleanup bill.

We argued the case to the state's highest court in September 5, 2002. As any lawyer will warn, predicting an appellate court's eventual ruling based on the judges' questions during oral arguments is about as scientific as reading tea leaves. We were encouraged, however, that the justices asked Marie Yeates tough questions that probed the weaknesses in Shell's arguments. Moreover, when I stood to argue our side, the seven justices seemed considerably more sympathetic, although they did give me a hard time about our punitive damages claim. Nonetheless, our group left the oral arguments in considerably better spirits than we had been when the high court first voted to hear the case.

It was nearly six months before the state supreme court ruled on the case. Finally, on February 25, 2003, the court issued its opinion in *Corbello v. Shell*. While the justices didn't agree to let us pursue our claim for punitive damages (with all the inflammatory evidence we had against Shell, I'd like to think we might've gotten another $500 million in a new trial), we were thrilled that the court basically left the other awards intact.

Remarkably, though, Shell wasn't through with its relentless campaign to avoid responsibility for the *Corbello* verdict. It filed a motion asking the court to rehear the case and argued that the court had been wrong to affirm the award for restoring the property because the contaminated groundwater was owned by the public, not the Heyd family. Thus, Shell argued, any damages for contaminated groundwater should go to the state, not to the landowners.

While that was pending, Shell also sent an army of lobbyists to the Louisiana legislature, which was meeting in the spring of 2003. With the support of Mike Foster, the state's Republican governor, Shell introduced a bill in the legislature that virtually nullified all claims against oil companies for oilfield pollution. The bill also provided that it would be retroactive in a way that rendered our judgment null and void.

The bill was in the nature of an *ex post facto* law and therefore unconstitutional. However, none of us wanted to spend the next two years in court proving the point. We reluctantly decided to hire lobbyists and join forces with land and timber companies and others to fight this "special favor" legislation.

There's an old saying that you should never watch law or sausage being made. When I got to Baton Rouge, I quickly learned why. The representative who introduced Shell's bill announced on the floor of the legislature that the *Corbello* decision was "the worst ruling in the history of the Louisiana Supreme Court." He later admitted that he had managed to reach this conclusion without ever reading the court's opinion.

Not that it mattered. Together with one of our lobbyists, I was eventually summoned to the governor's office on the fourth floor of the state capitol building. In a face-to-face meeting with the governor's executive counsel and chief of staff, I was asked to explain why we were so opposed to Shell's overreaching bill. Our lobbyist kicked me under the table when I looked at the two men sitting across from us and said, "You know, I voted for Governor Foster twice. I guess no good deed goes unpunished."

One member of the legislature later told us that "the anti-Corbello bill" was the single most heavily lobbied piece of legislation he had seen in his entire career. At one time, Shell had as many as a dozen lobbyists buttonholing ever legislator in Baton Rouge. While "the anti-Corbello bill" eventually did pass, it was watered down by numerous amendments, including one that made it apply only to future cases. This meant that it didn't affect our judgment.

Not long thereafter, the state supreme court granted Shell's application for rehearing, but only to emphasize in a new opinion how Shell's sins were too grievous to warrant the absolution it sought. In effect, the court's ruling meant that our judgment against Shell was now final. All that remained in the case were a couple of loose ends concerning the calculation of the trespass damages and the interest on the salt water disposal award. After a minimum of negotiations, Shell's lawyers finally agreed to see things our way. On September 10, 2003—roughly eight years after it reneged on a deal to settle the case for $300,000—Shell wired just over $76 million into a trust account at the Lake Charles office of Merrill Lynch.

The oil giant still would not go quietly, however. Apparently embarrassed by its beating, the company launched an intense public relations campaign across the state. With the assistance of a trade association called the Louisiana Independent Oil and Gas Association, Shell hired an economist from LSU named Loren Scott, who made speeches to civic groups around the state claiming that the *Corbello* decision had caused economic chaos and threatened the existence of the oil and gas industry in Louisiana.

This was a ridiculous claim, and Scott had no evidence to support his propaganda. As subsequent events showed, the number of drilling applications filed with the Louisiana Office of Conservation in 2005—two years *after* the *Corbello* decision—was roughly double the number filed in 2002—the year *before* the *Corbello* decision. In short, twice as many people applied to drill oil and gas wells in Louisiana after the *Corbello* decision than had done so before.

In the fall of 2004, I was invited by John Weimer, one of the justices on the Supreme Court of Louisiana, to appear before a committee he chaired that was reevaluating the disciplinary system for judges in Louisiana. I was among several lawyers asked to share our views with the committee, presumably because I had represented several judges before the Louisiana Judiciary Commission.

I went to New Orleans for the meeting. Before things got started, Justice Weimer made his way around the meeting room, shaking hands and welcoming everyone. I was in the back at the coffee service, and he came over and shared a cup of coffee with me.

I had worked on a case with Justice Weimer years before, when he was a practicing lawyer. The case involved an injury on a golf course, and because of my experience as a golf rules official I had served as an expert witness for the defendants. Justice Weimer also happened to be familiar with my golf novels, so he asked me if I was working on a new book. I told him that my agent had persuaded me to do a book on the Shell case. He smiled, looked at me thoughtfully, and said quietly, "'Clean up your own mess.' I liked that." Without saying anything more, he then walked back to the front of the room.

He was referring, of course, to the line I had inserted in our brief to the supreme court. Of the hundreds of pages of briefs written in the case, that was what Justice Weimer remembered most.

The simplest message is often the most powerful one.

INDEX